REMEMBRANCES OF THINGS PASSED

by Bonnie S. Bailey

Illustrations by
Melissa Luhn

THE HIGHLAND GOURMET, INC.
Birmingham, Alabama

Library of Congress Cataloging-in-Publication Data

Bailey, Bonnie S.
REMEMBRANCES OF THINGS PASSED
Includes index.

ISBN No. 0-9634316-0-9

LC Card No. 92-073647

First Printing, May, 1993

Photography by Karen Barnes
Birmingham, Alabama

Cover by art and science, inc.
Birmingham, Alabama

Printed in the USA by

WIMMER
The Wimmer Companies, Inc.
Memphis • Dallas

CONTENTS

DEDICATION

This book is dedicated to my grandparents,
Ellie Hillin and John Faison Oates,
and to my parents,
Virginia Oates and Jack Gates Shaw, Jr.:

"I thank my God upon every remembrance of you."
Philippians 1:3

Splintered wood, rusty chains,
This old front-porch swing remains.
The pendulum of memories
Blows back and forth on a summer's breeze...

Look how far I've had to come
to get back where I started from...

Waylon Jennings
From his album, *Waylon: The Eagle*
(Beth Neilsen Chapman)
CBS Records, Inc./Epic Records
Copyright © 1990

PREFACE

Originally the collection recorded here of family remembrances and recipes was to have been a private collection for my sons, my nieces and nephews, their families and families-to-be. Over time others have encouraged me to share this book with "the public." I do so with joy. The following is a letter to my sons and nieces and nephews that was to accompany this book, but it is now an open letter to you and to your families to share something of our past with us. It is our hope that it may be in some way a part of your own heritage as well. We need to know where we came from in order to understand where we are going.

To my sons, Charles, John, and Evans
and to my special children:
Virginia, Gates, Ben, and Christopher:

As you and your families and families-to-be face a new millennium, you are moving farther and farther away from a past that can never be recaptured.
It is my hope here to record something of my childhood and the past fifty years of my life to help you to reflect on your own personal histories as they are being lived out now, particularly in the light of the importance of family as a vehicle to love and serve each other, the world in which we live, for the glory of our Heavenly Father.

These remembrances of mine are none of them particularly unique, I'm sure, but they are a collection of thoughts and memories centered around two of our favorite subjects: family and food.

They remind me of what my Daddy long ago told my husband (your father and your uncle) about some of our off-beat relatives. Daddy said. "Now, Bill, they are a little funny, but they're family."

Well, so are these remembrances, but they are recorded here for you as you know, in love.

INTRODUCTION

Out of all the many pages in Marcel Proust's multi-volume tome, *REMEMBRANCES OF THINGS PAST*, perhaps the single most popular connotation his work still provokes today is of *madeleines*, those ethereal little shell-shaped cookies from Aix-en-Provence in Southern France. Truly, our remembrances of things past are so often things *passed*: warm gingerbread, fragrant teas and chocolate cakes, homemade breads and all the comfort foods of our own personal pasts. Here is a collection of some of my family's *remembrances*, in the hopes that it will not only bring back fond memories of your own past, but also, and more importantly, help you to establish new memories for future generations.

Ours now is not a generation of taking time, making memories, smelling the flowers, or the coffee or the bread. This is a time of impatience, when *knowledge has increased, and people run to and fro*. It is an era of *one-minute managers, fast foods,* and instant gratification. Is it any wonder then that those of us in the food business who have made our own breads, soups, mayonnaises, and the like, have actually burned out from trying to meet the demand for our products. As *we run to and fro* ever faster and faster, our hearts—physically and figuratively—need, long, seek and even occasionally find that inner peace of home in some outlet. Vegetable and flower gardens are springing up on square-foot gardens in penthouses and weekend houses; bagel shops, bistros, bakeries are making a comeback from the days of our childhood.

In our take-out shop in the '80s, the *down-home* foods such as meat loaf, chicken pot pie, homemade chicken salad, fresh (really fresh, not ersatz-fresh) fruit salad, even our lasagnas, and especially our homemade soups were almost impossible to keep in stock, although we produced a lot every day. It was not unusual to have the first customers of the day buy every take-out meal we made that day before they even knew what we had prepared for that day, or before we put them out in the refrigerator cases to sell. They called and bought them *sight unseen*. The soups went equally as fast. These were not *fancy* foods; these were simply *remembrances* foods—foods of our childhoods and youth.

Now, hopefully, you can make some of these yourselves. None of them are difficult. All of them are *pure* in that you KNOW what goes into each one. They have definitely stood the test of time in that these remembrances are our treasures, our memories—part of the past we want to pass on to our children and grandchildren.

Our *REMEMBRANCES OF THINGS PASSED*: God had blessed them for us, and may He for you and your loved ones too.

THE 1940s

When World War II began in 1940, my grandparents had lived through one world war, the Roaring Twenties, and the Great Depression, all before their fiftieth birthdays. They lived in Birmingham, Alabama, where I was born in 1940, on July 4th, the coldest July 4th in our history. My parents, my older sister, and I moved to Tampa, Florida, that year until the bombing of Pearl Harbor. After that, most of the men, fathers included, were being sent "overseas."

It wasn't long before my mother and my sister and I had to come back home from Florida to live with my grandparents in Birmingham until the war was over. Now, fifty years later, I often find my heart wandering back to those days in Forest Park.

There was no air-conditioning then, just a big rhythmic attic fan that caused the thin summer curtains to billow out like clouds around my bed. The streetlights came on automatically every night at dark: a perfect night-light for a child. I called my grandfather "Daddy," and my father, who was in the Philippines in the Navy, and whom I didn't know at that time, I called "Papa."

Every morning that I can remember, Daddy and I had a real breakfast together, and to this day, I love long-cooking, thick oatmeal with lots of unsalted homemade butter, brown sugar made with dark molasses, and cream off of the top of the neck of the glass milk bottle. Our butter and our milk stayed in the coldest part of the "ice box", right by the big block of ice that the iceman put on the shelf. He delivered the ice several days a week on big, black tongs, hollering all the way down the steps from the alley, "Iceman! Iceman!" The ice was packed in straw and burlap in the back of a wonderful slat-backed truck.

Just as our butter was homemade, so were all of our breads and preserves. In fact, we "put up" everything we ate with only a few exceptions. My grandmother and Stella Lockwood, our next-door neighbor, called it "canning," but we only used glass jars with funny-looking lids. I never saw a can until years later.

The summers were the best times: with the doors and windows all open for the breezes which carried the wonderful fragrances of gardenias that Daddy grew, of bread baking, coffee brewing, fruits stewing on the back of the stove. Somewhere there was always the quiet sound of a roller lawn mower and a rooster crowing somewhere in the distance. There was a wonderful quiet in those days without television or blaring music from today's boom boxes or car radios. There was no traffic noise, because gas was rationed. We walked to the drug store or to the neighbors' houses, and we played in our own yards. Polio was such a tremendous threat that we didn't go to movies or public places in the summers if we could avoid it, and we had to take naps every afternoon "in the heat of the day."

If the doors were locked at all, it was only the screen-doors that we locked. Visitors never rang the doorbell, which was too bad because ours sounded like the Doxology. If someone came to borrow or repay, they too, just like the iceman, hollered in the door for us.

Mrs. Lockwood would say her recipe said "Go next door and borrow a cup of sugar." Sugar was rationed during the War, but Daddy was in the soft-drink business, so we always had plenty of white and dark sugar. We even had a candy drawer in our dining room which made us the most popular children in the neighborhood. Interestingly enough, no one in my family, then or now, eats candy.

Our garden had fruit trees, vegetables, and flowers of all kinds. We got our corn and other vegetables that we didn't grow ourselves from the Farmers' Market. That, as I have mentioned later in this section on the '40's (See: Fried Chicken, Southern Style), was the highlight of my summer. There were other trips for foods, and because gas was rationed, we packed as many people as we could into the old clunker cars that we drove. We went to Leeds, Alabama, to visit relatives, pick fruits off of their trees, and best of all, bring home a real homemade fresh coconut cake from the famous Leeds cake-lady, Mrs. Lewis.

The windows were all down in the car, and the car was packed with food and people, or else I would have been into that coconut cake. My grandmother carried it on her lap, and it was safe there, despite the heat, the wind, and the children. We sang "God Bless America" all the way home, and to this day, I get hungry for coconut cake whenever I hear that anthem.

Things were indeed different in the '40's, especially during the War. We only ate out if we were going to The Temple Theatre downtown to a play, and then we ate Chinese food at a restaurant that had curtained-off booths and beige food. It looked and smelled like a diner on a train, which was a wonderful memory actually, even if Chinese food does occasionally still make me motion sick.

Other dining-out occasions were rare. There was "Chicken in the Rough" on an occasional Sunday night: this was a "take-out" kind of place with fried chicken, homemade biscuits, and little pots of honey. We ate a lot of fried chicken topped with honey in those days, because the honey invariably spilled all over the boxes on the way home.

There were no night parties at our house. Sometimes there were teas and ladies' church luncheons, but not often. A visitor was special if they had driven over to your house using up precious gasoline, so they usually stayed for dinner. All of our meals were served "family-style" with beautiful bowls of all shapes and sizes filled with three or four vegetables, a platter of meat or meats, biscuits or cornbread wrapped in linen napkins to keep them hot, and exquisite cut-glass dishes with homemade preserves, pickles, and relishes. My favorite of all of the glittering dishes and colorful array on our linen-covered table were the cut-glass pitchers filled with milk and "ice-water" that adorned each end of the table. They looked like liquid diamonds and pearls to me in the daytime in the sunlight or at night in the light of the chandelier overhead. They were beautiful and dependable, because they were always there.

We had linen napkins that were kept in silver napkin rings that have long since been rubbed clean of any legible names, but originally, they each one had our respective names on them. Usually there were flowers in the middle of the table. There was always laughter, warmth, and kindness around that table just as there was in that kitchen on Clairmont Avenue. It was hard work for my grandmother and my mother, but they never begrudged it, and I never heard them complain once. What a heritage!

The recipes under this section of the '40's lack "appetizers" as we know them today, because, for us, there were no "cocktails" or alcohol of any kind at my grandparents' house. The food came all at once to the table. Occasionally, on the train to Florida or in the restaurants, "appetizers" were offered, but they were most often fruit juices in little glasses set in ice-lined bowls. Most of these juices were fresh, because there were so few cans during the War. The fruits were juiced by hand in wonderful contraptions that strained out the seeds of the fruit but not a lot of the pulp. There were also glass "reamers" that are today labeled "antique reamers," and some of us still use them.

The section on the '40's is a collection of recipes that my grandmother, my mother, our neighbor, Mrs. Lockwood, and many other friends from that era have given to me over the years. I even got Mrs. Lewis' coconut cake recipe which everyone vowed she took to the grave with her. It has been a special time of choosing the recipes that we can and do still use today. Throughout this book, I have "up-dated" almost all of the recipes to fit our faster lifestyles somewhat by calling for food processors or blenders where possible, and fewer white sauces than were used so often back then.

Sometimes I have called for more modern "exotic" fruits and vegetables than we had back then, such as tomatillos instead of green tomatoes, or vegetable spaghetti squash instead of "noodles." These changes were made in order to be helpful to our present-day lifestyles, not to be merely esoteric. Sometimes in a salsa or relish, for example, the green tomatillos available today taste better than a sorry green tomato grown in chemical-laden soil; vegetable spaghetti squash is lower in calories and higher in nutrition than most pastas.

Someone has said, "If we only look back, we'll plow a crooked row." Looking back at the past and "passed" is futile if we don't learn from our mistakes, assimilate the best of then and now, and put people first, not food. These recipes are easy, tried, tested, and adaptable to each of us. My hope is that these gifts from our past will be gifts for your present and your future.

APPLE, GRAPEFRUIT, RAISIN, & ORANGE SALAD

This is a good salad all year around, but we especially liked it with quail which we only had at Christmas and on March 23, Daddy's birthday.

6 apples, pared and diced
4 stalks celery, chopped
1 cup golden raisins
1 large grapefruit (pink if possible), sectioned (save the juices)
2 large oranges, sectioned (save the juices)
1 cup of the following homemade mayonnaise:

Fruit Salad Mayonnaise:
4 whole eggs
1 teaspoon salt
1 teaspoon dry mustard
2 cups salad oil
1 tablespoon lemon juice
3 tablespoons juices from the grapefruit and oranges

1. Put the eggs, salt, and dry mustard in a blender or food processor. Turn on high or process until the eggs turn a light yellow color.
2. With the machine running, carefully, one teaspoon at a time at first, add the oil, until ⅓ of it is incorporated into the eggs.
3. With the machine still on high, add the rest of the oil in a steady stream.
4. Stop the machine and add in the lemon juice and 1 tablespoon of the orange and grapefruit juice. Turn the machine on high for the count of 10. Turn off and taste. Add more lemon, grapefruit or orange juice to taste. The lemon juice will make it more acid. Add more salt if necessary.
5. Combine the fruits and 1 cup of the homemade mayonnaise, reserving one of the oranges for garnish. Season to taste with salt and cracked pepper. Serve chilled.
6. As an alternative, arrange the fruits in an attractive pattern on Boston or Bibb lettuce on individual salad plates or on one large serving platter. Serve 2 tablespoons of the mayonnaise on the side of each salad plate or in a separate bowl on the side of the serving platter.

Serves 4 to 6

FROZEN FRUIT SALAD

If there were one recipe that turned up most often in all of the hundreds and hundreds of recipes for this book, the recipe for frozen fruit salad would get first place. Miniature marshmallows had just surfaced in the 40's, and the recipes from the 20's and 30's had us cutting the large ones with "scissors dipped in hot water and dried to keep the marshmallows from adhering to the scissors." Often, whipping cream was substituted for either the mayonnaise or the cream cheese in this salad, but the following version is the one that we like the best, and that appeared more often. The cream cheese today is not quite as rich as it was in the 40's, and the salty taste of today's, we think, gives a better flavor to the frozen fruit salad than the whipping cream. Our family used fresh fruit, but many recipes used "canned fruit cocktail" (or "cottontail" as we used to call it as children). The fresh is immensely better than the canned.

> **2 cups fresh fruit (Bing cherries pitted, sliced green and red grapes, orange slices, banana slices dipped in lemon juice, fresh pineapple cut in small chunks)**
> **1 cup fresh fruit juice**
> **16 ounces cream cheese, softened**
> **¾ cup mayonnaise (commercial)**
> **2 cups miniature marshmallows**
> **2 tablespoons powdered sugar**
> **½ cup whipping cream, whipped**

1. Soften the cream cheese and add the powdered sugar and fruit juice in a mixer or a processor. Add the mayonnaise and blend well. Fold in the fruit and the ½ cup whipped cream.
2. Freeze in an 8" square pan for 4 hours or overnight.
3. Serve on Boston or Bibb lettuce as a salad.

Serves 4 to 6

Note: At Christmas or Valentine's, sprinkle pomegranate seeds over the salad just before serving.

GERMAN POTATO SALAD

During The Highland Gourmet years (the 80's), we served this salad so often that we tend to forget it came from the '40's. It's wonderful served hot, and of course, cold and left-over the next day. Gwen, our catering director and co-teacher at the shop is of German descent, and one of the best cooks we know. This is her recipe, but it is just like I remember my grandmother's.

> ½ **pound bacon, cooked and crumbled**
> 6 **medium-size potatoes, peeled and sliced**
> 2 **cups chicken broth**
> 1 **tablespoon salt**
> 2 **tablespoons vegetable oil (or 2 tablespoons bacon drippings)**
> 1 **onion, chopped**
> 3 **stalks celery, chopped**
> 2 **teaspoons sugar**
> **salt and cracked pepper**
> ½ **cup cider vinegar**

1. Boil the peeled and sliced potatoes in the 2 cups chicken stock, salt, and enough water to cover the potatoes. When the potatoes are tender, drain, and reserve ½ cup of the broth.
2. Cook the bacon, and remove from the skillet. Reserve 2 table-spoons of the bacon drippings or replace them with 2 table-spoons vegetable oil. Break the bacon into pieces and set aside on paper towels to drain.
3. Heat the bacon drippings or the oil, and add the chopped onion, and celery to the drippings or oil in the skillet and sauté until barely sweated.
4. Mix the 2 teaspoons sugar and the vinegar to the ½ cup broth from the potatoes and add to the onions and celery in the skillet. Cook for 5 minutes over high heat. Pour over the cooked pota-toes. Taste and add salt and cracked pepper.

4 to 6 servings

Note: Gwen mixes hers up so well at this point that they almost look like mashed potatoes. My grandmother carefully folded all in so that the potatoes were still chunky. Either way, they are perfect!

LOBSTER (OR CRABMEAT) SALAD

2 cups diced cooked lobster
2 tablespoons French dressing (see Index)
1 tablespoon Worcestershire sauce
¼ cup stuffed olives
2 tablespoons lemon juice
½ teaspoon salt
3 tablespoons mayonnaise
½ cup chopped celery
3 hard-cooked eggs (optional)
3 tomatoes, peeled and quartered

1. Marinate the lobster in the French dressing in the refrigerator for 30 minutes.
2. Mix together with all of the other ingredients, except for the optional hard-cooked eggs and the tomatoes. Taste for salt and pepper and add if necessary.
3. Garnish with the tomatoes and if used, the hard-cooked eggs.

Serves 4 to 6

MACARONI & TOMATO SALAD

In the 40's, pasta was called "macaroni" or "noodles", and the only "noodles" we had then were our own homemade "dumplings" to accompany chicken. Once when I visited a friend from New York, her mother served this, and I have never forgotten it. You New Yorkers out there should be proud to have been so "with it" so early! Now Pasta and Tomato Salad is in every take-out shop.

1 package (8 ounces) macaroni pasta
3 medium tomatoes, peeled and seeded, chopped or diced
   small
4 stalks celery, chopped
1 cup commercial mayonnaise
1 tablespoon Dijon mustard
2 green onions chopped with some of the green
½ cup diced bread and butter pickles
salt and cracked pepper

1. Boil and drain the pasta. Run cold water over it while it is hot to cool it quickly. Drain it well.
2. Add the mustard to the mayonnaise.
3. Mix all of the ingredients together until just moistened. Add salt and pepper to taste. Chill and serve with additional sliced tomatoes.

Serves 4 to 6

MY MOTHER'S CHICKEN SALAD

> **3 cups cubed cooked chicken**
> **3 hard-cooked eggs, mashed**
> **3 stalks celery, chopped**
> **2 teaspoons salt (or more if necessary)**
> **1 cup mayonnaise**
> **4 sweet gherkins, chopped**

1. Combine all ingredients and moisten with the mayonnaise. Be stingy with the mayonnaise.
2. Season to taste with fresh lemon juice, salt, and pepper.

Serves 4 to 6

OLD-FASHIONED CABBAGE SLAW, NO. 1

Cole slaw in the '40's was served with a boiled dressing because we didn't have bottled dressings then like we do now. Boiled dressing was wonderful, and no purchased slaw "dressing" can compare. Add whatever other chopped vegetables you like such as today's yellow and red peppers, green peppers, shredded carrots, even red cabbage all or in part. Garnish with sliced tomatoes.

> **1 large green or red cabbage (green is traditional), outer leaves removed**
> **1 small mild onion, sliced very thin**
> **salt and pepper**
> **"Cooked Mock Mayonnaise" to bind**

1. Shred the cabbage with a knife or with a shredder. Chill in the refrigerator.
2. One hour before serving, add the onion and any other vegetables as mentioned above, and enough of the "Cooked Mock Mayonnaise" to bind. Taste and season with salt and pepper. Chill thoroughly.

Serves 4 to 6

COOKED MOCK MAYONNAISE

2 tablespoons salad oil
2 tablespoons flour
2 tablespoons lemon juice
boiling water
1 egg yolk, beaten
1 cup salad oil
1 tablespoon salt
1 teaspoon each: dry mustard, paprika, dill and black pepper
1 egg white, beaten

1. Blend the first three ingredients in a one-cup measuring cup, and fill cup with boiling water. Mix well.
2. Cook over medium heat, stirring constantly, until mixture thickens.
3. Put the thickened mixture in a blender, and with the motor on, add the beaten egg yolk. Blend until the mixture begins to cool.
4. Gradually add in oil, then add seasonings, and blend. Remove from the blender to a bowl, and fold in the stiffly beaten egg white.

Makes 2 cups

OLD-FASHIONED CABBAGE SLAW #2: SWEET & SOUR

The vinegar in this cole slaw makes it a good accompaniment to fried chicken.

> 1 large head cabbage, outer leaves removed
> 1 medium sweet onion, sliced thin
> 1 tablespoon sugar
> 2 teaspoons salt
> 2 teaspoons celery seeds
> 2 teaspoons dry mustard
> ¾ cup vegetable oil
> 1 cup cider vinegar

1. Shred the cabbage and add to the onion. Chill well.
2. Bring all of the other ingredients to the boil and boil stirring constantly until the sugar and mustard are melted.
3. Pour over the cabbage mixture a little at a time until thoroughly moistened. Toss. Chill or serve hot.

Serves 4 to 6

Note: Chilled is more traditional. Add salt and pepper to taste.

OLD-FASHIONED CHICKEN SALAD

**1 4-pound hen
celery leaves
1 small onion, peeled and cut in quarters
2½ teaspoons salt
1½ cups celery, chopped
1 cup fresh pineapple, cut into chunks
2 tablespoons salad oil
2 tablespoons orange juice
2 tablespoons vinegar
1 egg, well beaten
¼ cup lemon juice
¼ cup pineapple juice
½ cup sugar
½ cup toasted, slivered almonds**

1. Put chicken in pot and cover with water. Add celery leaves and onion, and 2 teaspoons salt. Cook uncovered until chicken is tender. Cool in broth.
2. Debone and dice or "pull" chicken into coarse pieces. Combine chicken, chopped celery, and pineapple in a large bowl.
3. Combine oil, orange juice, vinegar, and ½ teaspoon salt. Pour over the cooked chicken, tossing to mix well. Refrigerate for 1½ hours or overnight.
4. Combine egg, juices, and sugar in top of double boiler. Place over boiling water on medium heat. Cook, stirring occasionally for 15 to 20 minutes or until thickened. Chill.
5. Drain chicken mixture thoroughly. Combine the marinated chicken that has been drained with the pineapple dressing a half cup at a time, adding more if necessary to moisten. Chill and serve with Boston or Bibb lettuce. Top with the toasted almonds.

Serves 4 to 6

OLD-FASHIONED POTATO SALAD

Marinating the cooked potatoes while they are still hot enables them to absorb the vinaigrette, so that when they are cold, the potatoes have a wonderful flavor. There are many variations on this salad, but this was and is our favorite. Keep it cold.

6 large potatoes, peeled, sliced, and cooked until tender
1 onion, chopped
3 hard-cooked eggs, mashed
1 cup celery, chopped
½ cup green olives, chopped (with or without the pimento)
½ cup chopped bread and butter pickles
½ cup vinaigrette (see below)
1 cup commercial mayonnaise
2 teaspoons yellow mustard
juice of 1 small lemon
paprika
salt and pepper

Vinaigrette:
½ cup olive or vegetable oil
1 tablespoon cider vinegar
salt and pepper
1 fresh basil leaf or 1 teaspoon dry basil

1. While the potatoes are still hot but well drained, put them in a bowl and pour the vinaigrette over them. Chill them in the refrigerator, turning them occasionally.
2. Remove from the refrigerator, and add the rest of the ingredients.
3. Taste and season with salt and cracked pepper. Remove the basil leaf before serving.

Serves 4 to 6

RUSSIAN CHICKEN SALAD

1 cup diced, cooked ham
2 cups diced, cooked chicken
½ cup vinaigrette (see Index)
1½ cups diced, cooked potatoes
½ cup diced, raw peeled apple
⅓ cup chopped sweet pickles
½ cup diced celery
¼ cup diced sweet onion (or green onions)
1½ teaspoons salt
½ cup mayonnaise
3 hard-cooked eggs, quartered
2 tablespoons capers, optional

1. Marinate cubed cooked meats in vinaigrette for 1 hour in the refrigerator.
2. Blend all the rest of the ingredients except the hard-cooked eggs and mix well. Taste for salt and pepper and add if necessary.
3. Top with quartered hard-cooked eggs, and the optional capers. Serve chilled on Boston or Bibb lettuce.

Serves 4 to 6

SALMON SALAD

*The old cookbooks tell us that if we are to use canned salmon, drain it and
"scald it." Fortunately, today, if fresh cooked salmon is not available, we
need only use a high quality canned salmon, and carefully remove all of
the skin and bones. No "scalding" is necessary. Whole broiled fresh
salmon chilled is decidedly better than any canned salmon. Steaming fresh
salmon, a few green onions, and herbs in tightly wrapped foil in a 325°
oven for 10 to 15 minutes per pound or until it is firm to the touch, is
almost as easy as opening a can. The following salad is a "Salmon
Niçoise" like a fresh Tuna Niçoise, and we think it is equally as wonderful.
Naturally, we have taken some liberties with the 40's, because my grandmother bound her salad in "red-eye gravy" from the bacon drippings and
cider vinegar. With cholesterol and all, we have used only low-fat sour
cream mixed into a light vinaigrette. If you prefer the original version, and
are in good enough cholesterol health, make the red-eye gravy vinaigrette
for the cooked salmon with 4 tablespoons bacon drippings (part can be
vegetable oil) to 1 tablespoon cider vinegar, 1 teaspoon sugar, and mix
with a whisk or shake thoroughly in a small jar.*

> **3 cups cooked salmon (fresh or canned)**
> **3 cooked red potatoes, cut into slices**
> **2 tablespoons vinegar**
> **½ cup light vegetable oil**
> **2 tablespoons sour cream (low fat may be used)**
> **1 teaspoon each: salt, cracked pepper, dill**
> **¼ to ½ cup fresh blanched snow peas or cooked green beans,**
> **   chilled**
> **1 red onion, sliced thin and in rings**

1. Mix together the oil, vinegar, and spices and whisk in the sour
   cream and mix well.
2. Arrange the salmon, green beans (or snow peas), and red potatoes on Bibb or Boston lettuce on a serving platter or individual
   plates. Arrange the raw red onions on the top. Sprinkle with
   more cracked pepper and dill (dry or fresh) and chill.
3. Serve about 3 tablespoons of the sour cream-vinaigrette on the
   side of each salad or in a bowl on the side of the platter.

Serves 4

SHRIMP SALAD

2½ pounds cooked medium-size shrimp, peeled and deveined
1 cup commercial mayonnaise
½ cup commercial chili sauce (spicy)
1 cup chopped celery
juice of a small lemon
1 small avocado, peeled and cut in slices
1 small grapefruit, sectioned

1. Combine the mayonnaise, chili sauce, and celery.
2. Mix the grapefruit, and avocado very carefully, and add the lemon juice. The lemon juice and the grapefruit will prevent the avocado from turning dark. Just before mixing, remove the grapefruit and avocado with a slotted spoon into a bowl.
3. Fold in the rest of the ingredients. Season to taste with the lemon juice and cracked pepper if desired. Serve very cold on Boston or Bibb lettuce.

Serves 4 to 6

SWEET POTATO SALAD

4 medium sweet potatoes, peeled and diced
¼ cup vinaigrette (see Index)
2 cups diced cooked ham or smoked turkey
1 cup chopped celery
3 green onions, chopped
salt and pepper

1. Cook the sweet potatoes in hot water to cover until tender and drain, or microwave covered in a Pyrex dish until thoroughly cooked.
2. While the potatoes are still warm, marinate them in the vinaigrette. Chill.
3. Blend all of the rest of the ingredients, and add to the marinated sweet potatoes with the marinade, being careful not to mash the potatoes, but to retain their shape. Taste and season with salt and pepper.

Serves 4 to 6

TOMATO ASPIC

This is the only "congealed salad" that I have included in the entire book, although all of the heirloom recipe boxes given to me are loaded with gelatin salad recipes. Gelatin has been around since before Escoffier's days in the form of calves' feet, and yet somehow, the Knox gelatin people really made an impression during the 40's and 50's. It was something of a challenge in the un-air-conditioned South in the summer to gel something in an "ice box," so maybe, it was a mark of a great cook to congeal every-thing, and they sure did. Tomato aspic was and is different, somehow more acceptable, and endearing than all those shimmering light green and purple things that surrounded chicken salad every summer. Maybe since tomato aspic is similar to a spicy Bloody Mary (something that was unheard of in the 40's) is why we still accept this one congealed salad. If you do put vodka in your aspic, you will have to call it "Gazpacho", because vodka doesn't congeal too well, thank goodness.

>   3 envelopes unflavored gelatin
>   ½ cup cold water
>   3 cups V-8 juice (or tomato juice, or seasoned Bloody Mary
>   mix)
>   1 can beef consommé
>   leaves from 1 bunch celery
>   1 bay leaf
>   8 peppercorns
>   6 whole cloves
>   1 medium onion, sliced
>   1 tablespoon sugar
>   1 teaspoon salt
>   2 teaspoons Worcestershire sauce
>   2 teaspoons A-1 Sauce
>   3 stalks celery chopped
>   1 cup sliced olives with pimento, drained
>   1 can artichoke hearts, sliced and drained well

1. Soften gelatin in cold water.
2. Put juices and consommé in boiler and add the celery leaves, bay leaf, peppercorns, cloves, onion, sugar and salt, and bring to a boil. Cook over low heat for 10 minutes. Strain.
3. Add the softened gelatin, stirring all the while until it is com-pletely dissolved.
4. Add the rest of the ingredients and chill in a lightly oiled 8" ring mold. Serve unmolded with homemade mayonnaise on the side.

Serves 4 to 6

TOMATOES, CUCUMBERS, & VIDALIA ONIONS

When we served this salad, it meant summer had arrived: Real summer with all of its cold foods, iced tea with mint, open doors and windows that made the gardens seem so near. This salad was more like a "relish" in that we had it on the table in a little blue and white bowl at every meal except breakfast. Chopped and drained, it makes a perfect "salsa" for fish or black-eyed peas.

3 large perfect tomatoes, peeled and sliced
1 Vidalia or sweet onion, peeled and sliced
2 cucumbers, peeled, seeded, and sliced
½ cup cider vinegar
2 teaspoons sugar
3 or 4 leaves of fresh basil

1. Marinate the vegetables in the sweetened cider vinegar for at least two hours.
2. Refrigerate any left-over. They will keep about 24 hours.
3. To make a "salsa": drain the vegetables out with a slotted spoon, and chop them very coarse. Serve over grilled or broiled fish or over black-eyed peas.

VEGETABLE SALAD

> 1 clove garlic
> ¼ cup vinaigrette (see Index)
> 4 stalks celery, chopped
> 1 bunch fresh watercress, washed, and drained
> 3 tomatoes, peeled, seeded, and chopped
> 2 stalks white endives, chopped
> 1 bunch radishes, washed and chopped
> 3 raw carrots, peeled and chopped or shredded
> 3 green onions, chopped with some of the green
> 1 head Boston or Bibb lettuce, washed and drained
> 3 ounces Roquefort cheese
> 3 slices cooked bacon, drained and broken into pieces

1. Crush the garlic clove slightly and put into the vinaigrette while preparing the rest of the salad.
2. Put all of the vegetables into a salad bowl. Tear the watercress and the lettuce into small pieces and add to the vegetables. Refrigerate until serving time.
3. Just before serving, toss the vegetables, watercress, and the lettuces with the vinaigrette from which the garlic clove has been removed and discarded. Taste for salt and pepper, adding if necessary.
4. Break the cooked bacon and the Roquefort cheese into pieces over the salad.

Serves 6 to 8

WALDORF SALAD

Whether or not Waldorf Salad originated at The Waldorf Hotel in New York, it certainly is a traditional American salad today. The ingenious and creative "Silver Palate" of New York led by Shiela Lukins and Julee Rosso in the 80's, made a wonderful Waldorf salad with a vinaigrette of walnut oil, olive oil, and lemon juice, walnuts, and the like. My C.E.O. friend from The Highland Gourmet days, Mr. Richey of Torchmark, Inc., of Birmingham, liked blue cheese and fresh pineapple in his Waldorf salad, which is also our family's favorite. During the War years of the 40's, everything in the salad was bound up with lots of mayonnaise, but here we have used less mayonnaise, and Julee and Shiela's walnut idea.

APPLE & PINEAPPLE WALDORF SALAD

1 fresh pineapple, cut in bite-size pieces
1 pound firm apples (Delicious or York) diced (This should be about 4 cups)
1 cup celery, chopped
½ cup (4 ounces) walnuts, toasted
juice of one lemon
1 cup golden raisins
½ cup homemade mayonnaise
4 ounces blue cheese, crumbled (optional)

1. Bind all the ingredients except the lemon juice and cheese, using only ½ cup of the mayonnaise.
2. Taste and season with salt and the lemon juice adding more if necessary. This will depend on the sweetness of the pineapple and the apples: the sweeter they are, the more lemon juice you may need.

Serves 4 to 6

HOMEMADE MAYONNAISE

2 whole eggs
2 teaspoons salt
2 teaspoons dry mustard
1½ cups light vegetable oil
1 tablespoon cider vinegar
2 teaspoons chives

1. Process or blend the eggs, salt, dry mustard until light in color.
2. With the machine running, add the oil 1 teaspoon at a time until 1 cup oil has been added, then add the rest in a steady stream.
3. Turn off the machine, add the vinegar and chives. Turn the machine back on and process or blend until the vinegar and chives are well incorporated. Add more salt if needed. This keeps refrigerated in a glass jar for 3 days.

Makes approximately 2 cups

BEEF

BEEF STEW

> 1 tablespoon corn or vegetable oil
> 3 pounds beef stew meat, cut small
> 4 carrots, peeled and sliced in chunks
> 4 celery stalks, peeled and sliced in chunks
> 3 onions, peeled and sliced in quarters
> 2 baking potatoes, peeled and sliced in chunks
> 1 pound fresh mushrooms, washed and sliced
> 3 cups red wine or beef stock (or half and half)
> 1 large can stewed or whole tomatoes with the liquid
> 1 can shoepeg corn, drained, or 2 ears fresh, cooked
> 1 can large size English peas or 2 cups fresh
> 1 tablespoon A-1 Sauce
> 1 tablespoon Worcestershire sauce
> salt and pepper

1. Heat the oil in a Dutch oven or casserole, and add the beef cubes and potatoes and sauté until they are both browned.
2. Add the carrots and cook stirring for another few minutes to soften the carrots and potatoes a little more. Add the fresh mushrooms, onions, and celery and cook for an additional few minutes, stirring constantly.
3. Add the rest of the ingredients. Cover the casserole with foil and a heavy lid, and stew it in a 350° oven for 3 to 4 hours. This is best the next day.

Serves 6 to 8

Note: Serve with cornbread and a green salad.

CHILI

What a surprise it was to find a recipe for chili in my grandmother's box of recipes. I remember a few Sunday nights when we had chili and corn-bread, but we almost always had "left-overs" from Sunday noon on Sunday nights. This chili was wonderful, however, and I can still hear the background music from "One Man's Family," a Sunday night radio program, whenever I taste it. In our lower-fat world of the 90's, I have often substituted ground turkey for the ground pork, or used all lean ground beef, and it is just as good. This recipe makes a lot of chili, which freezes well, but you can divide it in half if you feel like it.

**3 pounds lean ground beef
3 pounds lean pork, ground twice (or see above)
3 red onions, chopped
3 large cans tomatoes
2 small cans tomato paste
3 cloves garlic, minced
3 cans red beans or "chili beans"
1 teaspoon cloves
2 bay leaves
dash of red pepper
chili powder to taste (about 1 tablespoon or more)**

1. In a large Dutch oven or casserole, sauté the meat(s) and onions until the meat browns. Pour off the excess fat. Add the rest of the ingredients except the beans, and cook covered over low heat, stirring occasionally for 2 to 3 hours or until the meats are well flavored.
2. Add boiling water as it is cooking only if the liquid cooks out.
3. Add the beans, and cook uncovered another 30 minutes, stirring occasionally.
4. Serve plain, over rice or spaghetti, with grated Cheddar cheese, chopped green onions, and (low-fat) sour cream.

Makes about 3 quarts

MEAT LOAF

*When Julia Child's books and television programs emerged in the 60's
with her wonderful French cooking for Americans, meat loaf became
"pâté," which greatly elevated its lowly status. We loved it then and now,
regardless of its status. Substitute all ground beef, veal, or even today's
low-fat ground turkey. Season it highly, and you won't miss the fat it used
to contain. The onions, celery, and tomatoes give off a lot of liquid of their
own, keeping it moist.*

> **3 pounds ground round (or see above)**
> **2 large onions, chopped coarse**
> **4 stalks of celery, chopped coarse**
> **4 medium fresh tomatoes, peeled, seeded and chopped coarse,
> or 1 can, drained, whole tomatoes, chopped coarse**
> **2 eggs, beaten (today we can use just the egg whites if
> cholesterol is a problem, but add one extra white for each
> yolk omitted)**
> **¼ cup milk (regular or low-fat)**
> **2 cups dry bread crumbs**
> **1 tablespoon Worcestershire sauce**
> **1 tablespoon A-1 Sauce**
> **1 clove garlic, minced**
> **2 teaspoons each: salt, oregano, thyme and tarragon**
> **2 teaspoons salt and pepper**

1. Sauté the onions and celery together. Let cool and add to the
   raw ground meat with all of the rest of the ingredients except
   the milk and the bread crumbs.
2. Soak the bread crumbs in the milk for a few minutes and add to
   the rest of the mixture. Mix well.
3. Shape into one large loaf or 4 smaller ones. For the large loaf,
   bake in a Pyrex loaf pan for 30 minutes at 325° or until the juices
   are clear. For the smaller ones, bake in four small mini-bread
   pans for 15 minutes at 325° or until the juices run clear.
4. Let rest 15 minutes, remove from their pans and serve with
   mashed potatoes and stewed tomatoes. A cold green bean salad
   with a vinaigrette is wonderful with this.

Serves 4 to 6

POT ROAST WITH VEGETABLES

1 5-pound pot roast (7-bone, chuck, or sirloin tip)
4 onions, sliced thick
5 carrots, peeled and left whole
8 baking potatoes, peeled and left whole
3 tablespoons corn oil
2 tablespoons Worcestershire sauce
2 tablespoons A-1 Sauce
4 cups hot water
1 cup red wine
1 8-ounce can tomato paste
2 cloves garlic
2 teaspoons each: thyme and tarragon
salt and pepper to taste

1. In a heavy Dutch oven or casserole, brown the pot roast on every side in the hot oil. Remove temporarily to a platter.
2. Heat the oil in the Dutch oven, and add the sliced onions, carrots, potatoes and cook until the onions are limp. The carrots and potatoes will still be hard.
3. Add the hot water and the rest of the ingredients, including the pot roast. The roast must be covered with the liquid. Add more if necessary.
4. Cover the casserole with heavy foil and a lid or two layers of heavy foil. It must be airtight.
5. Roast covered in a 325° oven for 3 hours or until very tender.
6. Let rest for 10 minutes. Remove cover and serve with the roasted vegetables.

Serves 4 to 6

"STEAK-ON-A-STICK"

In today's lingo, this is, of course, "Shish Kabob". During the War in the early 40's, we hardly ever went out to eat, and "Shish Kabob" was a flaming mystery seldom seen in those days. We put our "steak on a stick," and marvelled at our daring. Actually, it was our gourmet neighbor, Mrs. Lockwood, who fixed this, but then she was a real gourmet because she also served eggplant. Mrs. Lockwood's eggplant casserole goes well with the beef kabobs, or you can use lamb in place of the beef. "DINNER ON A DAGGER" can be chicken, pork, fish, veal, or lamb. The cooking time is very short, so this can be a very quick dinner. The assembling doesn't even take too long.

> **2 pounds beef tenderloin, sirloin, or 2 pounds either: chicken, veal, lamb, or fish cut into 16 chunks of approximately ⅛ pound (2 ounces) each. This allows ½ pound meat per person for 4 people.**
> **16 large fresh mushrooms**
> **16 cherry tomatoes**
> **16 small white onions, peeled, or 4 medium onions cut into 4 slices each (16 slices)**
> **4 skewers or wooden kabob sticks with pointed end**
> **¼ cup vegetable oil mixed with 3 tablespoons red wine vinegar**
> **2 teaspoons each rosemary and thyme**
> **salt and pepper**

1. Lightly sauté the onion slices and the mushrooms in 2 teaspoons oil just to barely wilt and cook them, but not until they lose their shape. Let cool.
2. On 4 skewers alternate 4 slices each: tomato, onion, meat, (or fish), mushroom, repeating each until the skewer is full.
3. Brush with the oil, vinegar, and herbs, and broil for 3-6 minutes, turning once until the juices run clear. (The fish will have opaque milky protein instead of the clear juices of red and white meats). Salt and pepper to taste.

Serves 4

Note: Any other raw vegetables may be substituted, even all raw vegetables (with no meat or fish), including: squash, zucchini, parboiled fresh carrots, parboiled red potatoes, green, red, or yellow peppers, keeping in mind that any of the harder vegetables must be parboiled in order to cook in the same amount of time as the softer ones. These can also be done on the grill.

CHICKEN

Some futuristic generation may unearth bones from the 20th century in America and find as many chicken bones as human bones! During the war years of the early 40's, a drive to the Farmer's Market in "Lizzie", Mrs. Lockwood's Ford, to pick out live, squawking chickens was the highlight of my life back then! We couldn't go until late in the afternoon, when the farmers were ready to go home, because the chickens were cheaper then. Mrs. Lockwood would carefully select the best ones, and then the most amazing thing would happen! The farmers would tie the chickens together by the leg, and the chickens would lie down, and they stayed quiet in the trunk of that tank of a car all the way home! My grandmother and Mrs. Lockwood would put the chickens in my grandmother's garage with the doors closed, and my little four-foot-ten-inch grandmother would disappear into the garage and ring the necks of the chickens! My grandmother always came out as spotlessly clean as she went in. Even her beautiful white hair all knotted up on her head would still be in place! What a lady! The next day, the garage was as clean as my grandmother, and no one missed a beat. It was all in the day's work. It was a good thing too, because we ate chicken every possible way: boiled, roasted, baked, fried, stewed, sauced, creamed, hashed, pulled, barbequed and croqueted. Later when I was in the restaurant business, we cooked between three and four hundred pounds of chicken breasts a week, every week for 7 years. That's why I think futuristic generations will find more chicken bones in Alabama than people bones. Maybe one day, we'll get tired of it!

CHICKEN & DUMPLINGS

"Dumplings" were our 40's version of pasta. They were usually big, wide noodles poached in the chicken broth itself. They had chopped green onions which we called "scallions" over them for taste and color, and we loved them. Chicken and Dumplings was a cold winter's night dish, and it made me love winters even more. I have made this a 90's version with less chicken fat than we used back then, but it doesn't compromise the taste, in our opinion.

> **4 to 6 chicken breasts, skinless, but with the bones**
> **1 cup dry white wine and enough water to cover**
> **4 celery stalks, cut in half with some of the leaves**
> **1 large onion, peeled and cut in half**
> **2 whole cloves**
> **1 tablespoon salt**

1. Cook the chicken breasts uncovered in the water, wine, vegetables, cloves and salt, until the chicken is done. This takes about 30 minutes.
2. Remove the breasts from the hot liquid with tongs or a slotted spoon and keep on a plate with ½ cup of the broth until they are cool.
3. Remove the flesh from the bones and add the bones back to the stock. Reduce by half, strain. Bring the strained stock to a boil, then lower heat.
4. Add the dumplings a few at a time to the strained stock and cook until they float easily, about 5 to 8 minutes.
5. Remove the dumplings from the liquid with a slotted spoon, and drain them on a plate. See directions for dumplings.
6. Reduce the chicken broth over high heat to about 2 cups liquid. Strain into a sauce boat and keep warm.
7. Put the sliced chicken breasts and the poached dumplings on a platter, and spoon ½ cup broth over them. Sprinkle with the tops of 3 or 4 green onions, chopped. Salt and pepper to taste. Heat covered until very hot or microwave carefully. Serve the rest of the sauce separately.

Serves 4 to 6

DUMPLINGS FOR CHICKEN BROTH

1 cup flour
1 teaspoon thyme
1 egg
1 teaspoon salt
1 tablespoon milk
1 tablespoon good olive oil (Tuscan, if possible)
2 tablespoons Parmesan or Romano cheese, grated

1. Mix the egg, salt, milk, thyme, and enough white flour to make a stiff dough.
2. Roll out thin and cut in strips about ¼ inch wide and 3 inches long.
3. Let dry in a warm 200° oven for 15 to 20 minutes while the chicken is cooking.
4. Drop into boiling broth, lower heat to medium, and cook until they float easily, about 5 to 8 minutes.
5. Remove from the broth with a slotted spoon and drain. Sprinkle the 1 tablespoon olive oil over the dumplings. Add salt and pepper.
6. Serve with chopped green onion tops and the grated cheese sprinkled over them.

CHICKEN HASH

Corned beef could be added instead of chicken, but we found corned beef to be too salty for our family, so we kept with the chicken, occasionally substituting left-over roast beef.

> 1 tablespoon vegetable oil
> 3 stalks celery, cut up
> 3 carrots, peeled and cut up coarse
> 1 medium onion, chopped
> 1 garlic clove, minced
> 2½ cups cooked chicken
> 3 cups cooked Irish potatoes, peeled, cubed, grated or cut-up coarse
> 1 cup chicken broth (or 1 can good chicken broth)
> ½ cup dry white wine or vermouth
> salt and pepper
> fresh or dried basil, thyme, and tarragon to equal 1 tablespoon

1. Sauté the onion, celery, carrots and garlic clove in the vegetable oil.
2. Add the rest of the ingredients except for the chicken broth. Stir well and heat slowly over medium heat.
3. Add the broth and white wine a little at a time to incorporate it well. Cook over medium heat stirring occasionally until all of the liquid is gone. Taste for seasonings, adding salt and pepper if necessary.

Serves 4 to 6

CHICKEN SPAGHETTI

All of my grandmother's recipes for chicken (and there are many) call for "one 5-pound stewing hen cooked in 1 quart water, celery leaves, etc." Most of us today have no clue what a "stewing hen" is, and it seems like young people may believe that chickens, beef, pork, and the like somehow come into this world "cryovacked" with no skin, no bones, no fins or feathers. To simplify these chicken recipes for any future generations of cooks, I have simply called for "3 cups cooked, cut-up chicken." This would be about 6 or 8 single, boneless, skinless breasts, which would, of course, give you all white meat, or a whole chicken of about 4 to 6 pounds, cooked in water and celery, onions, salt, pepper, cooled in the broth, fat then removed, and the cooled flesh cut up or "pulled." It is not hard to

cook a whole chicken, but I would do it the day before assembling any of
these dishes. Of course, to get dark and white meat, you could add a few
boneless, skinless chicken thighs to the boneless, skinless chicken breasts,
but do explain to your future generations that chickens do have bones and
feathers.

CHICKEN SPAGHETTI

> 3 cups cooked, cut-up chicken
> 1 tablespoon vegetable oil
> 2 stalks celery, chopped
> 1 medium onion, chopped
> 2 green onions, chopped (reserve the green for the garnish)
> 1 package fresh mushrooms, washed and sliced
> 1 medium red sweet pepper, chopped
> 1 tablespoon vegetable oil
> 2 cups chicken broth
> 1 teaspoon each oregano, basil, thyme, to equal 1 tablespoon
>   total
> salt and pepper to taste
> 1 package vermicelli, cooked and drained
> 2 teaspoons good olive oil (Tuscan, if possible)
> 2 of the reserved green onion tops
> grated peel of 1 lemon
> 1 tablespoon Parmesan or Romano cheese, grated

1. Sauté the vegetables in the hot vegetable oil until they are limp,
   but not over-cooked, using only the whites of the green onions.
2. Add the chicken broth, herbs, salt and pepper and stir well.
   Reduce by half over high heat.
3. Lower the heat to medium and add the chicken, and mix well.
   Taste for salt and pepper. Cook over medium heat for 8 to 10
   minutes or until the chicken is thoroughly heated.
4. Heat in a skillet the olive oil or unsalted butter and add green
   onion tops and the lemon peel. Cook only long enough to heat
   the green tops. Toss with the cooked and drained vermicelli and
   add the grated cheese. Add salt and cracked pepper to taste.
5. Serve the chicken, its broth and the vegetables over the spaghetti with additional herbs sprinkled on top.

Serves 4 to 6

CHICKEN RINGS WITH MUSHROOMS

3 tablespoons unsalted butter or margarine
3 tablespoons flour
1½ cups milk
salt and pepper
5 egg whites
6 cups, cooked chicken, cut up very fine
5 hard-boiled eggs
1 cup cracker crumbs

1. Mix the butter and flour in a small saucepan over low heat. Stirring all the while, add the milk, and whisk until all lumps are gone. Add the salt and pepper.
2. Whip the egg whites with a pinch of salt until the whites are stiff, but not separated.
3. Fold the egg whites into the butter-flour-milk mixture.
4. Mix the chicken with the mashed hard-boiled eggs and fold into the egg white mixture. Season highly with salt and pepper.
6. Fill 8 well-oiled rings (or 1 8-cup oiled ring mold) with the chicken mixture. Bake in a pan of hot water ⅔ full for about 15 to 20 minutes or until firm.
7. Loosen the sides with a knife carefully. Turn out and serve with sautéed garlic mushrooms in the center.

SAUTÉED GARLIC MUSHROOMS

1 tablespoon vegetable oil
1 package fresh mushrooms, sliced
2 cloves garlic
1 teaspoon each: salt, pepper and thyme
½ cup dry white wine or vermouth

1. Heat the oil and sauté the sliced mushrooms, garlic, pepper and thyme for several minutes.
2. Add the dry white wine or vermouth and cook on high heat for 5 minutes. Remove and discard the garlic.
3. Taste for seasoning, adding salt and pepper if necessary.

FRIED CHICKEN, SOUTHERN STYLE

There are all kinds of ways to "oven-fry" and "no-fat-fry" chicken these days. Fried chicken is chicken that is fried, and there is no getting around it. There are a few hints to make it less fatty, with less cholesterol, and a little less caloric. Vegetable oil has less cholesterol than solid shortening, and some vegetable oils have none. The chicken skin and the flour from the breading also adds the fat and calories. You cannot successfully fry chicken without its skin, but you don't have to eat it once the chicken is fried. Always get the oil hot before adding the food to be fried, or the food will absorb too much oil. This is true even of stir-frying or tempura. Always drain the fried food on absorbent paper towels when it is done.

> **1 medium 4 to 6 pound chicken, cut up**
> **1 paper or plastic bag**
> **2 cups white flour**
> **1 teaspoon thyme**
> **salt and pepper**
> **2 cups vegetable oil**

1. Wash and dry the chicken pieces. Put the flour in the bag with the salt and pepper and thyme, and shake well. Add the dried chicken pieces, the largest pieces first, and shake well to coat.
2. Heat the oil until a bread piece turns brown before the count of ten. The oil must not be smoking or it will be too hot, and the chicken will not cook all the way through.
3. Add the largest pieces to the hot oil first, turning often. When the pieces are browned, lower the heat to medium and continue cooking. Each large piece will take about 5 or 6 minutes. Remove to paper towels and drain well.
4. Salt and pepper while hot. Herbed or garlic salt sprinkled on while the chicken is still hot is wonderful.

Serves 4 to 6

"WHITE" GRAVY OR "CHICKEN" GRAVY

1. After all of the chicken is fried, turn the heat off and pour out all but 2 tablespoons of the fat, leaving the unburned residue. Add an equal amount of flour to the skillet (2 tablespoons), and stir with a whisk until the fat and the flour are incorporated. With the heat still off of the skillet, add 2 cups milk to the flour and the fat and whisk thoroughly to remove all lumps. Turn the heat back on to medium, and heat to the boiling point, whisking constantly. Cook one or two minutes until the raw smell of the flour is gone. Cool and serve over rice or over biscuits.

ROASTED CHICKEN

We roasted chicken the same way we cooked turkeys for Thanksgiving, and it makes a nicer, more evenly moist bird. During the War years of the early 40's, there was no tinfoil, but today's aluminum foil is readily available, and it works far better than the old roasters we had for our chickens and turkeys. The size chickens we get today are generally all about the same, usually 4 to 6 pounds each. There is something more festive about a whole roasted chicken than its roasted parts, especially if the whole chicken is on a platter with lots of fresh herbs and cherry tomatoes garnishing it. It is quite easy to do too, and it's not very expensive.

> **1 medium to large chicken, whole**
> **1 medium onion, peeled and cut in half**
> **3 stalks of celery, cut in half**
> **olive or vegetable oil**
> **salt and pepper**

1. Remove the neck and giblets from inside the bird and for this recipe, discard them. Fill the cavity with the onion and celery. Pour a little oil over the chicken and rub it all over the bird. Salt and pepper on top of the oil.
2. Wrap the chicken very tight in foil and put in a heavy pan in the oven. Roast at 350° for approximately one hour or until the juices run clear when the leg is moved.
3. Remove the foil from the breast of the chicken, and turn the oven to 375°. Roast the chicken until the breast is nice and brown, basting occasionally with a large kitchen spoon with some of the juices.
4. Remove from the oven and let rest 10 minutes before carving.

Approximately 4 servings

LAMB

My grandfather raised sheep when he was a boy, so we couldn't have lamb in the house. Occasionally, my grandmother would roast a lamb leg early in the morning in the summer, leaving all the doors and windows open and an electric fan on, and we would have roast lamb with barbeque sauce for lunch. Our next-door neighbor would get the left-overs. My grandmother said that without the big lamb bone in it, the lamb would not smell and taste as strong as if it were cooked in it, so it helps to know your butcher or your bones and remove it. It cooks faster too without the bone. It was our secret lunch, and we wonder if my grandfather ever really knew.

ROASTED LEG OF LAMB WITH BARBEQUE SAUCE

6 to 8 pound boneless leg of lamb
4 cloves of garlic, peeled and left whole
salt and fresh cracked pepper

1. When the bone is removed from the lamb leg, it will lie flat. Lightly salt and pepper it. Insert the garlic cloves in the flesh in the fattest parts, and roll it back up as though it still had a hip bone. There is no need to tie it.
2. Roast it uncovered at 375° for 20 minutes to the pound. Remove from the oven and let it rest for 10 minutes. Slice thin and serve with the following barbeque sauce.

Note: Some meat departments sell boneless whole lamb legs already tied up in netting. Don't untie the netting, just roast the lamb at 20 minutes per pound. Remove the netting 15 minutes after you take the cooked lamb from the oven, and slice the lamb thin.

BARBEQUE SAUCE

2 cups ketchup
2 cups hot water
1 lemon, cut in slices
1 whole onion, peeled and chopped
1 tablespoon brown sugar
1 tablespoon dark molasses
1 tablespoon smooth peanut butter

1. Mix the ketchup and hot water. Squeeze the juice of the lemons through your hands, catching and discarding the seeds. Drop the lemon slices in the sauce and the peeled and chopped onions.
2. Add the rest of the ingredients, including the peanut butter, stirring well.
3. Cook over medium to low heat uncovered until it is reduced by half and very thick, stirring occasionally. Remove the lemon slices with a slotted spoon. Serve the sauce over the roasted lamb slices.

Note: This is a great sandwich on toasted homemade bread or you can give the leftovers to your neighbor.

LAMB STEW

*Our neighbor made a wonderful stew with the left-over roasted lamb.
Everything that went into the stew was itself a left-over: cooked cubed
potatoes, cooked carrots, and cooked English peas. She used lots of curry,
chutney, and golden raisins. We thought she was amazing. She never
travelled back then like she does now, but she had all these wild ideas!
These portions are easily changed should you not happen on all these left-
overs. Just be sure that all the ingredients you add to the cooked lamb are
also cooked. I have here substituted sweet red peppers for the carrots, both
for taste and for color.*

        2 teaspoons vegetable oil
        1 red onion, chopped
        2 cups fresh mushrooms, chopped
        1 medium red bell pepper, sliced or chopped
        2 cups cooked lamb cut in small pieces
        2 cups cooked potatoes (approximately), cubed
        1 cup cooked English peas
        1 jar Major Grey's mango chutney
        1 cup golden raisins
        1 tablespoon curry powder
        1 teaspoon dry mustard
        8 to 10 ounces beef stock, or beef consommé
        salt and pepper to taste

1. In a large Dutch oven, heat the oil and add the onions, mush-
    rooms, and red bell pepper to the oil, and sauté until the veg-
    etables are wilted.
2. Add the lamb, potatoes, chutney, and golden raisins, and cook
    over medium heat stirring occasionally for 8 to 10 minutes or
    until hot.
3. Add the curry powder and dry mustard to the beef stock or
    consommé, and stir until the dry ingredients are dissolved. Add
    to the lamb and vegetables, and mix well.
4. Continue to cook uncovered over medium heat, stirring occa-
    sionally until the liquid is reduced to ¼ cup or less. Season with
    salt and pepper.

Serves 4 to 6

*Note: If you didn't use potatoes, serve over cooked white, brown, or
yellow rice.*

PORK

PORK CHOPS ALABAMA

6 large center-cut pork chops
1 medium onion, sliced medium thin
2 cloves garlic, minced
6 large tomatoes, peeled, seeded, and chopped, or 1 large can
  crushed tomatoes, drained
1½ cups chicken broth
1 tablespoon thyme
salt and pepper to taste

1. Brown the pork chops on all sides. Drain off any rendered fat.
2. Add the rest of the ingredients to the skillet or Dutch oven, cover and cook over medium heat for one hour or until very tender. Can be done ahead and reheated later.
3. Serve over rice.

Serves 6

PORK CHOPS AND APPLESAUCE

It was unusual in our family to have pork chops and anything else but applesauce. Pork was readily available during the war for our family, and I still serve it today. It certainly is one of the most versatile meats there is, easily being adapted from Oriental to Alabama. It cooks quickly and easily, and it isn't very expensive.

> **6 large center-cut pork chops**
> **4 Granny Smith apples, chopped coarse**
> **3 cups apple juice**
> **juice of one lemon**
> **1 medium onion, chopped**
> **1 clove garlic**
> **salt and pepper to taste**

1. Brown the pork chops on both sides in a hot skillet. Remove to an oven-proof dish.
2. Sauté the onions and apples in the fat that is rendered, or pour off the pork fat and add 1 tablespoon vegetable oil. The apples and onions should be limp, but not stewed.
3. Add with the rest of the ingredients to the pork chops. Cover very tight with foil or foil and a lid and bake at 325° for one hour or until the chops are very tender. (The larger they are, the longer this will take).
4. Serve the pork chops and applesauce with boiled or baked potatoes or rice or pasta.

Serves 3 to 6

SEAFOOD CASSEROLE

"Casseroles" were typically in the post-war 50's, but the one here for a "seafood casserole" was the forte of a local caterer, and no ladies' luncheon was complete without it. Seafood or fish (except for salmon) in my grandmother's house was unusual, because only the very rich and the very poor ate seafood, and we were neither. During the war, there were very few freezers even in the grocery stores or what we called the "markets". Fresh fish were sold at The Redmont Market where we shopped, and except for this seafood casserole, I never knew anyone who really ate the fish or shellfish displayed in the cases there. The Redmont Market was a treat to visit. It had sawdust on the floor, and a clerk waited on you. There was a woman there whose name was Sally, and while Mother and my grandmother shopped, Sally explained to me about the fish, which were trout mostly, and since I came to about eye-level with the iced, wide-eyed

trout (and occasionally a red snapper or two), I found them pretty scary. Sally, in her worldly wisdom, always reassured me not only of their demise, but also of their being "good eatin' ", something years later that has served me well. Thanks, Sally.

SEAFOOD CASSEROLE

2 pounds uncooked small scallops
2 pounds cooked shrimp, medium size
2 pounds cooked lobster meat, cut into bite-sizes
1 package (about 4 cups) fresh mushrooms, sliced
1 onion, chopped
1 stick unsalted butter
2 cups white flour
1½ cups chicken broth (or 2 cans of good chicken broth)
¼ cup dry white wine
1 can tomato paste
1 tablespoon Worcestershire sauce
1 tablespoon nutmeg
few dashes of Tabasco sauce
¼ cup dry sherry
1 cup toasted sliced almonds

1. Cook the scallops in 3 cups of water with 1 teaspoon salt for about 2 to 3 minutes or until the scallops are opaque. Remove with a slotted spoon to a platter to cool, and reserve the liquid.
2. Cook the mushrooms and onions in 1 tablespoon butter (or vegetable oil) in a Dutch oven or large casserole. With a slotted spoon, remove to the pan with the scallops.
3. Melt the rest of the butter in the casserole over medium high heat. Add the flour all at once, and stir well with a whisk or a fork to incorporate. Cook the flour and butter for about 5 minutes, being careful not to brown it.
4. Add the chicken broth, the dry white wine, and 1 cup of the reserved liquid from the scallops stirring or whisking constantly to prevent lumps. Add the tomato paste, Worcestershire, nutmeg, and Tabasco, stirring constantly. Cook for several minutes. Let cool completely.
5. Add the cooked, cooled seafood, the sautéed mushrooms and onions, and refrigerate overnight. If the mixture has absorbed all of the liquid, add ½ cup additional chicken broth with the dry sherry, and stir in carefully. Top with the almonds. Heat in a 350° oven 30 to 45 minutes or until bubbling.

Serves 10 to 12

Note: Serve on toast points or rice.

DESSERTS

APPLESAUCE CAKE

Originally, this was made with our own homemade applesauce, but the chunky kind in the markets today works fine. This is a quick-mix cake that is not too sweet.

>   **2 cups flour**
>   **1 teaspoon soda**
>   **1 teaspoon salt**
>   **1 cup sugar**
>   **1 teaspoon each: cinnamon, nutmeg and allspice**
>   **½ teaspoon ground cloves**
>   **½ stick unsalted butter, softened**
>   **1 cup sweetened applesauce (chunky)**
>   **1 egg**
>   **1 cup golden raisins**
>   **½ cup chopped pecans**

1. Mix the dry ingredients together in a mixer, then add the butter, and applesauce, and continue to beat on medium speed for 2 minutes, scraping the bowl often.
2. Add the egg, raisins, and chopped nuts and beat 1 minute or until well mixed.
3. Pour into an oiled loaf pan or an oiled 8" square pan, and bake at 350° for 45 minutes to 1 hour, or until a straw in the middle comes out clean.
4. Cool and ice with the following 7-minute icing.

Seven-Minute Icing:
1. Over boiling water in the top of a double boiler put: 1 egg white, ¾ cup sugar, pinch of cream of tartar, 3 tablespoons water, and beat for 7 minutes or until icing "peaks." A hand-held electric mixer can be used instead of the whisk.
2. Let cool. Fold in ¼ cup chopped raisins, ¼ cup pecans, and 1 teaspoon vanilla.
3. Ice cooled cake.

BRIDE'S CAKE

If you want a white cake, use vegetable shortening, because the unsalted butter will turn the cake a light yellow. If it doesn't matter to you, use the butter because the taste is much better than the shortening.

> **1 cup vegetable shortening (or butter: see above)**
> **3 cups sugar**
> **grated peel of one lemon**
> **grated peel of one orange**
> **1 teaspoon almond flavoring**
> **1 cup water**
> **6 cups sifted flour**
> **1 cup cream**
> **2 teaspoons baking powder**
> **1 teaspoon salt**
> **6 egg whites**

1. Cream the shortening and sugar. Add the flavorings and ½ cup of the water, and beat for another 5 minutes.
2. Sift 2 cups of the flour into the mixer and beat for 5 minutes.
3. Alternate the water and cream and the remaining flour sifted with the baking powder and salt until they are all incorporated.
4. Beat the egg whites in a separate bowl, and fold into the cake batter taking care not to deflate the whites, but mixing well.
5. Pour into two oiled 8" cake pans, and bake at 325° for 45 minutes or until the cake tests done in the middle. Let cool in the pans 10 minutes, then remove from the pans and let cool on an oiled rack.

Note: This cake can be iced with any white icing, including "Seven-Minute Icing."

ANNIE'S FIVE-EGG CAKE (GOLD CAKE)

The cake recipe here was the recipe from our friend, Mrs. Lewis, from Leeds, Alabama. Everyone swore she would take the recipe to the grave with her. Years ago she left it to her sister-in-law who just recently sent it to me. Mrs. Lewis made wonderful cakes: coconut, Lane, and caramel — all with this yellow cake.

> **2 sticks unsalted butter**
> **2 cups sugar**
> **1 cup milk**
> **3 cups flour, sifted**
> **3 teaspoons baking powder**
> **5 eggs, separated**
> **1 teaspoon vanilla**
> **1 teaspoon lemon extract**

1. Cream butter and sugar, and add milk, flour, egg yolks and flavorings. Beat on low speed 3 to 4 minutes or until all is well incorporated, scraping down the bowl several times.
2. Beat the egg whites until they are stiff but not separating and fold into the cake batter.
3. For layers: put in 3 floured 9" cake pans and bake at 325° for about 30 minutes or until a straw in the center comes out clean.
4. For one single cake to be split and filled: put in floured 9" cake pan and bake at 325° for about 1 hour or until a straw in the center comes out clean.
5. Let sit in the pans for 10 minutes before unmolding onto a greased rack.

CARAMEL ICING

1. Melt 1 stick butter and add 1 cup dark brown sugar. Bring to a boil, and stir for 2 minutes or until thick.
2. Lower heat and let cool slightly. Add ¼ cup cream, and beat with a whisk until smooth. Add in 3 cups confectioners sugar and blend until smooth and of spreading consistency, adding more cream if necessary.

CHOCOLATE ICING

1. Stir together 4 cups sugar, 2 tablespoons white corn syrup, 2 sticks unsalted butter, 1 cup milk, 5 squares Bakers chocolate, until melted.

(Annie's Five-Egg Cake, continued on next page)

(Annie's Five-Egg Cake, continued)

2. Cook over very low heat, stirring for 4 minutes. Let cool and beat until spreading consistency.

LANE CAKE FILLING

1. Put all of the following in a double boiler and cook stirring occasionally until thick: 8 egg yolks, 1 stick melted unsalted butter, ¾ cup sugar, 1 teaspoon cornstarch, 1 cup golden raisins, 1 cup toasted pecans, 4 ounces port or cream sherry or bourbon and 2 teaspoons vanilla.
2. Fill the cake with Lane Cake Filling and ice with Seven-Minute Icing mixed with 2 cups coconut.

MRS. LEWIS' COCONUT CAKE

This meant a holiday to all of us. Christmas, Easter, and even Thanksgiving were all the better because of Mrs. Lewis' coconut cake coming from Leeds. In those days in the 40's, coconut was hard to come by, especially during the war, so this was a very exciting dessert. It still is special to me now even in the middle of the summer. Mrs. Lewis made the coconut milk by steeping chopped coconut in milk, then straining it, reserving both the coconut and the milk. Today coconut milk is available in the grocery stores usually by the cocktail bar supplies.

5 cups flour
3 cups sugar
2 teaspoons baking powder
1 teaspoon baking soda
1 teaspoon salt
1 cup buttermilk
1 cup coconut milk
1½ cups vegetable shortening
1 cup egg whites (about 8)
grated peel and juice of 1 lemon
1 teaspoon vanilla

1. Combine the dry ingredients in a mixer bowl and mix thoroughly on low speed.
2. Add the shortening alternately with the milk and coconut milk and beat on low for several minutes, stirring down the sides occasionally.
3. With the mixer running, add the unbeaten egg whites to the batter and continue mixing until the batter is smooth. Add the lemon peel, lemon juice, and vanilla, and beat for another 3 minutes.
4. Divide the batter between three 9" cake pans that have been greased and floured. Bake at 350° for 30 to 45 minutes or until a straw inserted in the center of each cake comes out clean. Let cool in pans for 10 minutes, then unmold on a greased rack.

Lemon Filling:
1. Mix 2 cups sugar, 2 tablespoons unsalted butter, ¼ cup fresh lemon juice and some of the grated lemon peel, and 4 whole eggs.
2. Cook in the top of a double boiler, stirring occasionally until thick enough to coat a spoon.
3. Chill before spreading in between the layers.

(Mrs. Lewis' Coconut Cake, continued on next page)

(Mrs. Lewis' Coconut Cake, continued)

Icing:
1. A Seven-Minute Icing can be used here, or the following whipped cream icing can be used. Keep the cake in the refrigerator if using the whipped cream.
2. Beat 1 quart whipping cream with ½ cup confectioners sugar and 2 teaspoons vanilla until stiff. Ice the filled and stacked cakes at once and keep refrigerated.
3. If desired, sprinkle coconut over the tops and sides of the icing and decorate the top with mint, lemon slice or strawberries.

DEVIL'S FOOD CAKE

This was my grandmother's recipe, and on the bottom of the worn 3" x 5" card, she had written, "This is very good." She glazed it with a rich chocolate glaze and served it with homemade peach ice cream in the summers. Daddy was in the soft-drink business during the War, so we always had sugar and chocolate. This cake was very popular in the neighborhood since chocolate was so seldom seen.

> **2 cups sugar**
> **¾ cup butter (1½ sticks)**
> **5 eggs, separated**
> **1 scant teaspoon baking soda dissolved in 1 tablespoon hot water**
> **1 teaspoon baking powder**
> **2½ cups flour**
> **¾ cup buttermilk (or sour milk)**
> **1 teaspoon vanilla**
> **8 ounces Baker's chocolate, melted**

1. Cream butter and sugar and add beaten yolks and the dissolved baking soda. Mix flour with the baking powder and add to the batter alternately with buttermilk; add vanilla.
2. Add the melted chocolate to the cake mix and beat for several minutes until all is incorporated.
3. Beat the egg whites and fold into the cake mixture.
4. Divide the batter between 3 greased and floured 9" cake pans, and bake in a 350° oven for 25 to 30 minutes or until the cake begins to pull away from the sides and a straw in the middle of the cake comes out clean.

Chocolate Glaze:
1. Melt 1 bag mini-chocolate chips (12 ounces) and stir to smooth out all chips.
2. Add ¼ cup boiling water all at once and stir with a whisk for several minutes until it stops "seizing." If it does not smooth out after several minutes, add more boiling water by the tablespoon, mixing after each addition until it becomes smooth and glossy.
3. Pour over the cooled cake layers while the glaze is still slightly warm. Let the glaze drip down the sides of the cake in a random pattern.

GINGERBREAD CAKE WITH MAPLE GLAZE

The original for this moist gingerbread called for lard and butter. I have deleted the lard, and it still tastes great. This is a winter dessert to me, but I have friends who make it year round. In the summer, glaze it with a little frozen lemonade concentrate mixed with confectioners sugar to a smooth white glaze instead of the maple syrup. If you put the confectioners sugar in the bowl first and add the melted, undiluted lemonade to the sugar, you will find it is easy to mix together to a glaze. The boiling hot water is what makes this cake so moist and tender, but once you pour it into the batter, turn the machine on low to incorporate the hot water or it will splash out all over the counter. Stir it all up from the bottom with a big spoon before pouring it into the cake pan.

> 1 stick unsalted butter
> ½ cup dark brown sugar
> 3 eggs, beaten
> 1 cup dark molasses (unsulphured is best)
> 2½ cups flour
> 2 teaspoons ground cinnamon
> 2 teaspoons ground or grated fresh ginger
> 1½ teaspoons baking soda
> 1 teaspoon salt
> 1 cup boiling water
> ¼ cup real maple syrup

1. Cream butter and sugar, and add beaten eggs and molasses. Mix well on low speed.
2. Mix together all of the dry ingredients and add to the batter. On low speed, carefully add the boiling water into the batter and mix well. Stir once or twice with a large spoon before pouring into the greased 8" square pan.
3. Bake at 325° for 30 minutes or until the middle springs back to the touch and a straw inserted into the cake comes out clean.
4. While still warm, glaze with ¼ cup Vermont maple syrup, poking small holes into the cake for the syrup to go into. Serve warm with sweetened whipped cream.

Note: This recipe can easily be doubled. Bake in a 10" x 13" greased baking pan or Pyrex dish. For Pyrex, lower the heat to 300°.

APRICOT DREAMS

These were a lot harder to make before the days of food processors. We had to use a grinder and grind the ingredients several times. A food processor will turn it to mush if you process it for too long, so be sure to get it to a chunky consistency or it won't stick together.

> **1 pound dried glazed apricots**
> **1 medium orange, cut into thick slices, seeds removed**
> **juice of one orange**
> **juice of one lemon**
> **2 cups sugar**
> **pecan halves**

1. Process the apricots and whole orange together. Add the orange juice, lemon juice and sugar and process just until mixed.
2. Cook over low heat, stirring until the juice has cooked out. Cool.
3. Drop from a teaspoon on a mound of granulated sugar. Roll into a ball and place on a cookie sheet lined with waxed paper. Top each ball with a pecan half and let dry at room temperature overnight.

CHOCOLATE DROPS

These are very easy, and practically everyone made them for Christmas after the War was over in the 40's, but I never tired of them. The type of cocoa makes all the difference. Be sure to get a good quality Dutch-process cocoa which is not so bitter as the plain.

> **3 heaping tablespoons flour**
> **2 heaping tablespoons Dutch-process cocoa**
> **1 can condensed milk**
> **1 package coconut**
> **1 cup pecans**

1. Mix all ingredients and drop on a wax-paper-lined cookie sheet and bake in 300° oven for 15 to 20 minutes or until set.
2. Cool and just before serving, sift Dutch-process cocoa through a tea-strainer onto the cookies. Keep tightly covered.

OTHER DESSERTS FROM THE '40's:

APPLE BROWN BETTY

This was one of my favorite desserts as a child, and in grade school at the old Brooke Hill School for Girls, I would trade away my recess snack, and two desserts for one extra Brown Betty. My teachers never knew this, or I would not have gotten away with it. We ate at tables with a teacher at the head of each table, so trading away had to be done very surreptitiously. Occasionally, some wise teacher would suspect my wiles, and I would be assigned to Miss Ordway, the headmistress's, table, which meant all trades were off. I like Brown Betty today, but without the inherent thrill of the trade, something seems to be lacking in it. It's actually a very wholesome dessert and would make a wonderful breakfast or brunch dish. Oatmeal is quite in vogue today, and that is what really makes this so good, not the trading.

    6 large baking apples (Granny Smith, York, etc.)
    1 cup dark brown sugar
    ½ stick unsalted butter, melted
    1 teaspoon each: cinnamon, nutmeg and cloves
    2 teaspoons vanilla
    pinch salt
    2 cups rolled oats
    ½ cup dark brown sugar
    ½ cup flour
    ½ stick unsalted butter, melted
    pinch salt
    1 teaspoon vanilla, additional

1. Peel and slice the apples into small chunks. Combine the apples, brown sugar, ½ stick melted butter, spices, vanilla, and salt in a large oven-proof bowl and mix thoroughly.
2. Combine the oats, flour, ¼ cup dark brown sugar, ½ stick melted butter, and pinch of salt and mix with a fork until the mixture is very crumbly. Spread the mixture over the apples.
3. Bake at 325°, uncovered, for 30 to 45 minutes or until the apples are tender and the oatmeal mixture is golden brown. If the topping browns too fast before the apples are tender, cover the baking dish loosely with foil and continue baking.

Serves 6 to 8

Note: Serve with sweetened whipped cream or sweetened vanilla yogurt.

BANANA PUDDING

*For as long as I can remember, banana pudding was made with either
vanilla wafers or toasted lady fingers. The vanilla wafers are probably the
most classic. But a homemade custard rather than the packaged custard
mix is immensely better, and not at all difficult to do. I would rather eat
the eggs and milk of the real custard than all those chemical names on the
instant custard and pudding boxes. If you have some banana liqueur, add
a little after the custard is cooked, if you want to gild the lily a bit.*

½ **cup sugar**
2 **tablespoons flour**
3 **cups milk**
3 **eggs, beaten**
1 **tablespoon vanilla**
1 **tablespoon banana brandy, optional**
5 **medium bananas, very ripe with brown sugar spots**
1 **package vanilla wafers (12-ounce size)**
1½ **cups whipping cream, whipped with 1 tablespoon**
   confectioners sugar

1. Put the sugar, flour, and eggs in the top of a double boiler and
   mix well with a whisk. Add in the milk gradually and continue
   mixing over medium heat until the mixture thickens and coats a
   spoon. Add in the vanilla and banana brandy and mix well.
   Remove from the heat. Let cool with a piece of plastic wrap
   touching the custard to prevent a film from forming.
2. Whip the cream with 1 tablespoon confectioners sugar and
   gently fold into the cooled custard mixture.
3. In a glass bowl, slice ⅓ of the bananas to make the first layer
   and top with a layer of vanilla wafers. Add ⅓ of the custard,
   and repeat with the bananas, wafers, and custard until they are
   all used up, ending with the custard. Refrigerate covered for at
   least 4 hours to chill thoroughly. Just before serving, sprinkle
   the top with freshly grated nutmeg.

Serves 6 to 8

FRUIT COBBLERS

Cobblers can be made with fresh peaches, strawberries, blueberries, black-berries, or any combination of fresh fruits, like strawberries and rhubarb, apple and cranberries, etc. My grandmother always made her fruit pies and cobblers by cooking the fillings separate from the crust and then combining them later to keep the crusts and dough crisp and the fruits properly cooked. She even did her pecan and lemon pies this way, and her pies and cobblers were always perfect. Cooking the filling separately helps too if you have a lot of fruit to get rid of and no time to make cobbler or pie dough. Just cook the fillings, put in Ball or Mason jars with headroom to swell, and freeze until the baking day comes along.

6 cups peeled and sliced peaches (apples, etc.)
2 whole lemons, sliced thin, and seeds removed
2 cups white sugar
1 cup brown sugar
½ stick unsalted butter
2 teaspoons each: cinnamon, nutmeg and cardamom
2 teaspoons vanilla
pinch of salt

Cobbler:
1 cup sugar
2 cups flour
2 teaspoons baking powder
1 teaspoon salt
1 teaspoon each: cinnamon, nutmeg and vanilla
½ to 1 cup milk

1. In a boiler on top of the stove, cook the peaches (or other fruit) with the butter, cinnamon, nutmeg, and salt until the fruit is just barely tender. If the fruit does not produce enough liquid, add up to 1 cup of apple or white grape juice. Remove from the heat into a baking dish
2. Combine the sugar, flour, baking powder, salt, cinnamon, nutmeg, and vanilla in a bowl. Add enough milk to make a very moist biscuit dough. Put the dough by large tablespoons on top of the fruit and bake at 350° for 30 to 45 minutes or until the biscuits are done and are golden brown.

Serves 8 to 10

Note: for strawberries and softer fruits, this stove-top cooking time will only be a few minutes; for apples and quinces and the hard fruits, it can take as long as 8 or 10 minutes.

THE 1950s

The 50's brought a whole new generation of "baby-boomers", a direct result of the end of World War II. Fathers were home from the War, and new houses were being built everywhere. Businesses flourished with their new employees. Soon there were new automobiles, and television came into its own. Our lives began to change drastically. We didn't seem to have time or the need to "can" fresh vegetables; freezers were the new thing, and frozen foods were readily becoming available. A new breezy style of entertaining called "Open Houses," and "Cocktail Parties" became quite in vogue, and recipes for "finger foods" quickly replaced Fannie Farmer, and "Mrs. Allen". Since the 50's were my teenage years, the hallmark of the era in my mind was always the "Casserole": that hodgepodge of everything imaginable in one dish, served with a green salad, and still, in my home, cornbread.

Most of us shudder at the thought of a "Casserole", and I had quite a few friends, boys mostly, who would not eat any food that "touched" another food. I think this was a rather harsh reaction to an overly-ambitious "Casserole Mother", but it is understandable.

There were, however, a few good "Casseroles", not many, but a few, that have lasted, and not those with the crushed potato chips on the top, thank goodness. The few that commemorate here that decade of change, the 50's, are still agreeable, still timely, and even good and good for you. They are mostly vegetable casseroles, and we usually would have a whole ham, or a lamb leg, or a turkey or roast beef, and then the ubiquitous "casserole." You could add a simple roast chicken, or broiled fish, or even a steak now and then to make matters a little more rounded. But one thing "touching" is enough at any one meal.

BAKED BEAN CASSEROLE

This was my mother's hallmark. She was always asked to bring it or fix it or tell it to someone. It went with our barbeques, whether they were the real outdoor barbeques in those huge chimney pits that we all had in the backyard, or an "oven-barbeque" such as our barbequed leg of lamb that we had every Thursday night. The big "lima beans" are totally different in taste and appearance from the Boston or New Orleans beans, and I always thought it had to be cooked in a red casserole dish, because that is the way I saw it for decades. You can use any large casserole dish, even Pyrex if you can cover it. The key to these was the long, slow, slow cooking.

4 cans large lima beans, reserving liquid from 2 of them
2 cups ketchup
¼ cup molasses
2 medium onions, chopped fine
salt and pepper
4 to 6 pieces of rendered bacon

1. Cook the bacon in a skillet long enough to render most of the fat off, but not to crisp the bacon.
2. Put all ingredients in a casserole with the bacon on top.
3. Cook tightly covered in a 325° oven for 2 hours. If more liquid is needed as they cook, you can add chicken broth. If the casserole is tightly covered, the liquid should not cook out during the 2 hours.

Serves 8 to 10 generously

BEETS & BEANS

This was not a "casserole" per say, but they went together in our family like salt and pepper. I used to keep my love of pickled beets to myself, but once in the shop we ran in the 80's, two of us decided to try pickled beets out on the customers instead of just eating them ourselves. They were enormously popular among men. We served them a lot after that, and they remained on our all-time-favorites list. We baked them at the shop in tinfoil in the oven, but now at home, I microwave them in a covered Pyrex dish until they are tender, and they keep their pretty red color better than boiling them.

> **1 bunch red beets (about 2 pounds)**
> **2 tablespoons sugar**
> **1 cup red wine (or balsamic) vinegar**
> **salt and pepper**
> **1 bunch fresh green beans, the baby-ones preferably**
> **2 cups chicken broth or 1 cup broth and 1 cup water**
> **1 medium onion**
> **fresh thyme or 1 teaspoon dried**

1. Scrub, trim, and peel the beets. Slice into half-dollar-size slices. Bake or microwave until a knife is easily pierced through the fattest part.
2. Add the sugar to the vinegar.
3. Remove the beets from the oven and immediately pour the vinegar-sugar mixture over it while the beets are still hot. Let cool.
4. Wash, trim and, if necessary, string the green beans. Cook them over high heat uncovered in the chicken stock and water mixture to which you have added the onion and the thyme. This should take about 20 minutes depending on the size of the beans. They should be fork tender, but not limp.
5. Let cool in the liquid. Drain before serving.
6. Serve the beets and beans in the same dish or platter adding salt and pepper as necessary. Sprinkle both with fresh thyme, and serve hot or cold.

CABBAGE CASSEROLE

This is probably my favorite vegetable, and years later Evans, my youngest child, still would ask for "some more cabbage rather than dessert." Cabbage is always in the market, always inexpensive, low-calorie and filling, and it is good for you. You can vary this recipe by using red and green cabbage or all red, or even Savoy cabbage, but its original self was plain, garden-variety green cabbage. We always had it with an all-vegetable-meal, but you can serve this with pot roast, ham, chicken, and of course, with corned beef.

> **1 large head of cabbage, outer leaves removed**
> **2 cups chicken broth**
> **2 cups water**
> **1 medium onion, chopped**
> **2 stalks celery, chopped**
> **1 clove garlic, smashed**
> **1 tablespoon fresh herbs: basil, thyme, caraway**
> **salt and pepper**

1. Chop or shred the cabbage just until coarse.
2. Heat a 2-quart casserole and add the onion, celery, and garlic, stirring constantly to prevent burning. Cook until they are just limp and sweated.
3. Add the chicken broth and the rest of the ingredients. Cook uncovered over medium to high heat until all of the liquid is evaporated. Salt and pepper to taste. The cabbage should be tender and not raw. Cook a little longer if it is still crisp and raw.

Serves 4 to 6

Note: This can be done a day in advance and reheated later.

CABBAGE: SWEET & SOUR

This is usually done with red cabbage, and we usually had it in the winter months though today quite a few excellent restaurants like Jeremiah Towers' STARS and Wolfgang Puck's SPAGO have been serving this old favorite all year round; but with them, this vegetable is all dolled up in balsamic vinegar and goat cheese for a warm salad. It is delicious like that. Balsamic vinegar is aged in balsam wood in one place in Italy, and we never heard of it until the 70's, but it is a wonderful, woody, deep flavor that holds up perfectly against this strong member of the vegetable family.

1 large head red cabbage, outer leaves removed
4 slices of bacon
1 tablespoon brown sugar
1 teaspoon salt
¼ cup vinegar (red or balsamic)
additional salt and pepper to taste

1. Fry the bacon until it is crisp.
2. Remove from the skillet and drain.
3. Let the bacon drippings cool a bit, and add the brown sugar, vinegar and salt, stirring until the sugar is dissolved.
4. Shred the cabbage until it is still just coarse.
5. Add it to the skillet and heat through.
6. Add additional salt and pepper to taste.
7. Garnish the top with the crumbled bacon.

Serves 4 to 6

Note: Optional: Top each salad plate with 1 ounce goat cheese, and let it melt into the warm salad. Serve at once.

CORN CASSEROLE

You can lighten this up by using skim milk and a light bread, and even though it won't have the richness of taste of the original recipe from my grandmother, it will still be good if your corn is the best quality white corn, like Silver Queen or Truckers' Favorite. In the winter, you could use a good brand of canned white corn. My grandmother used Pet milk and homemade bread crumbs. You can easily double or triple this recipe.

> **3 cups white corn**
> **1 cup milk**
> **1 cup bread crumbs**
> **1 red bell pepper, chopped**
> **1 medium onion, chopped**
> **2 tablespoons oil or margarine or butter**
> **2 whole eggs, beaten**

1. Sauté the bell pepper and the onion in the oil or butter. Add the corn and the rest of the ingredients. Salt and pepper to taste.
2. Add the beaten eggs and stir well. Bake at 325° for 20 to 30 minutes or until set.

Serves 4 to 6

CORN FRITTERS

These are corn versions of the French beignets, and we actually did eat them with confectioners sugar sprinkled on them even though we served them as a vegetable.

3 cups white corn
4 tablespoons flour
4 tablespoons butter or margarine
½ cup milk (or skim milk)
salt and pepper
dash Tabasco sauce

1. In a bowl with the back of a fork, blend the flour and butter or margarine to a paste, add the milk gradually stirring vigorously with the fork or with a whisk to prevent any lumps. It should be quite thick.
2. Add the corn, salt and pepper to the mixture and incorporate together, adding the drop of Tabasco sauce.
3. Bring about 3 inches of oil in a boiler to bubbling, but not smoking, temperature. Add rounded tablespoons of the fritter batter several at a time, but not overcrowding the pan. Let cook until golden on all sides.
4. Remove and drain on paper towels. Keep warm on paper towels in a low oven while the others are cooking.
5. Serve with confectioners sugar or with just additional salt and pepper.

Serves 4 to 6

CORN-OFF-THE-COB

We had this during those no-front-teeth years, and we called it "Baby-Tooth-Corn", but somehow, I think "Corn-off-the-Cob" is a better name.

6 ears white corn
½ cup milk (regular or skim)
4 tablespoons butter or margarine
salt and pepper
dash of Tabasco sauce

1. Cook the corn husked and in water to cover or in the husk in the microwave until it smells and feels cooked. It will not be tough when it is done, but give in to a fork pressed in one "tooth." Cut the kernels off of the cobs.
2. Scrape the cobs to get the corn milk. Add all except the cobs to a skillet and cook covered over low heat only until good and hot. This can be done ahead and heated later.

Serves 4 to 6

EGGPLANT CASSEROLE

Stella Lockwood, my next-door neighbor in my childhood days, was the only person I knew who ever had eggplant, and we thought she was THE gourmet of the neighborhood (She was, too). Later, in my New Orleans years, I was glad I had become acquainted with eggplant, because it is really a Creole and Cajun staple. The small, home-grown ones are best, but you can use the big ones during the winter when eggplant is hard to find. Eggplant tends to be very bitter, so it is necessary to boil it in salted water to calm it down a bit. It's worth the effort.

> 1½ to 2 pounds eggplant
> 2 eggs, beaten
> 1 cup milk
> 2 tablespoons olive oil, butter, or margarine
> 1 medium onion, chopped
> 1 large clove garlic, minced
> 1½ cups cracker or bread crumbs
> 1 can stewed tomatoes, drained
> salt and pepper

1. Peel the eggplant and cut into cubes. Boil in salted water (1 tablespoon per quart) for 8 to 10 minutes. Remove from heat and drain.
2. Sauté the onion, garlic, drained eggplant in the oil or butter until the onions are limp. Let cool slightly.
3. Add the beaten eggs and the rest of the ingredients, reserving ½ cup cracker crumbs for the top.
4. Bake in a 325° oven for 30 minutes or until it is bubbling in the center.

Serves 4 to 6

OKRA, TOMATOES, & CORN

The oft-maligned vegetables, okra and eggplant, are really wonderful if they are cooked right. Maybe it's just the name: "okra," that conjures up something weird, but I loved it as a child, loved it in New Orleans, and love it today because it is so versatile. If you boil it, it becomes gummy, hence, "gumbo" must always have okra to be real gumbo, but sautéed quickly, breaded and fried, in a casserole like this, okra is trustworthy, because you're not boiling it for a length of time. It's very easy to grow in the south in the summer, just be sure to cut it when it's small, or you can't cut it at all.

> **2 pounds fresh okra**
> **6 ears white corn**
> **6 to 8 fresh tomatoes (or 1 large can crushed tomatoes)**
> **1 can tomato paste**
> **1 medium onion, chopped**
> **2 stalks celery, chopped**
> **1 large clove garlic, minced**
> **fresh or dried basil, about 4 leaves fresh, 2 teaspoons dried**
> **salt and pepper**

1. Cut the okra into dime-size pieces, discarding the ends.
2. Cook the corn and scrape all of the kernels and the milk from the cob into a bowl.
3. If using fresh tomatoes, peel and seed them by cutting the tomato in half and pushing the seeds out with your thumb.
4. Chop the tomatoes.
5. Heat a deep casserole or Dutch oven and add the onion, celery, garlic, and let these sweat until they are limp, but not burned, stirring constantly.
6. Add the rest of the ingredients. Stir well.
7. Add more salt and pepper if necessary.
8. Bake covered for 30 minutes at 325° or until bubbling hot.

Serves 4 to 6

ONION BAKE

This is a Thanksgiving symbol for us today in our family. It is not the heavy, creamy thing that the 50's seemed to promote, but it is pure onion flavor, and we all love it because it is "real" and not "smothered." It's also good with barbeques or, for a dieter, we serve it instead of potatoes. Vidalias, of course, are the queen of onions, but any yellow onion will do. If you use great big ones, cut them in fourths. The medium to small onions are the easiest to work with and to serve.

> **12 medium to small yellow onions, peeled**
> **2 tablespoons olive oil (or butter)**
> **3 tablespoons Worcestershire sauce**
> **salt and pepper**
> **grated Parmesan cheese**

1. Put the onions on a baking sheet with sides or on foil-lined cookie sheet with a foil lip around the edge.
2. Sprinkle with the olive oil, Worcestershire sauce, salt and pepper. Bake at 325° about 35 to 30 minutes or until the onions are cooked throughout.
3. Serve with the juices, sprinkled with Parmesan cheese.

6 servings

PEAS

FRESH ENGLISH PEAS

Once fresh English peas have been shelled, they quickly lose their sugar content, and thus, most of their wonderful taste. When we were little, we grew peas in early spring, and no one objected to shelling them, because they were so good raw. After all, this is where Mr. Carver got the "peanut". Years later, we had a Vietnamese woman live with us for about a year when Saigon fell in the 70's, and she used to cook raw peas and green beans in sugar, and they were wonderful. The peas tasted like the sugared peanuts that are so readily available today in America. The "English-peas-Vietnamese" and the breaded and sugared "Green Beans Vietnamese" were always served by our Vietnamese friends with the ubiquitous Vietnamese "fish sauce": a wonderful little bowl of 2 tablespoons cider vinegar, 1 teaspoon Vietnamese fish sauce, and a teaspoon of sugar, and one tiny hot pepper floating in it. They ate the English peas with chop sticks, but we could barely keep them on a fork after they were dipped in the fish sauce vinaigrette. The green beans were easier to dip and eat, but we Alabamians still used a fork. Keep an eye out for fresh English peas in the spring, snow peas almost all year around, sugar-snap peas in the summer. Remember to string the snow peas and sugar snaps, or they are a nuisance to eat, chop sticks or forks.

BLACK-EYED PEAS

These are as important to our southern family as red beans and rice to a New Orleanian, or pea soup to a New Yorker, or baked beans to a Bostonian. You will find in this book not only this basic recipe, but a black-eyed pea soup, pâté, cold salad, and if I could, I would make a dessert with them! Recently at a local cafe, I watched how many people ordered black-eyed peas as a side-order with hamburgers, sandwiches, salads, or just black-eyed peas alone with cornbread and ketchup. The owner of the cafe said that at least one-third of his customers order black-eyed peas in some form. Why not? They speak of home, they are easily digested for legumes, they are real food, and fortunately not easily disguised. That's food.

> **1 pound dried or fresh black-eyed peas**
> **4 cups water**
> **4 cups good chicken broth**
> **3 onions, chopped coarse**
> **3 cloves of garlic, chopped or smashed with the side of a knife**
> **ground fresh pepper**
> **salt to taste at the end of the cooking time**

1. If using dried peas, wash them and soak them in cold water overnight.
2. Drain the peas the next morning and proceed with the recipe. If using fresh black-eyed peas, omit the soaking and begin cooking them as directed here.
3. Put all of the ingredients, with the exception of the salt, in a large pot and bring to a boil with the lid on.
4. Remove the lid, lower the heat to medium, cook until the peas begin to soften and burst.
5. If the water evaporates too low, add hot, boiling water to keep the peas at a low boil. Cold water will stop the cooking and toughen the peas. You should have peas that are cooked and soft, slightly bursting, and about one-third of the entire liquid left in the pot.
6. Watch carefully the last hour, and stir the bottom of the pot to keep the peas from sticking.

Serves 6 to 8

Note: Serve with "Black-eyed-pea Relish, following page"

BLACK-EYED-PEA RELISH

This is a "salsa" in today's vernacular. We called it "relish", and if we ever have almost equal amounts of cooked black-eyed peas and this relish left over (an unlikely happenstance, but it can happen), we mix the two, and THEN we call it " black-eyed-pea salsa". What's in a name? This recipe comes from one of our dearest family friends, Carol Graham, who is among the best cooks in our world. She calls it a "topping."

1 or 2 tomatoes, peeled and chopped fine
1 bunch green onions, chopped fine
⅓ cup cider or white vinegar
2 tablespoons sugar
salt and pepper to taste

1. Mix all together. Taste and add whatever is needed of any more of the ingredients.
2. Serve over black-eyed peas. Keep the relish in the refrigerator.

   6 to 8 servings, 1 or 2 tablespoons each

POTATO CAKES

These actually could be included in every decade of these memoirs, but the 50's were such "casserole-and-cocktail" years that I am adding this old favorite, friendly potato cake in the decade of the 50's so that I can give us all kinder memories of the 50's. Actually, in the late 80's and 90's, potato cakes, crab cakes, even black-bean cakes have become quite the darlings of the early 80's "Beurre Blanc Bistros", at least, of the better bistros of that era that lasted by standing the test of time. Potato cakes with sautéed green onions, chopped green tomatoes, and fresh mushrooms on top was and still is one of my favorite Sunday night suppers in my favorite month of January. It would be equally as wonderful in the summer with shrimp or crabmeat instead of the green tomatoes, but we didn't have a lot of shellfish in the 50's, and we had lots of green tomatoes all year round.

> **4 large Idaho potatoes, peeled**
> **¼ cup light olive or vegetable oil**
> **1 medium onion, chopped**
> **4 ounces Parmesan cheese, grated**
> **½ box fresh mushrooms, chopped**
> **3 small green tomatoes, unpeeled and chopped coarse**
> **1 teaspoon each fresh or dried thyme, basil and tarragon**
> **salt and pepper to taste**

1. Grate the potatoes in a food processor grater or on the longest shred possible on a metal grater so that they are thin shoe-strings. Soak the shredded potatoes in cold water to cover for about 10 minutes. Drain and dry well on a clean dishcloth, squeezing out all of the water.
2. Heat the oil in a skillet until it is hot but not smoking. The oil must cover the entire surface of the skillet.
3. Add all of the potatoes to the skillet in a large patty. Press it down with the back of a pancake-turner and cover the skillet with a lid or foil. Salt and pepper lightly.
4. Cook over medium high heat for 15 minutes or until golden. Turn and cook the other side covered for an additional 15 minutes or until this side too is golden. Remove from the skillet onto an oven-proof platter and keep warm in a low (250° oven) while you are sautéeing the tomatoes.
5. Sauté the green tomatoes, fresh mushrooms and the onions in the hot skillet until they begin to wilt. Add the herbs, salt and pepper. Taste carefully for seasoning.
6. Serve over the potato pancake topped with 3 tablespoons sour cream (regular or low-fat), additional fresh or dried herbs and the cheese sprinkled over the top.

Serves 4 to 6

POTATO CROQUETTES

4 large Idaho potatoes, peeled
3 eggs, beaten
3 tablespoons bread crumbs
2 tablespoons milk (regular, low-fat, or skim)
1 small onion, peeled
2 teaspoons chives, fresh or dried
1 small clove garlic, smashed

1. Grate the potatoes and onion into a large bowl. Add the rest of the ingredients to make a thick batter. If the batter is too liquid, dry it out by adding more bread crumbs until you can pick the batter up in your hands.
2. Form into 4 to 6 pancakes depending on the size you want to serve.
3. Heat a skillet with 2 tablespoons unsalted butter or regular margarine or vegetable oil until the fat is hot. Add the potato pancakes a few at a time in order not to crowd the skillet.
4. Cook on both sides until brown and the middle is well cooked. Salt and pepper. Keep warm on paper towels in a very low (200°) oven.

Serves 4 to 6

POTATOES, MASHED

4 large Idaho potatoes, peeled and cut into cubes
2 cups milk (regular, low-fat, or skim)
3 tablespoons unsalted butter or regular margarine
salt and pepper to taste

1. Boil potatoes in enough water to cover. Drain completely. Put them back in the boiling pan with no water and shake over high heat to remove all water from them.
2. Press through a ricer or mash with a potato masher, adding hot milk a little at a time until the potatoes are fluffy and not at all soupy. Season to taste with the butter or margarine, salt and pepper. Keep hot over very hot water with the potatoes partially covered with a lid.

POTATOES ROASTED & TOASTED

6 Idaho baking potatoes, peeled
2 tablespoons vegetable oil (corn or good olive oil) or unsalted
   butter
2 cups crushed plain corn flakes (unsugared)
salt and pepper

1. Cut the peeled whole potatoes into fifty-cent-size circles.
2. Dip the raw potato circles in the olive oil or melted butter and roll the slices in the crushed corn flakes to coat thoroughly.
3. Put the coated potatoes on a lightly oiled foil-lined cookie sheet and roast for 30 minutes at 325° or until the potatoes are tender in the middle. The thickness of the potatoes will determine how long they need to roast.

Serves 4 to 6

SPINACH & TOMATO SCALLOP

2 packages frozen spinach, cooked and drained well
4 to 6 medium tomatoes, peeled, seeded, chopped coarse or
   canned tomatoes (8 to 10 ounces), drained well
2 medium onions, chopped coarse
1 clove garlic, chopped
4 slices rye bread without crusts, toasted
2 tablespoons light olive oil or vegetable oil
½ pound Havarti and dill cheese, regular or low fat in thin
   slices
salt and pepper to taste

1. Sauté the onions, garlic, and tomatoes in 1 tablespoon of the olive oil. Add the spinach and cook over medium to low heat uncovered for 10 to 15 minutes, stirring often and until most of the water left clinging to the spinach has cooked out.
2. Rub the bottom surface of an oven-proof baking dish with the other tablespoon of the olive oil and put the toasted rye bread on the bottom of the dish, completely covering the bottom.
3. Put the tomatoes and spinach mixture on top of the rye toast, season with salt and pepper, and top with the cheese. (Can be done ahead to this point.)
4. Bake uncovered at 350° for 30 minutes or until bubbling.

Serves 4 to 6

SQUASH CASSEROLE

*This was and is probably the Queen of All Casseroles, then and now.
There are many versions of it: some with frozen dried soup mixes, red and
green peppers, cheeses of every variety, and every kind of bread crumb
imaginable. The one included here is just the basic one. In the 50's, despite
all of the social changes of faster lifestyles than the 40's, and the resultant
processed cheeses, dried and canned soups, and the general loss of the true
meaning of "homemade", our family was still eating only fresh vegetables,
real cheeses, and our own soups. Even our bread crumbs, which were no
longer the homemade yeast breads of the 40's, were homemade "quick"
breads: Mama's biscuits, her skillet cornbread, and occasionally, a loaf
from the bakery down the street. That is the way squash casserole is best,
and today, our bread crumbs come from our homemade breads or once
again a wonderful local bakery, or when we had the gourmet shop and
bakery ourselves in the 80's, from croissants and our own real French
bread. Let your conscience be your guide.*

> **3 to 4 pounds fresh yellow squash, washed and sliced in thick
>   slices**
> **2 large onions, chopped**
> **1½ cups bread crumbs**
> **4 to 6 ounces Romano, Parmesan, or Cheddar cheese, grated**
> **1 cup sour cream (regular or low-fat)**
> **salt and pepper to taste**

1. Boil the squash and chopped onions in enough water to cover
   for 20 minutes. Drain well.
2. Put the well-drained squash, onions, and all the rest of the
   ingredients except the cheese in an oven-proof dish. Mix well.
   Season to taste with additional salt and pepper if necessary.
3. Sprinkle the top of the squash with the cheese. This can be done
   ahead up to this point.
4. Bake at 350° for 40 minutes or until very hot and bubbling.

Serves 4 to 6

SQUASH CROQUETTES

3 cups cooked squash, drained well, and mashed
1 medium onion, chopped fine, or 2 or 3 green onions
   chopped with some of the green
1 teaspoon each: thyme and basil
2 eggs, beaten
1 cup good bread crumbs, fairly coarse
salt and pepper to taste
2 cups vegetable or peanut oil

1. Mix all of the ingredients except the oil. You should have a fairly thick paste, if not, add more bread crumbs until you can pick up the paste and form balls easily. Season to taste with salt and pepper.
2. Heat the oil until a tiny bit of batter floats quickly to the top of the hot oil. The oil should not be smoking.
3. Cook 3 or 4 golf-ball size croquettes in the hot oil, being careful not to overcrowd the pan. If the oil is not hot, and the pan is over-crowded, the croquettes will absorb a lot of oil, and they will not be good. Drain on paper towels, keep warm uncovered in a low (200°) oven.

Serves 4 to 6

TOMATOES: FRIED GREEN

6 to 8 green tomatoes, washed and not peeled
2 cups flour seasoned with salt, pepper, and basil
salt and pepper

1. Slice the green tomatoes in ½" slices.
2. Dredge one slice of green tomato at a time in the seasoned flour, coating both sides evenly.
3. Heat between 1 and 2 inches of light vegetable oil in a skillet until a small sprinkle of flour sizzles. Add the coated green tomatoes a few at a time to the hot oil, not over-crowding the skillet. Turn when one side is golden and no flour shows and cook the other side.
4. Drain the cooked green tomatoes on paper towel and keep warm in a low oven (200°) uncovered. Salt and pepper to taste.

TURNIP GREENS

If you can buy turnip greens already washed and cleaned, you have saved a lot of time and water. They grow in cold weather, close to the ground, and usually after a lot of muddy rains. A grocery sack full of turnip greens will cook down to about 3 cups, so don't be misled. They must be washed repeatedly in cold water, even if you bought them "pre-washed." Gritty greens are enough to turn anyone off of all greens forever. Remove the hard, tough stems, and soak the large cleaned leaves in a sink full of cold water. Change the cold water several times, shaking all of the grit and sand off each time. Drop the greens in a large pot of boiling water seasoned with 1 whole onion, peeled and cut in half, 1 tablespoon salt, 1 large clove garlic (or 2 or 3 smaller ones), and a tablespoon of good, light vegetable or olive oil. Cook over high heat for about 45 minutes or until the greens are cooked thoroughly and the liquid is reduced to about 1 cup. If you must add more liquid as the greens cook down, be sure to add boiling water so that the cooking is not stopped by cold water which would make the greens tough. Season individual servings at table with either pepper-vinegar, or any vinegar sweetened with 1 teaspoon sugar. Balsamic vinegar is excellent, or any cider vinegar.

Note: You can cook these greens in part de-fatted chicken stock for a less traditional taste. In the 50's we added a ham hock to the pot, or some left-over smoked turkey. Either are very good additions.

VEGETABLE SAUSAGES

This is really a left-over vegetable croquette, but my grandmother called them sausages because she loaded them up with sage that made them taste like pork sausages. Years later, I omitted the sage, and added lots of basil and thyme, and called them "Nunna's Sausages." Today, decades later, I have reverted back to calling them by their original 40's and 50's name, because, guess what? Sausages and vegetables are back in vogue. We could have predicted it. These proportions depend on your own taste. I never use the stronger vegetables like broccoli, Brussels sprouts, and asparagus, because they are also very fibrous when processed. Some green beans can be very fibrous, too.

> 1 cup cooked carrots
> 1 cup English peas, cooked
> 3 or 4 red or Idaho potatoes, peeled and cooked
> 4 green onions, cleaned and trimmed
> 1 clove garlic, peeled
> 2 eggs, beaten
> 1 cup dry bread crumbs (can be from any toasted bread)
> 2 teaspoons dried sage, or 1 teaspoon each: basil and thyme
> salt and pepper to taste

1. Process all of the cooked vegetables and the green onion and garlic. Taste for salt and pepper. Add the herbs.
2. Form into either flat or oblong sausage shapes. Chill if necessary. (If your vegetables were cold to begin with, they may still remain chilled even after the heat of the processor).
3. Beat the eggs with 2 tablespoons milk. Put the bread crumbs in a shallow dish. Dip the "sausages" in the milk and egg mixture, then in the bread crumbs.
4. Heat enough oil in a skillet to cover the bottom of the pan. When the oil is hot, add the sausages, being careful not to overcrowd the pan. Cook on both sides until the sausages are golden.
5. Serve with or without peeled, chopped, fresh tomatoes, cut into small dice.

4 to 6 servings of about 2 small sausages per serving

ZUCCHINI FRITTATA

3 cups thinly sliced zucchini (slightly peeled)
1 medium onion, chopped
½ bunch fresh, washed parsley, chopped fine
1 clove garlic, chopped
½ cup grated Parmesan cheese
4 eggs, slightly beaten
1 cup Bisquick
½ cup good, light olive oil
2 teaspoons oregano
salt and pepper to taste

1. Mix all the above ingredients together. Spray a 9″ X 13″ oven-proof pan and add all of the above.
2. Bake at 325° for 30 minutes until bubbling in the center.

DESSERTS FROM THE 50'S:

The 50's brought about many changes in our lives socially after the years of World War II, for, suddenly, our fathers were home, families grew bigger with the "baby boom", people moved more and more from the cities to the suburbs, and a whole new way of life began. Television began its impact. It was an effort to have a family dinner with every one going and wanting to go in so many different directions. We always had family dinners, and we welcomed them. Every one could report on his or her day, and catch up with the others' lives, but we all knew that the closeness of the 40's was long gone. These desserts that I remember the most from the 50's are probably not totally representative of that decade any more than the ubiquitous "casserole" was the sole fare, but these old-fashioned pies were always in the refrigerator or in the bread-box, and Mother made them. Homemade pies were a lot quicker than the old-fashioned cakes and layered puddings of the past, and we see far too few of them today. Often when asked to bring a dessert to a dinner, I bring a fresh peach or blackberry pie, and it is usually one of the first desserts on the table to be eaten. Maybe others share the fond memories of "just a piece of pie" that my family and I hold. Years later in New Orleans, when I was the mother, and I had to get up for the 4:00 a.m. feedings, I felt much better warming the bottle, knowing that a piece of chess pie awaited me in the refrigerator, and while I fed that little boy, I blessed whoever had brought that pie. It was a real comfort food then, and it still is now when I get up with my grandson.

BLACK-BOTTOM PIE

The Toddle House served this pie along with a lot of other wonderful cream pies: butterscotch, chocolate, coconut. I wore braces back then, and as soon as I had them tightened, I wanted to go get a piece of pie from the Toddle House. There was something about going to the dentist and orthodontist that made me want sugar, but I never told them that. Black Bottom Pie was flavored with rum, which is a very hard flavor to get without over-loading the custard with so much rum that it won't set up. We tried rum flavoring, but it is more of a butter-rum than a real rum, so the best flavor we can get is with a very dark rum and some vanilla. The white rum is not strong enough.

BLACK-BOTTOM PIE

1 8″ crumb crust
1 tablespoon gelatin
¼ cup dark rum
1 cup milk
1 cup cream
½ cup sugar
1 heaping tablespoon cornstarch
4 egg yolks
2 ounces melted dark chocolate (not milk chocolate)
1 teaspoon vanilla
1½ tablespoons dark rum
4 egg whites
pinch cream of tartar
¼ cup sugar
1½ cups whipping cream
2 tablespoons confectioners sugar

1. Soak the gelatin in the ¼ cup dark rum until the gelatin is dissolved.
2. Bring the milk and cream to a boil with the ½ cup sugar.
3. Beat the 4 egg yolks until light and slowly add in the milk, sugar, and the cornstarch, beating on low speed or whisking constantly. Put in the top of a double boiler over boiling water, and cook, stirring constantly until the mixture coats a spoon.
4. When the custard is thick, remove 1 cup to another bowl and to that 1 cup add the melted chocolate, stirring well to make the custard a smooth chocolate color. Add the vanilla. Pour the chocolate custard into the bottom of the pie crust. Chill.
5. Add the gelatin that has been dissolved in the rum to the rest of the hot custard and stir well to dissolve the gelatin in the custard. Add in the 1½ tablespoons dark rum and stir well. Allow to cool but not set.
6. Beat the egg whites with the cream of tartar and gradually add in the ¼ cup sugar and beat until stiff. Fold the stiffly beaten egg whites into the cooled custard and spread on top of the chilled chocolate mixture. Chill.
7. Just before serving, whip the cream with the confectioners sugar until stiff and spread on the chilled and set custard. Decorate the top with shaved chocolate.

Serves 6

CHESS PIE

When we had The Highland Gourmet, Inc., in the '80's, our chess pie was featured in FAMILY CIRCLE BEST-EVER BAKING, 1984. We were so proud, because we really love this pie ourselves, and they called it "Highland Chess Pie."

**1 9" unbaked pie shell
2 cups sugar
4 eggs
1½ sticks unsalted butter, melted
2 teaspoons vanilla
2 tablespoons cornmeal
1 tablespoon plus 2 teaspoons cider vinegar**

1. Beat the sugar and eggs in a bowl with a fork or whisk until they are well mixed. Add the melted butter and beat together thoroughly.
2. Add the vanilla, cornmeal and vinegar, and mix all together. Pour into the 9" pie shell and bake at 350° on a cookie sheet for 45 to 50 minutes or until the custard is set, and a knife in the center comes out clean.
3. Chill to set. This can also be served at room temperature, slightly warmed, or cold.

Makes one 9" pie

EGG CUSTARD PIE

This is another favorite of many, many of our family and friends. It has to be chilled to set up, but after that you can warm it slightly if you prefer.

1 9" unbaked pie shell
2½ cups milk
4 eggs, beaten
¾ cup sugar
1 tablespoon flour
2 teaspoons vanilla
2 teaspoons freshly grated nutmeg
pinch salt
1 tablespoon melted unsalted butter

1. Bring the milk to a boil and let cool slightly.
2. Mix the eggs, sugar, flour, vanilla, nutmeg and salt in a bowl, and gradually add the scalded milk, stirring or whisking it all together. Add in the melted butter, and mix well.
3. Pour into the unbaked pie shell and bake on a cookie sheet at 375° for 25 to 30 minutes or until a knife in the center comes out clean.
4. Chill the pie for several hours to set the custard. Sprinkle the top with more grated fresh nutmeg.

Makes one 9" pie

LIGHT LEMON PIE

1 baked 9" deep-dish pie crust
1 8-ounce package lemon gelatin
1 cup hot water
1 cup sugar
1 small can Pet milk
3 tablespoons fresh lemon juice

1. Dissolve gelatin in hot water and sugar. Let set until syrupy, then beat until very thick.
2. Whip Pet milk and add lemon juice. Beat all together.
3. Pour in baked pie shell and chill. Serve with sweetened whipped cream or vanilla yogurt.

Makes one 9" pie

PEACH-ALMOND PIE

1 unbaked 9" pie shell or graham cracker crust pie shell
4 cups fresh peaches, sliced
½ cup brown sugar
juice of 1 lemon
3 eggs
2 tablespoons flour
¾ cup white sugar
½ stick unsalted butter, melted
1 teaspoon vanilla
⅓ teaspoon almond flavoring
½ teaspoon salt
½ cup sliced, blanched almonds

1. Put the sliced fresh peaches in a bowl with the brown sugar and lemon juice and toss to coat. Let sit for 15 to 20 minutes or until juices form from the peaches. If the peaches are very hard and dry, add ¼ cup apple or white grape juice to the bowl.
2. Beat the eggs, flour, white sugar, and melted butter together until smooth. Add the vanilla, almond and salt, and mix well.
3. With a slotted spoon, put the peaches in the unbaked pie shell reserving any liquid. Add the liquid to the egg mixture and mix well.
4. Pour the egg mixture evenly over the peaches, and top with the ½ cup blanched almonds.
4. Bake at 400° for 15 minutes, then lower heat to 300° and bake for another 45 minutes. If the crust or the almonds begin to darken, cover them loosely with foil, and continue cooking until the pie is set.
5. Serve with vanilla ice cream or vanilla yogurt.

Makes one 9" pie

PEACH CUSTARD PIE

1 9" unbaked pie shell
⅔ cup Eagle Brand milk
2 cups hot water
3 eggs, slightly beaten
½ teaspoon salt
1 teaspoon vanilla
1 teaspoon fresh grated nutmeg
10 fresh peach halves, peeled and drained on paper towels

1. Combine milk and hot water. Stir into eggs and add salt, vanilla, and nutmeg. Put in 9" unbaked pie shell.
2. Bake at 400° for 20 minutes, then lower heat to 325° and bake for 15 or 20 minutes more or until the custard is set. Remove from oven and let cool.
3. Garnish the top of the cooled custard with the peach halves, cutting some to make a design if desired.

Makes one 9" pie

PECAN PIE

1 baked 9" pie shell
3 egg yolks
1 cup sour cream
1 cup sugar
4 tablespoons cornstarch
¼ teaspoon grated lemon peel
pinch salt
3 egg whites
1 cup brown sugar
1 cup chopped pecans
2 teaspoons vanilla

1. Cook the egg yolks, sour cream, sugar, cornstarch, lemon peel and the pinch of salt together in the top of a double boiler until thick enough to coat a spoon.
2. Pour the mixture into the cooled pie shell.
3. Beat the egg whites and a pinch of salt together until they begin to stiffen, then add the brown sugar and pecans gradually, beating all the time.
4. Spread the pecan meringue over the custard in the pie shell and bake at 400° or until the top browns. Watch carefully to prevent its burning.

Makes one 9" pie

PUMPKIN CHIFFON PIE

1 9" baked pie shell
1 envelope gelatin
¼ cup cold water
2 eggs, separated
1½ cups cooked pumpkin
⅔ cup milk
½ teaspoon salt
¼ cup sugar
2 teaspoons pie spices
½ teaspoon orange extract
1 cup whipping cream, whipped with 3 tablespoons
   confectioners sugar

1. Soften gelatin in cold water.
2. In the top of a double boiler, heat egg yolks, add sugar and beat well. Add sugar, pumpkin, milk, and salt. Cook for 10 minutes over hot water. Remove from heat.
3. Stir gelatin into the hot pumpkin mixture, stirring constantly to dissolve the gelatin. Let cool until partially set.
4. Beat the egg whites until foamy, and add ¼ cup sugar, the pie spices and the orange extract, beating until stiff.
5. Fold the cooled pumpkin mixture into the egg white mixture and pour into the baked pie shell. Chill. Garnish with sweetened whipped cream.

FRESH STRAWBERRY PIE (OR TARTS)

2 9" baked pie shells or 10 small (4") baked tart shells
1 quart fresh strawberries, sliced
1 cup sugar
3 tablespoons cornstarch
pinch of salt
1 tablespoon fresh lemon juice
2 cups whipping cream, whipped with 3 tablespoons
  confectioners sugar

1. Crush one-half of the berries. Bring to a boil, stir in sugar combined with cornstarch and salt, and cook stirring constantly until thick, about 10 minutes. Add the lemon juice.
2. Spread the other half of the berries in the baked pie or tart shells. Pour hot cooked filling over the top. Cool and refrigerate.
3. When cold and set, top with the sweetened whipped cream.

WHISKEY PIE WITH CHOCOLATE SAUCE

1 9" pie shell
1½ tablespoons plain gelatin
7 egg yolks
1 cup sugar
grated peel of 1 lemon
½ cup bourbon
2 egg whites
2 tablespoons sugar
1 cup whipping cream, whipped

1. Sprinkle 1½ tablespoons of the plain gelatin over 2 tablespoons cold water to soften. Stand the container of gelatin in simmering water and heat it stirring constantly, until the gelatin is melted.
2. Beat the 7 egg yolks until they are creamy and gradually beat in 1 cup sugar. Add the grated lemon peel and the juice of 1 lemon, the dissolved gelatin, and ½ cup of bourbon and stir the mixture thoroughly. Cook in a double boiler until the mixture thickens and coats a spoon. Let cool.
3. Beat the 2 egg whites until they begin to hold shape. Gradually beat in 2 tablespoons sugar and continue to beat until they hold a shape.
4. Fold in the egg whites and whipped cream. Pour into the pie shell and chill until firm.
5. Serve with chocolate sauce on the side.

Makes one 9" pie

Chocolate Sauce:
3 cups sugar
1 cup Dutch process cocoa
6 tablespoons unsalted butter
1 large can evaporated milk

1. Heat all in a double boiler until smooth.

Makes 1½ cups

THE 1960s

The decade of the 1960's was the decade of my 20's, and now, looking back some thirty years and more later, I am still amazed at all of the changes that took place during that turbulent period of history. Most of the changes in society were hundreds of years over-due: in the early 60's, segregation in the South was a sickening disgrace. Our era was one in which my friends and I were the "women, blacks, and other undesirables." We were told "Do not fold, bend, spindle, or mutilate", which meant we had somehow become computer numbers, not people. The world was seeing us in such a distorted fashion that we had to make sense out of it somehow. Our friends were being shipped off to Viet Nam, many never to return, and yet, our younger siblings and cousins who were fighting so far away were not even allowed to vote until the 1970's, when the voting age was lowered from 21 to 18 years of age. They could be killed for their country, but they could not vote for their leaders.

Those of us who were married in the '60's in the South were married in the midst of the race riots in Birmingham, Selma, and other cities. We felt like something out of the Bible for we "were marrying and being given in marriage" while the world we lived in was aflame.

My grandparents had long since prayed for the injustices to be ended in our city and in our nation. I was taught as a child that all women are as valuable as all men, and that "success" depended on character based firmly on Biblical principles, not on skin color or gender. Our family didn't trade with people who had "colored" and "white" waiting rooms, not even a doctor. We were taught that even small, personal changes would someday, somehow make a difference. We said "Yes, M'am," and "Yes, Sir" to all adults, and just as all children were treated with dignity, so were all adults. We prayed for a new day for all of our beloved South. We hated the way it did come about, but it had to come.

It was a new era: My friends and I had new names, new homes, even lived in different cities. For my new husband and me, it was New Orleans, where he attended medical school. We made $125 a month from my job, we paid $75 a month for rent, and we were deliriously happy.

As K. T. Oslin sang years later in her '80's Ladies" country music hit, "We burned our bras, and we burned our dinners, and we burned our candles at both ends...and now we have children who look just like we did back then."

The first of our three sons was born in January, 1965, and we brought him "home" to a two-room apartment with 19-foot-high ceilings. Our grocery bill was $17 a month, because we ate most of our dinners at Charity Hospital where the students and staff could eat for free and together; also, the new "formulas" that the drug companies were producing were free to medical students' children. There were some oddities in our lives that even we saw: Charity Hospital had great Cajun and Creole food, but even little babies two and three months old reeked of garlic. We also had things like red beans and rice for Thanksgiving, and lasagna for Christmas dinner at Charity, but we loved it. And, of course, our children were allergic to the drug companies' free formulas. Their first food was lasagna, red beans and rice, and skim milk.

Hurricanes were almost an annual affair for us in the 1960's in New Orleans. I held a 9-month-old baby boy throughout the whole night of Hurricane Betsy's fury, hearing the calm of the eye, and then the reversal of the whole thing as it swept Lake Ponchartrain to meet the Gulf. My husband was so busy working in the Emergency Room at Charity Hospital during the hurricane that he didn't get home from working at the hospital for three weeks: he had an 80-year-old patient who had been standing on a table in her home up to her neck in water for one week; he quit counting how many babies they delivered during that period of time. He saw cases of animal bites, encephalitis, meningitis, and even leprosy cases that were sent down from the old Carville Hospital near Baton Rouge, Louisiana. There were no telephones, no airplanes, no busses, no electricity after every hurricane.

Hurricanes tore up the Mississippi River and Lake Ponchartrain so that all of our water was to be boiled for 30 minutes at high heat. Those were the days that I blessed natural gas stoves, and I hope always to have one. I boiled and boiled and boiled and boiled. Every baby food jar that wasn't finished had to be thrown out, because there was no refrigeration and very little ice. The late-summer heat in New Orleans was stifling. Hurricanes don't occur in nice, cool, pleasant weather.

We lived across the street from New Orleans' only above-ground cemetery, and I thankfully report and record that we had no unwanted visiting neighbors after any of the many hurricanes or at any other flood-level season.

Our food budget in those early days of being a new bride and then a new mother meant I HAD to be innovative, and New Orleans, Louisiana, is at its best for a low-budget cook. Catfish were abundant. An eighty-nine-cent package of catfish filets would feed us for a week. We sautéed it, stewed it, and gumboed it, always with rice. The Irish Channel fishermen sold the best redfish ("spots" to us, because they had a spot on their tail) which we stuffed and baked with French bread stuffing, tomatoes, our own fresh basil which we grew in pots, onions, and, of course, lots of garlic.

Every Monday in New Orleans, every household, including Charity Hospital's, had red beans and rice. It was wash-day at home, and the beans could cook almost unattended. When Leitner's bakery behind Charity Hospital had their light flashing, we knew that the French bread had just come out of the ovens, and a long, hot loaf only cost a dime. The left-over, if there ever was any, was our French toast, "Pain Perdu", for the children's breakfast the next day or bread pudding the next night.

In New Orleans, there were really only three months out of the year when you could not grow anything in the garden, and during that time, the French Market sold "greens", usually collards, spinach, or kale. We ate those at home while the great restaurants downtown called our homely greens by such wonderful names as "Rockefeller". Oysters Rockefeller usually are spinach, collards, or kale, or a mixture of these and any other greens, sautéed with lots of onions and garlic, and a hint of Pernod. It is then cooked down to make a thick mixture to put atop raw oysters and baked until bubbling hot. Often, at home, we omitted the oysters and used the Rockefeller part heated as a "dip" for French bread.

Creole Tomatoes were plentiful, herbs grew like crazy, and loquat plums and banana trees were abundant. Rice was, and is still today, in New Orleans a mainstay. We ate rice with everything. We ate it sweetened or salted or baked or boiled or fried. We ate it if we were well, if we were sick, if we were old, if we were young. Leftover-cold rice was made into croquettes with meats, into rice pudding, or leavened and fried into cakes called "calas".

For a new bride, a young mother, in her twenties in New Orleans in the 60's, with a limited budget, the abundance of natural and indigenous bounty of that area and that era was far more of a blessing than even we could have realized at the time. The 1960's ushered in probably the greatest changes in culinary America ever. Julia Child began on WGBH, and on black and white t.v., she led us to great culinary freedom. Who can forget her dropping the omelettes on the floor, picking them up, and reassuring us that no one would be any the wiser about the floored omelette if we kept it quiet. Who can ever want to forget the lesson on the whole pig where she told us of a "convenient little place to store the pig's tail", while the whole pig was cooking. "The Joan of Arc of American kitchens," our beloved "Julia." She taught us classical cooking methods, not just recipes. She deplored food snobbery, and encouraged us to try new things, new ideas, while keeping our heads about us. "The point of a soufflé," she told us in that wonderful Julia-voice, " is for the soufflé to collapse before the hostess does."

Thirty minutes of Julia once a week was not enough. We bought her books, followed her directions and advice, and we never, almost never, failed. We merely called the dish by another name. Julia gave us the greatest gift of all: the gift of love and laughter and confidence.

There were "Julia Groups" from New York to New Orleans and all in between: men and women met once a week to go over either her last t.v. class or her latest book step-by-step in our tiny kitchens. Our families and friends were delighted with our new confidence and our new gift of serving them and others.

Someone had given my husband and me THE JOY OF COOKING by Irma S. Rombauer and Marion Becker for a wedding present, and had inscribed inside the book: "I have been looking for the joy of cooking for 30 years, and I sure hope YOU find it. Love, Aunt Some-one." Irma Rombauer and Marion Rombauer Becker gave us the facts (lots and lots of them), and Julia Child gave us the joy.

People often ask me how I got started in the food business. Some of my friends years later are still astounded that I care about food, enter-taining, baking, wedding cakes, and food writing, when I could be doing other things. Maybe the decade of the 60's is to blame! It was a wonderful time to enter the culinary world. The "food business" is one of the most rewarding of vocations or avocations of which I know. After all, a poorly prepared dish is soon a thing forgotten, whereas a poorly painted portrait is hung on a wall for years only to haunt you. I'll take the culinary arts any day!

Julia Child, Irma Rombauer, and Marion Becker were not the only strong influences of the decade of the 1960's. Dione Lucas, James Beard, Julie Dannenbaum, Pierre Franey, and many others came on the scene as the political and social climate of the early '60's began to cool off. The young Kennedy family and their chefs and elegances began to make front pages of our newspapers. Color television began its invasion by the end of the 60's for some households, and many other "t.v. chefs" began to appear. It was far more appetizing to view a colorful Cobb Salad than a gray chopped glob, Julia's or anyone else's. Ditto, the roast pig.

One of the all-time favorites of the media celebrities and authors in the culinary arts for many of us in the 60's and still today was Peg Bracken and her I HATE TO COOK COOKBOOK. She gave us enough recipes to get us out of that kitchen and into whatever other calls of the wild were so rapidly coming our way. With her wonderful sense of humor, she, like Julia Child, warned us not to take our culinary selves too seriously.

She told us we might as well develop a repertoire of some sort, because, sooner or later, the jig is going to be up, and you and I are going to have to entertain "to pay people back or to honor them, or both, as well as to get the silver polished once in a while, and you cannot honor people with a pride of hot dogs. Some work is expected of you and perhaps something a little unusual." (pg. 157, THE COMPLEAT I HATE TO COOK COOKBOOK.)

As Peg Bracken herself says (though about someone else), so I say about her: "Bless her and bow low." After all, cooking is "so daily," and even though there are a few people who have managed to avoid it totally, eating out all the time is expensive, impersonal, and fattening. Some of the worst cooks I know have come up with some of the best meals I've ever had (though they made me swear not to tell how good the meal really was), and usually by sheer accident.

The white rémoulade sauce that we still use for shrimp and for our pasta salad came from a kitchen-illiterate cook who, out of total happenstance one day, had to move something around in her refrigerator door to keep the jars from falling on her kids' feet every time they opened the refrigerator, so she mixed the mayonnaise with the Zatarains' Creole mustard, and voilà! White Rémoulade!

I saw this lovely woman for the first time in twenty years a few years ago, and I mentioned this to her, and she was aghast. "I thought I had a cook back then!" Imagine her, opening up the refrigerator! But CLEANING it?! She promptly dismissed my white-rémoulade remarks, so I feel rather free in saying what a horrible cook she was/is. She's told me often that she would be delighted to be thus labelled.

Actually, she is not a rara avis. There are plenty of people out there who despise the kitchen, food, and all the hoopla about it. There are days when I, too, would rather be in a hammock in Tahiti, and that is when my culinary skills are the most welcomed. I know how to get in there and get out to the green pastures or to the hammock even if it isn't Tahiti.

These New Orleans-in-the-60's recipes are good for entertaining as well as for every day family fare. They are fairly easy, not too serious, and Cajun and Creole foods will always be popular. My family has always been as important to me as my guests, and even now, thirty years later, I fix these recipes and ideas with a lot of faith and confidence. You can, too.

APPETIZERS, SOUPS, & GUMBOS

OYSTERS & ARTICHOKES

3 large artichokes, boiled until a leaf comes out easily
¼ cup good olive oil (Tuscan, if possible)
¼ cup flour
½ cup dry white wine or vermouth
3 dozen oysters (reserve the liquor from them)
4 stalks celery, chopped
6 green onions, chopped with some of the green
1 box fresh mushrooms, sliced and slightly chopped
3 cloves garlic, smashed
½ bunch fresh parsley, washed and chopped fine
2 teaspoons thyme
1 tablespoon Tabasco sauce
2 tablespoons Worcestershire sauce
juice of 1 lemon
salt and pepper to taste
1 cup fresh grated Parmesan cheese
1 cup fresh dry bread crumbs

1. After the boiled artichokes have cooled enough to handle, remove the leaves and scrape them, reserving the scraped flesh. Remove the "choke" from the artichoke and discard. Wash the heart to remove all fibers from the choke and chop the hearts of each artichoke into medium-size chunks. Add to the scraped flesh from the leaves and set aside.
2. Heat the oil in a skillet and when hot, add the flour all at once and stir with a whisk or wooden spoon until the roux turns the color of peanut butter, being careful not to let it burn or it will be bitter. Remove from the heat.
3. Strain the oyster liquor through a strainer into the cooked roux. The oyster liquor will be cool enough to stop the cooking of the roux which will be very hot. Whisk until all lumps are gone, and add the ½ cup of the white wine or vermouth, again whisking until smooth.
4. Return to the heat, and add the rest of the ingredients except the artichoke flesh, oysters, cheese and the bread crumbs. Cook over medium heat until bubbling and the onions and celery begin to wilt.
5. Add the oysters and cook until their edges just begin to curl. Add the reserved chopped artichoke flesh. Remove from the

(Oysters and Artichokes, continued on next page)

(Oysters and Artichokes, continued)

heat and put into an oven-proof serving dish. Taste and correct seasonings. You can do ahead to this point.
6. Top with the bread crumbs and the cheese and heat at 325° in the oven until very hot and bubbling. This should take about 20 minutes.

This serves about 4 to 6 people

Note: If you prefer to use canned artichokes, or if fresh ones are not available, use 2 cans artichoke BOTTOMS, drained, and chopped coarse, and 1 can artichoke hearts, drained and chopped fine to substitute for the 3 large whole artichokes.

OYSTERS EN BROCHETTE

"En Brochette", or "on skewers", has usually been a New Orleans restaurant tradition, and I am not too sure why it was not served at home as much in our New Orleans' 60's days, because it is easy, and it looks like it isn't. Traditionally, Galatoires, especially, served Oysters En Brochette lightly battered and fried and on toast-points. The oysters were alternated with partially pre-cooked bacon. At home, we simplified the frying part somewhat, and added our own flavors of onions and mushrooms and omitted the bacon. This cuts down on the fat quite a bit for today's low- and no-fat generation, and still makes an "oysters-are-good-for-you" statement. Maybe we should call it "Oysters En Brochette Birmingham," because the New Orleans restaurateurs of the 1990's certainly won't recognize this rendition of their old tune. Actually, Galatoire's was originally begun in Birmingham, Alabama, in the 1890's by Jean Galatoire, and Birmingham has had a "John's Seafood Restaurant" in almost the same location as the original Galatoire's in downtown Birmingham ever since. This, then, is the "Centennial Celebration of the Oysters en Brochette from the Original Galatoire's, Birmingham-Style." With a name like that, and this long list of directions, you are probably already intimidated, but, it is a very uncomplicated recipe, despite its appearance, that is a lot easier to do than to say. I promise.

¼ **cup good olive oil (Tuscan, if possible)**
2 **dozen raw oysters (for 6 people this is 4 per person as an appetizer or lunch, allow 6 per person for dinner-size portions, which would be 3 dozen oysters for 6 people)**
6 **medium red onions (or Vidalias if available), each cut into 4 chunks**
24 **medium fresh white mushrooms, washed and dried, and left whole**
3 **cloves fresh garlic, peeled and smashed flat**
6 **pieces brioche, or good homemade-type bread, toasted and cut in half**
4 **green onions, washed and chopped with the green tops**
¼ **bunch fresh parsley, chopped**
¼ **cup dry white wine or vermouth**
1 **tablespoon Worcestershire sauce**
1 **tablespoon Dijon mustard**
salt and pepper to taste
6 **skewers at least 6" long**

1. Heat the olive oil in a skillet and quickly dip the toasted bread slices in the oil to "butter" one side of each slice. Set aside on a platter.

(Oysters En Brochette, continued on next page)

(Oysters En Brochette, continued)

2. Add the onion chunks to the hot oil and sauté until they are sweated and not at all limp. You are going to skewer them so try to retain their shapes while sautéeing them in the hot olive oil. Remove from the skillet, and set aside to cool.

3. Allow the oil to stay hot in the skillet, and add the garlic and mushrooms, allowing these to heat completely and not become at all limp. Remove from the skillet, and set aside to cool.

4. Add the cleaned and drained oysters to the same skillet, and heat only until their edges barely begin to curl. Again, the oil must be hot for the oysters to heat and not absorb the oil. Remove the oysters from the skillet with a slotted spoon draining off all oil, and set aside to cool. If the garlic is not too brown, leave it in the olive oil and adjust the heat to high before the next step, otherwise, discard it.

5. Add the chopped green onions, parsley, Worcestershire sauce, and mustard to the skillet, and sauté until the onions are sweated. Add salt and pepper, stirring well. Add the white wine or vermouth carefully, and over medium heat, reduce to about half, stirring to prevent the garlic and onions from sticking and burning. Remove from the heat, and set aside while skewering the oysters and vegetables as in step 6 below.

6. Alternate the cooled oysters, onions, and mushrooms on the skewers, using 4 or 6 to a skewer as suggested in the above ingredients list. You can do ahead to this point, if desired. Refrigerate if holding for longer than 30 minutes.

7. On a broiler-proof pan lined with foil, put the "buttered" toast points, the skewered oysters, mushrooms, and onions, and run under a hot broiler until they are broiling hot but not burned.(!)

8. While the oysters and toast are heating, heat the white wine sauce in the skillet until bubbling.

9. Put the heated brochettes and the toast on a platter and pour the heated sauce over all, allowing about 2 tablespoons of sauce per serving. Serve at once.

Serves 4 to 6

OYSTERS ELLIS

Sidney, our waiter and friend at Antoine's for years, never asked us what we wanted to begin our meal because, he had already written our order for Oysters Ellis when we called for reservations. The recipe here is good, and a fair copy when we can't get back to New Orleans, but at home, we just don't have the glace de viande (meat "extracts") and stocks that a large, good restaurant keeps on hand. If you have access to good beef or veal stock or like to make your own, reduce them to several tablespoons over very high heat, and the resultant thick residue will give you the flavor and the consistency that comes nearest to the professionals'. There are some "beef extracts" that are for sale in gourmet grocery stores that are neither laden with salt nor MSG nor caramel coloring and are rather good. Look on the label to see what ingredient comes first: usually for the poorer quality ones, it is water, salt, or MSG, but for some of the better ones, beef extract comes first and no MSG is added. "Bovril" is one good brand, but it is very distinctive in its taste, and must be used judiciously. Making your own as described above is immensely better, but unfortunately, most of us do not have the time.

> **4 tablespoons good olive oil (Tuscan, if possible)**
> **4 tablespoons flour**
> **1½ cups beef broth**
> **Optional: 2 tablespoons beef extract, if available (see above)**
> **¼ cup red wine**
> **2 tablespoons tomato paste**
> **1 additional tablespoon olive oil**
> **1 tablespoon Worcestershire sauce**
> **1 box fresh mushrooms, washed and sliced thin**
> **4 green onions, chopped with some of the green tops**
> **3 cloves garlic, smashed flat**
> **2 dozen oysters, drained and cleaned of all shells**
> **6 slices good bread (Brioche or a homemade type), toasted and cut into triangles**

1. Heat the olive oil in a heavy skillet or sauté pan, and add the flour all at once. Cook over medium-high heat whisking or stirring all the time with a whisk or fork. Do not allow it to burn, or it will be bitter. Cook to the color of peanut butter. On medium-high heat, gradually add the beef stock, extract (if available), tomato paste, Worcestershire sauce and red wine, whisking constantly to a smooth consistency.
2. Raise the heat to high, and while stirring occasionally, reduce to half. You can do ahead to this point.

(Oysters Ellis, continued on next page)

(Oysters Ellis, continued)

3. In a separate small skillet, heat 1 additional tablespoon of olive oil and sauté the green onions, mushrooms, and garlic cloves until they are just limp and the garlic is not burned. Add the cleaned, drained oysters and heat thoroughly until the edges just begin to curl, but the oysters are not over-cooked.
4. If the toast points are cold, heat them in a toaster or oven.
5. The red wine sauce should be reduced and thick. If it is too thin, continue to reduce it over high heat stirring occasionally. Taste sauce and correct the seasonings with salt and pepper, if necessary. Add the oysters, mushrooms and green onions to the sauce and heat carefully in order not to cook the oysters.
6. Serve over the heated toast points, allowing 4 oysters per person.

Serves 6

OYSTERS ROCKEFELLER

As mentioned in the Introduction to the '60's, we often used the Rockefeller-part, i.e., the sauce for the oysters, as a "dip" with French bread. Years later, I even mixed the Rockefeller sauce with a dry cottage cheese, and put it in puff pastry, and we sold it at our shop as an accompaniment to our Christmas roast beef. That particular recipe of ours can be found in MAGIC, the Birmingham, Alabama, Junior League cookbook. For Oysters Rockefeller, or for a Rockefeller "dip", the dry cottage cheese is not necessary. Allow 4 oysters per person for an appetizer. Put the raw oysters in their half shells on a pan of ice-cream salt in a low oven (200°) to warm and not cook. The ice cream salt will help to retain the heat.

> *For the sauce:*
> ¼ **cup good olive oil (Tuscan, if possible)**
> **5 green onions, chopped with some of the green**
> **4 cloves garlic, smashed flat**
> **4 stalks celery, chopped fine**
> **1 bunch fresh watercress, washed and chopped with the stems**
> **1 tablespoon anchovy paste**
> **3 boxes frozen chopped spinach, cooked and drained**
>   **thoroughly**
> **2 tablespoons Pernod (anise-flavor liqueur)**
> ¼ **cup good dry bread crumbs**

1. Heat the olive oil in a heavy skillet and add all of the ingredients for the sauce *except* the spinach, Pernod and the bread crumbs.
2. Cook over medium-high heat stirring constantly about 10 minutes or until the vegetables are limp, but not stringy.
3. Add the chopped spinach, Pernod and bread crumbs to the above mixture and heat thoroughly stirring constantly to prevent burning. The alcohol in the Pernod will cook out and leave only the anise-flavor. Keep warm.
4. Remove the oysters on the ice cream salt from the oven and top each oyster with about 3 tablespoons Rockefeller mixture. Return to the broiler and heat until bubbling. Serve at once.

Note: This is enough sauce for about 36 oysters. The recipe can easily be halved. Allow 4 oysters per person for appetizers, 6 per person for a light supper or lunch. To keep the oysters warm while everyone is being seated, you can add some of the warmed ice cream salt to each plate and set the baked oysters in their shells on top of the salt. This not only helps to keep them warm, but it also keeps them from rattling around on the plate.

SHRIMP RÉMOULADE

There are two versions of this here in this book. The first one, the red rémoulade is the "real" or traditional one, the second was something of a mistake as I have mentioned in the Introduction to the '60's. Both are good, and neither one are written in stone so that you can vary proportions to your liking, especially with garlic and Tabasco sauce in the red rémoulade, and you can make the white one hotter or milder by adding more Creole mustard or mayonnaise, respectively. They are either one usually used on shellfish, but are very good binders for pasta salads as well.

RED RÉMOULADE SAUCE

1. Add all of the following ingredients to a processor or blender and process or blend thoroughly:

   1 cup chili sauce
   1 cup ketchup
   1 cup mild olive oil or vegetable oil (add ½ cup or so more if the finished sauce is too thick for your use)
   ¼ cup cider vinegar
   2 cloves fresh garlic (more if desired for a true New Orleans flavor)
   ¼ cup horseradish
   4 tablespoons Creole mustard (Zatarains)
   1 tablespoon anchovy paste
   3 chopped green onions
   3 stalks chopped celery
   ½ bunch fresh parsley, washed, drained, and torn in pieces
   2 teaspoons salt
   2 teaspoons pepper
   2 dashes Tabasco sauce
   1 tablespoon Worcestershire sauce

2. Blend or process all until blended but not totally liquid. There should be some large pieces of parsley, celery, and green onion visible.
3. Keep in a glass jar with a lid in the refrigerator. Keeps one week.

   Makes 4 cups

WHITE RÉMOULADE

This is a nice and easy change sometimes from the original red rémoulade, and often for a lot of people and a lot of shrimp, we will use both. They are not incompatible.

Mix:
½ cup Zatarains Creole mustard
1 cup commercial mayonnaise

1. Serve on or by any shellfish or use in pasta salad.
2. Keeps in the refrigerator in a glass jar for about 1 month.

Makes 1½ cups

SOUPS & GUMBOS:

ARTICHOKE SOUP

¼ cup good olive oil (Tuscan, if possible) or vegetable oil
4 green onions, chopped, with some of the green
4 stalks celery, chopped fine
4 cloves garlic, smashed
2 teaspoons tarragon
2 teaspoons basil
4 cups artichokes: about 4 large fresh cooked and chopped or 3
  cans artichoke hearts, drained, and chopped fine
5 cups chicken broth
¼ cup dry white wine or vermouth
juice of 1 lemon
salt and pepper to taste

1. Heat the oil in a skillet and add the green onions, celery, garlic, and sauté until they begin to wilt or "sweat."
2. Add all of the rest of the ingredients except the lemon juice and stir well. Cook over medium-high heat with the lid off until the soup is reduced by half. This should take about 30 to 40 minutes.
3. Add the lemon juice, salt and pepper. Taste and correct the seasonings, adding more thyme, basil, lemon juice if necessary.

Serves about 4 to 6 small bowls

BOUILLABAISSE

This is one of my family's favorite soups even today, 30 years and more later. It is a very fast soup to make as are all fish soups. Fish broth, or "court-bouillon" as we knew it in our New Orleans days, has to be cooked quickly or else it will turn very, very bitter. Fish bones and heads are obviously quite a bit more delicate than beef, veal, and even chicken bones, and thus, the faster cooking time. If you have a family member who is allergic to shellfish, as we do, you can make your fish stock (or broth) with any kind of fish, omitting shellfish completely. The best kinds of fish for a Fish Stew like this is always one of the whiter fish, rather than the heavier, more oily ones. Whiter fish are: redfish, scamp, trigger fish, trout, flounder, pompano, snapper, and lots of others. Some of the more oily fish are: salmon, tuna, and blue fish. The fish markets in our inland Alabama cities are teeming with beautiful fresh fish, and the personnel in these markets are exceptionally helpful. Frozen fish are just not the same, and I don't recommend them. They tend to lose their texture and taste, regardless of how they are frozen. The cost of fresh vs. frozen is almost always about the same, or often, even a little less for the fresh. Actually in this soup, any combination of the white fish, and shellfish will work beautifully. Shrimp, oysters, crab, and lobsters work well too. Remember that shellfish don't take a lot of cooking time either or they will turn out like rubbery rocks if you over-cook them.

¼ **cup good olive oil (Tuscan, if possible)**
¼ **cup flour**
4 cups liquid:
court-bouillon, as below, or in combination with: chicken broth, dry white wine or vermouth, veal stock
1 package fresh mushrooms, chopped
2 medium onions, chopped
4 stalks celery, chopped
3 cloves garlic, smashed
2 cans tomato pieces with their liquid
2 bay leaves
2 teaspoons thyme
2 teaspoons tarragon
3 pounds fish or fish and shellfish or shellfish, cleaned and shelled if necessary (the fish should be cut into 2-inch chunks)
½ **cup dry sherry (optional)**

1. Heat the olive oil in a boiler and add the flour all at once, cook about 5 minutes or until the flour no longer smells or looks "raw," but is not at all brown. Remove from the heat.

(Bouillabaisse, continued on next page)

(Bouillabaisse, continued)

2.   Add the 4 cups liquid gradually, whisking constantly to re-move all lumps. Return to the heat and cook over medium-high heat until the liquid is very hot. Add the bay leaf, thyme, and tarragon. Lower heat or set aside if doing ahead.
3.   In another pan, heat just enough oil to cover the bottom of the skillet and add the mushrooms, onions, celery, and garlic, fish and/or shellfish. Cook until the fish begins to turn opaque, and the shellfish, if used, begin to curl slightly. Add the tomatoes with their liquid, stirring carefully.
4.   Add the tomatoes, fish, and other vegetables to the first boiler, and stir constantly. You can do ahead to this point. Keep chilled if waiting longer than 45 minutes to 1 hour.
5.   Heat just until boiling, and test one piece of fish or shellfish. They should be cooked throughout. If not, raise the heat and cook no longer than about 5 to 8 minutes depending upon the thickness of the pieces of fish, shrimp, etc.
6.   To the completed stew, add the ½ cup dry sherry, salt, pepper, and correct the seasonings. Add more salt, pepper, or a little lemon juice if necessary.

Serves 4 to 6 regular-size soup bowls

Note: Serve with toasted (garlic) French bread rounds.

COURT-BOUILLON (Fish Broth)

1 to 2 pounds fish: small ones with head and skin on, if possible, lobster, crab, shrimp shells and large trimmings from other fresh fish
4 cups water
1 cup dry white wine
3 celery stalks, cleaned with the leaves still on
1 medium onion, peeled and cut into fourths
2 bay leaves
3 garlic cloves
2 teaspoons salt
1 lemon sliced into thick pieces
4 or 5 peppercorns, whole

1.   Bring all to boil, then lower to simmer, and simmer for 20 minutes.
2.   Strain and reduce over high heat for 10 minutes. Correct seasonings.

CRAB BISQUE

The following recipe came from my friend and teacher, Myriam Guidroz, who wrote for the New Orleans STATES-ITEM, and who was my first and favorite teacher. I took classes from her in her tiny kitchen in her home for almost two years, and what a blessing she has been to me then and over the years. She is from Belgium, and in those years, her classes and her newspaper articles were supporting her and her children. This made her an excellent first teacher for me in that she had to be, and was, a very economical cook. She taught me how to substitute ingredients if availability or budget necessitated it; how to get by with only three excellent, commercial pots and pans, and how to look for and get the freshest, finest ingredients by knowing a little bit more than the vendors. A pot of fresh basil that looked hopeless could be revived with just a little water and sunlight; a "spot" is a redfish, but you could get a better price by calling it a "spot" rather than a "redfish"; good leafy lettuce could substitute for poor fresh spinach in a soufflé or a Rockefeller-type sauce; an omelet pan can also be used as a sauté pan, and on and on. It's too bad that her book, ADVENTURES IN FRENCH COOKING, MacMillan, 1970, is out of print, because today it is still one of the basic teaching books and reflects her own wonderful sense of humor. Her teaching is the background of a great deal of my own food style, especially the basic, practical side of food as mentioned above.

    1 tablespoon oil
    4 fresh whole crabs (blue crabs)
    ¼ cup good brandy
    2 cups hot water
    2 cups dry white wine
    3 stalks celery, chopped
    3 green onions, chopped with some of the green
    3 carrots, peeled and chopped
    2 teaspoons thyme
    salt and pepper
    2 bay leaves
    4 cups broth from the above and enough white wine and hot
        water to make 4 cups liquid
    1 tablespoon tomato paste
    1 tablespoon Worcestershire sauce
    2 teaspoons Tabasco sauce
    3 cloves garlic, smashed
    2 teaspoons thyme
    salt and pepper to taste
    ¼ cup good brandy
    1 pound crabmeat, picked and carefully clean (lump, if
        available)

(Crab Bisque, continued on next page)

(Crab Bisque, continued)

For the broth:
1. In a large pot, heat the oil and add the fresh crabs, stirring them until they turn a bright red. Remove from the heat and add the ¼ cup brandy and let the brandy cook out in the hot pot, stirring for about 5 minutes. Return to a moderate heat. Add the hot water and wine, the celery, onions, carrots, thyme, bay leaves, salt and pepper, and let cook uncovered on medium heat for about 15 to 20 minutes. With a large spoon or potato masher, mash the crabs until the shells crack to release all of the "goodness" from the shells. Continue to cook until the 15 or 20 minutes is up. Strain the broth through a large strainer, mashing the shells and the vegetables, reserving the broth and discarding the rest.
2. To the broth, add the tomato paste, Worcestershire, Tabasco sauce, and the rest of the ingredients except the crab meat. Stir well to incorporate the tomato paste and bring to a boil. Let cook for about 5 minutes. You can do ahead up to this point. Add the crab meat and brandy and refrigerate.
3. To reheat, heat over medium-high heat to avoid cooking the crab meat. It should merely be heated and the brandy should not be cooked out. Taste and season with salt and pepper if necessary.

4 to 6 servings

GUMBO

There are entire books on gumbo, and many New Orleans' cookbooks have at least one chapter devoted to the subject, but the basis for any gumbo is generally the same: the roux, onions and garlic, usually tomatoes, and either a red or dark stock. In the homes, we usually had a red, tomato-based stock, but restaurants with all their broths and meat glazes usually produced dark stocks, either from beef, veal, duck, or other wild game stock. The base I use here is a combination of tomatoes and beef stock, and produces a good alternative. The "gumbo" part comes either from okra or "filé" powder, the latter being a product of the sassafras plant. In the 90's, and who knows how long this will last, "filé" powder has fallen into disfavor by some cooks. It may cycle back into favor, but in the meantime, okra treated fairly is just as authentic and certainly, as good. Okra should not be over-cooked, or it becomes too stringy to be good, so adding it at the end of the cooking will give you the consistency you want. If okra is out of season, and it usually is in the dead of winter when we crave a good hot bowl of gumbo, you can omit it altogether. Once again, be very careful not to overcook the seafood, especially. The seafood, duck, turkey, or chicken must be fully cooked before going into the gumbo, because once the meats go into the gumbo, no further cooking should be done, merely reheating. Obviously then, it is better made the day before and refrigerated.

½ cup oil
½ cup flour
1 quart or more beef stock or consommé
1 large can tomatoes with their liquid
1 small can tomato paste
2 medium onions, chopped
4 stalks celery, chopped
4 cloves garlic
thyme, bay leaf, Creole seasonings
2 pounds total of any cooked white fish, crawfish, shrimp, crab or any combination thereof, or 4 to 6 cups of cooked turkey, duck, chicken cubed or "pulled"
3 tablespoons Worcestershire sauce
Tabasco sauce to taste
salt and pepper
1 cup okra, cut in rounds and sautéed quickly in 1 teaspoon hot oil (optional)

1. Make a dark roux from the flour and oil in a hot skillet, cooking over medium-high heat until the color of tobacco.
2. Add all of the chopped vegetables, except the optional okra, and

(Gumbo, continued on next page)

(Gumbo, continued)

cook until just limp. (If you are using okra, sauté it in a separate skillet in 1 teaspoon hot oil until it is just limp. Set aside the okra until the very end.)

3. Add the tomatoes with their liquid, beef stock, tomato paste, seasonings and cook down until it is reduced by almost half. Taste and add more of the herbs and/or Creole seasoning if desired. Add the Worcestershire and Tabasco sauce, and correct the seasonings, adding salt and pepper as necessary.

4. Add the cooked fish, shellfish, or the duck, chicken, or turkey pieces. If using the okra, add it now. If doing ahead, you can refrigerate it overnight, putting the pot in a pan of ice to cool it down quickly.

5. Bring to a boil stirring, and lower the heat, cover and heat until bubbling hot, but the fish, shellfish or the meats are not overcooked.

Serves 4 to 6

Note: Serve over rice or plain with toasted French bread.

JERUSALEM ARTICHOKE SOUP

Hardly anyone knows what a Jerusalem artichoke is, but they are every-where along the highways in the South with a flower that looks just like one of the "Black-eyed Susans." They are hard to pick, and it is the tuber, or root, that is so good, so it is better to buy them at your grocer's than to risk life and limb on the highways and by-ways. They are very knobby-looking tubers about the size of a red potato, and they are brown and white like a wet baking potato. Jerusalem artichoke pickles are crunchy and perfect little condiments for Thanksgiving or any other "relish tray." But Jerusalem artichokes, in my opinion, star as a soup base. They are some-where near the taste of celery or celeriac, and watercress, combined. They will maintain their texture through a lot of cooking, and I think that is what makes them good, but you could puree it all if you're given to that kind of soup, and it will be just as good.

> ¼ **cup olive or vegetable oil**
> **6 to 8 medium-size Jerusalem artichokes, peeled and sliced**
> **1 medium yellow or Vidalia onion, chopped**
> **4 stalks celery, chopped**
> ¼ **cup dry white wine or vermouth**
> **4 cups chicken broth**
> ¼ **cup cream (optional)**
> **salt and pepper**
> **juice of 1 lemon**

1. Heat the olive or vegetable oil in the skillet, and add the sliced Jerusalem artichokes, the onion and celery. Cook over medium heat, stirring constantly until the vegetables are limp, but not mushy.
2. Remove from the heat and add the vermouth or white wine and the chicken broth. Return to the heat and cook uncovered over high heat until it is all reduced by one-half. This should take abut 30 minutes.
3. Add the optional cream. Season to taste with the salt, pepper, and lemon juice. Correct the seasonings, if necessary.

Makes 4 to 6 small soup bowls

OYSTER STEW

This is one of the easiest soups or stews to make, but the richer the ingredients, the better it is. Butter, cream, oysters, and the best white wine is really all that is necessary for a good oyster stew, and then season it with salt, pepper, and of course, garlic. In this day and time at the end of the 20th century, however, most of us avoid the fat and calories of the original and wonderful Oyster Stew, so I have greatly altered this recipe. It is nothing like the original, but it is still easy, and it is good, and we don't feel at all guilty serving it.

> 1 pint fresh oysters in their liquor
> ½ cup or more dry white wine
> 1 teaspoon tarragon
> 1 teaspoon thyme
> 2 tablespoons oil
> 4 green onions, chopped with some of the green
> 1 medium onion, chopped fine
> 4 stalks celery, chopped fine
> 1 small baking potato, peeled and cut into small dice
> 1 cup oyster liquor
> 1 additional cup dry white wine or vermouth
> 3 cups broth: court-bouillon (see Index) chicken or veal, or any
>   combination thereof
> 2 bay leaves
> ½ bunch fresh parsley, chopped very fine
> ¼ cup dry sherry
> salt and pepper to taste
> ¼ cup cream (optional)

1. Strain the oysters through a sieve into a measuring cup, reserving the liquor. Wash the oysters under cold water to remove all pieces of shells. Set aside.
2. Add enough white wine or vermouth to the liquor to make one cup liquid. Add 1 teaspoon each thyme and tarragon and the bay leaves. Bring to a boil and boil hard for 2 minutes. Remove from the heat and set aside.
3. In a saucepan, heat the oil and add the green and yellow onions, celery, garlic, peeled and diced potatoes. Sauté, stirring until the vegetables are wilted. The smaller the dice for the potatoes, the faster the potatoes will cook.
4. Add the oyster liquor, dry white wine, and broth. Cover and simmer for 20 minutes or until the potatoes are soft. If a smooth soup is preferred, you can puree the soup in a processor or blender at this point. For a heartier "stew", do not puree.

(Oyster Stew, continued on next page)

(Oyster Stew, continued)

5. You can do ahead to this point. Let the broth cool, add the oysters, and, if desired the ½ cup cream. Refrigerate in a bowl of ice not longer than overnight. Heat carefully over medium heat in order to heat only and not to overcook the oysters, stirring occasionally. Add the ¼ cup dry sherry. Taste for seasoning and add salt and pepper if necessary. Serve piping hot garnished with the chopped parsley.

6. If serving immediately, add the ½ cup cream if desired, bring to a boil, and add the oysters. As soon as the oysters begin to curl around the edges and are hot, remove from the heat. Add the ¼ cup dry sherry. Stir well and taste for seasonings. Add salt and pepper if necessary, and serve piping hot garnished with the chopped parsley.

4 to 6 servings

SHRIMP STEW

A good friend of ours in New Orleans made this stew for us so often that this became her signature dish during the medical-school days in the 60's in New Orleans. This was long before we had all the frozen shrimp that we have in today's markets. Our friend, Emilie, used to peel and devein the tiny, little shrimp called for in this recipe. She was, obviously, the only one who ever made this stew. It was a real labor of love, and we all loved her, not just for her stew, but for her perseverance. Today the smallest shrimp available are usually called "popcorn shrimp" or "salad shrimp". The "popcorn shrimp" are usually about 50 to a pound. The "salad shrimp" are about 100 to the pound, and they are too small for this recipe. One of the next size larger is called in the trade "36 to 40" (shrimp per pound), and they are a little more flavorful than the " popcorn shrimp". All of the small shrimp cook in literally minutes; too long and they toughen into little rubber bands. In order to flavor the shrimp with all of the wonderful stew ingredients, this recipe is much better served the next day. Make the stew, let cool, add the shrimp, refrigerate overnight. Reheat carefully over medium heat, stirring, and not allowing the little shrimp to overcook in the heating process.

> ¼ **cup oil**
> ¼ **cup flour**
> **2 cups beef broth, bouillon, or consommé**
> **1 tablespoon beef extract, if available**
> **2 tablespoons Worcestershire sauce**

(Shrimp Stew, continued on next page)

(Shrimp Stew, continued)

1 tablespoon tomato paste
½ cup red wine
2 teaspoons Tabasco sauce
salt and pepper
1 additional tablespoon oil
1 medium onion, chopped fine
3 stalks celery, chopped fine
2 cloves garlic, smashed
1½ pounds raw "popcorn" shrimp, or 36-40, peeled and
  deveined

1. Heat the ¼ cup oil in a large pot, and add the flour all at once. Stir or whisk constantly, cooking until the roux is the color of peanut butter. Remove from the heat and add the beef stock (bouillon, consommé, etc.) and the beef extract, if available. Whisk or stir thoroughly to remove all lumps. Return to medium heat, whisking constantly, and add the red wine, Worcestershire, tomato paste, Tabasco sauce, salt and pepper. Bring to a boil and cook for about 10 minutes. Remove from the heat, and set aside.
2. While the stock is cooking, heat the 1 tablespoon additional oil in another pot or deep skillet, and add the onions, celery, and garlic. Sauté until they just begin to wilt. Remove with a slotted spoon and add the vegetables to the beef stock, and stir well. Taste for seasonings.
3. If serving at once, bring the broth and vegetables to a boil, lower heat to medium, and cook for about 5 minutes, stirring occasionally. Add the raw shrimp to the hot stew, cover, and cook for another 5 minutes only so as not to overcook the shrimp. Correct seasonings, making it very spicy since it is to be served over rice.
4. If doing ahead, add the raw shrimp to the cooled broth and vegetables, refrigerate overnight, and heat the next day on medium heat until the shrimp are thoroughly cooked which will only take about 8 to 10 minutes. Taste for seasoning, adding more salt, pepper, Worcestershire, Tabasco sauce if desired. It should be very spicy since it is to be served over rice.

4 to 6 servings

Note: Serve over rice, sprinkled with chopped green onions.

NEW ORLEANS GLAMOUR EGGS

There are very few foods that appeal to my family and me as much as the egg dishes from New Orleans. Eggs have fallen somewhat out of favor with the low-cholesterol advocates, but we are all allowed one or two a week, I think. Give me mine dressed in New Orleans' garb! They are really not difficult to fix at home, are terribly inexpensive, and with the right sauces, are not even THAT fattening. During the '60's, Breakfast at Brennan's in New Orleans was about $5 a person, with everything, and today it is still not exorbitant. My oldest son and I used to go to Brennan's with the slightest excuse: just the two of us together. He was only 18 months old. We were treated royally every time. Eggs Benedict at Brennan's are nothing like the fast-food interpretation. The eggs can, however, be done ahead of time and kept without becoming rubbery, and the original Eggs Benedict of Brennan's in the '60's were always on a Holland Rusk, not a tough English muffin. Years later for this same son's prom breakfast at our house in Birmingham, we served 60 high school seniors Eggs Benedict at 4:00 in the morning. I think. The teenagers were in high gear, and I can't remember how we got the eggs and all on the table, and everyone served, but apparently, it was a great success. I would never recommend this to any sane parent, but the point is that everything CAN be done ahead and warmed the last 15 minutes or so, even at 4:00 in the morning. Make the sauce(s) up ahead of time, poach the eggs and hold them in ice water, have the Holland Rusks ready; mix a big green salad without the vinaigrette; and you can hold all of this overnight for a brunch or lunch the next day.

POACHED EGGS

1. Have a large bowl filled with ice and cold water beside the cooktop before you begin. This will hold the poached eggs and stop them from cooking.
2. Fill a skillet with fairly deep sides with hot water and 1 tablespoon white vinegar. Bring to a boil, lower the heat to a medium simmer. Too fast a boil will tear the eggs up rather than gently poaching them.
3. Slide 3 eggs into the hot vinegar-water taking care not to break the yolks. Slide a spatula gently under each egg to prevent its sticking to the bottom of the pan. "Baste" the eggs gently over the yolks with a spoonful of hot water. This will cook the top of the egg.
4. When the white is set on the eggs, and the yolks are poached, but not hard, remove the eggs with a slotted spoon to the bowl of ice water. Let cool completely. Gently pick up the cold poached egg and trim the white strands off to make a neater egg. Refrigerate until needed or continue to poach as many eggs as you need adding them to the ice water as they finish poaching.
4. Repeat the process by bringing the water once again to a boil, adding 1 additional tablespoon white vinegar, lower the heat again to a medium simmer, and slide three more eggs into the hot water. Repeat as above.

6 servings of one egg each

EGGS BENEDICT

3 Holland Rusks, buttered
3 slices ham, slivered
3 eggs, poached as above
1 cup Hollandaise sauce or "Mock Hollandaise"

1. Top the buttered Holland Rusks with the ham slivers and keep warm in a 200° oven.
2. Bring water to boil in a skillet with straight sides, lower the heat and let simmer.
3. Remove the poached eggs from the ice water and carefully slide them into the simmering water for a few minutes to warm them thoroughly.
4. Remove the warm Holland Rusks and ham from the oven. With a slotted spoon carefully remove each egg from the simmering water, and dry it well with a clean dish towel to remove all water. Put one egg on top of each Rusk.
5. Top with about 1 tablespoon (or more, if desired) warm Hollandaise (or Mock-Hollandaise sauce). Serve at once.

3 servings of 1 egg each

HOLLANDAISE SAUCE

4 whole eggs
juice of ½ lemon
2 sticks room temperature unsalted butter
pinch of salt

1. In a double boiler over simmering water, beat the 4 whole eggs with a whisk. Add the lemon juice.
2. Cook, whisking constantly, adding about 1 tablespoon butter at a time until all the butter is incorporated, and the eggs are thickened. Add salt.
3. Keep warm over very low hot water, whisking occasionally. It will thicken as it sits.
4. To do ahead: Chill the sauce in a bowl placed in a pan of ice. Return to the double boiler and bring slowly to warm, whisking constantly.

Makes about 1½ cups

MOCK HOLLANDAISE

This is really a homemade mayonnaise, but it keeps for three days in the refrigerator in an airtight glass jar. To warm it, put the jar in a warm pan of water for about 30 minutes.

> **4 whole eggs**
> **2 teaspoons salt**
> **1 teaspoon Dijon mustard**
> **2 sticks room-temperature unsalted butter**
> **¼ cup vegetable oil**
> **grated peel of 2 large lemons**
> **juice of 2 large lemons**
> **additional salt and pepper to taste**

1. Process or blend the whole eggs with the salt and Dijon mustard until the eggs are a very light yellow.
2. With the machine running add the room-temperature butter, one tablespoon at a time, letting each tablespoon incorporate into the eggs before adding the next tablespoon
3. When all of the butter has been added, and with the machine still on, add the ¼ cup oil a little at a time, and process or blend for several minutes. The sauce should be fluffy and smooth.
4. With the machine still running, add the lemon peel and juice all at once. Process or blend for another 3 or 4 minutes. Taste for salt and pepper and add if necessary.

Makes about 1¼ cups

Note: Keep in a glass jar in the refrigerator. Put in a pan of warm water to use over eggs, shaking or stirring well if it separates at all.

EGGS CREOLE

1 or 2 eggs per person
1 pound Cajun sausage or other highly seasoned sausage
   (Italian, veal, etc.)
1 medium yellow onion
1 red bell pepper, chopped
3 stalks celery, chopped
2 cloves garlic, smashed
1 tablespoon tomato paste
1 tablespoon Worcestershire sauce
2 teaspoons Tabasco sauce
4 cups fresh tomatoes peeled and chopped or 2 cans tomatoes,
   crushed with their liquid (if using fresh tomatoes, add 1 cup
   hot water to make up for the liquid)
2 teaspoons each thyme and tarragon
salt and fresh ground pepper
4 lightly buttered Holland Rusks or toast points (allowing one
   per egg)
1 bunch fresh parsley, chopped

1. Poach eggs as described under "Poached Eggs".
2. If the sausage is in casings, slit the casings with a knife and
   remove the sausage and discard the casings.
3. Heat a deep skillet and add the sausage, stirring until it is completely cooked. Remove the sausage with a slotted spoon onto
   paper towels to drain, and discard all but 1 tablespoon of the
   rendered fat. Heat and add the onions, celery, garlic, red pepper, and cook until the vegetables are wilted.
4. Add the tomato paste, Worcestershire sauce, Tabasco sauce,
   herbs, and 1 cup of the tomato liquid (or hot water) and cook
   over moderate heat for another 5 to 8 minutes stirring to keep
   from burning.
5. Add the sausage, tomatoes and the rest of their liquid and
   cook uncovered until the sauce is thickened, about 10 to 15
   minutes. Taste and correct seasonings adding salt and pepper
   as necessary.
6. Heat the poached eggs and dry them with a clean dish towel as
   described in the Master recipe for poached eggs, and put on
   lightly buttered toast or Holland Rusks, one egg per rusk.
7. Top with about 1 cup of the Creole sausage per egg. Serve hot
   sprinkled with chopped fresh parsley.

Makes about 4 cups Creole-sausage sauce, or enough for 4 eggs

EGGS HUSSARDE

This is a Brennan's specialty, too. It has the addition of sliced, fresh tomatoes, and 2 sauces (Hollandaise and Marchand de Vin) to the Eggs Benedict. Eggs Hussarde is probably our favorite of the Brennan's eggs.

1 poached egg per person
1 slice slivered baked ham per person, warmed
1 thick slice peeled fresh tomato per person, warmed
1 recipe Hollandaise sauce (see Eggs Benedict recipe)
1 recipe Marchand de Vin sauce (see below)

1. Poach eggs as described in the master recipe for "Poached Eggs." Re-heat and dry with a clean towel as described.
2. Put slivered ham on a lightly buttered Holland Rusk (or toast).
3. Top with 1 thick slice peeled tomato.
4. Top the tomato with 1 poached egg, and then put 3 tablespoons each of Hollandaise and Marchand de Vin sauce on the egg. Serve warm.

MARCHAND DE VIN SAUCE

4 tablespoons butter
4 tablespoons flour
1 bunch green onions, chopped with some of the green
1 package fresh mushrooms, washed and chopped
2 cloves garlic, chopped fine
½ bunch fresh parsley, chopped fine
1½ cups red wine
1 can (10 ounces) beef stock with 1 tablespoon beef extract
(Bovril, etc.) added
2 tablespoons cream
salt and pepper to taste

1. Brown the butter and flour together to make a roux. Whisk or stir constantly over medium-high heat in order not to burn the roux. It should be the color of peanut butter.
2. Add the chopped fresh vegetables and the parsley and cook over medium-high heat just to wilt the onions and mushrooms, stirring carefully to prevent the garlic from burning.
3. Add the red wine slowly, whisking or stirring carefully, until it is incorporated and there are no lumps from the roux. Gradually add the beef extract and beef stock, cover and let simmer about 15 minutes.
4. Remove the lid, and over medium-high heat reduce the sauce to about ½. Add the cream and whisk or stir thoroughly. Taste for salt and pepper, adding if necessary.

This makes about 2 cups

It will keep about 4 days in the refrigerator.

EGGS SARDOU

This is a welcome change from the classic Eggs Benedict and Eggs Hussarde, and it is a classic in its own. There are a lot of possible variations on Eggs Sardou. Instead of poaching the eggs, you can bake eggs in the spinach-artichoke heart mixture, omit the eggs altogether and have a great "side-dish" for a brunch; add a bit of anisette or Pernod, and call it Eggs Rockefeller; or put it in little ramekins, add a few raw oysters and bake them for a brunch, lunch, or breakfast. Spinach and artichokes just have an affinity for each other, and add a little lemony Hollandaise-like sauce, and it is a classic combination. Use your imagination here.

1 poached egg per person (see "Poached Eggs")
2 boxes frozen, chopped spinach, cooked and drained well
1 tablespoon good olive oil (Tuscan, if possible)
4 green onions, chopped fine
2 cloves garlic, chopped fine
1 small package cream cheese (4 ounces), softened
1 teaspoon each: thyme, tarragon and nutmeg
salt and pepper to taste
2 cans artichoke bottoms
1½ cups Hollandaise Sauce (see Eggs Benedict)

1. Heat the olive oil in a deep skillet, add the green onions and garlic, and sauté until the onions are limp. Add the chopped spinach that has been well drained, and cook over medium-high heat for about 8 minutes, stirring constantly.
2. Add the softened cream cheese, thyme, tarragon, nutmeg, and cook over low heat until the cream cheese is totally melted and incorporated into the spinach mixture. Taste and add salt and pepper as necessary.
3. Heat the artichoke bottoms in a separate pan in their own liquid. Remove with a slotted spoon to the warmed individual plates or serving platter. Pat each artichoke bottom dry with a cloth.
4. Place a warmed egg that has been dried with a clean dish towel in each of the artichoke bottoms. Arrange the warmed creamed spinach around the artichokes and eggs on the plates or platter. Top each egg with about ¼ cup Hollandaise sauce. Serve at once.

Serves 4 to 6

EGGS & TOMATO BAKE

Baking eggs in a casserole instead of poaching them is another easy brunch, lunch or Sunday night supper meal. Once the eggs are broken, however, it is best not to let them wait too long before baking them. Raw eggs without their shells pick up bacteria even in the refrigerator fairly quickly. You can make the sauce or base, refrigerate it, and then add the eggs just before baking by breaking them carefully into indentations in the sauce. Top the eggs with a little grated cheese before going into the oven, and the fat from the cheese will keep the yolks from getting leathery while baking. If cholesterol is a problem, a low-fat cheese works just as well as any other for this purpose.

> 1 tablespoon butter or good olive oil (Tuscan, if possible)
> 1 bunch green onions, chopped with some of the green
> 3 stalks celery, washed, and chopped
> 1 large cucumber, peeled, seeded, and chopped
> 3 or 4 medium size green tomatoes or tomatillos*, if available, chopped
> 1 bunch fresh basil, chopped fine (or 1 tablespoon dry basil)
> ½ cup vermouth or dry white wine
> 2 large (or 4 regular size) canned tomatoes, crushed, with liquid
> 1 tablespoon tomato paste
> 1 teaspoon each: thyme and tarragon
> 1 cup dry bread crumbs (homemade, if possible)
> 6 large eggs, raw
> 1 cup grated Romano, Monterey Jack, or Parmesan cheese

1. Heat the oil in a skillet with sides and add the green onions, celery, cucumber, chopped green tomatoes (or tomatillos, chopped). Cook until they just begin to wilt and sweat.
2. Add the chopped fresh basil, ½ cup vermouth or dry white wine, and stir well. Add the tomato paste and stir well to incorporate it. Add the tomatoes with their liquid, the thyme, tarragon, and bread crumbs. Cook for about 8 minutes uncovered over medium-high heat, stirring occasionally. Taste and correct seasonings, adding salt and pepper as necessary.
3. Put the sauce in a 9" x 13" oven-proof dish, adding more vermouth or white wine if the mixture is too thick. (Note: depending on the quality of the tomatoes that you used, you may have to add one more can of tomatoes and their liquid if the mixture at this point is still too thick.)
4. If doing ahead, refrigerate the mixture now, and add the eggs

(Eggs and Tomato Bake, continued on next page)

(Eggs and Tomato Bake, continued)

just before baking as in Step 5.

5. With the back of a serving spoon, make indentations in the tomato casserole, and put one egg in each indentation. Sprinkle with salt and pepper and grated cheese over the eggs. Bake at 325°, uncovered, for 35 to 40 minutes or until the eggs are completely done. Do not overcook or the eggs will be rubbery.

Serves 4 to 6

*Note: "Tomatillos" are small, green specialty "fruits" that you will find in the vegetable section of most grocery stores. They have a papery husk on the outside that is peeled off and discarded. Tomatillos are usually used in salsas, and they tend to have a much better flavor than most green tomatoes. You can substitute green tomatoes here, as we used in New Orleans, but the green tomatoes today are nothing like the green Creole tomatoes of the past.

BAKED INDIVIDUAL EGGS & HERBS

For each serving:
1 teaspoon fresh or dried basil (1 leaf fresh)
1 tablespoon chopped fresh parsley
2 eggs
1 tablespoon cream
½ tomato, peeled and chopped into dice
2 tablespoons chopped cooked ham or 1 piece cooked, drained bacon, crumbled
salt and fresh cracked pepper

1. Stir basil, parsley, ham (or cooked bacon), tomatoes in 3" custard cups or individual ramekins.
2. Break eggs over tomatoes, add cream over the eggs, and salt and pepper.
3. Bake in another pan ½ filled with hot water in a 400° oven for 20 to 25 minutes or until the egg is set.

FISH & SHELLFISH MAIN COURSES:

CREOLE-BAKED FISH

We used to call this "Planked Red Fish", and we really did "plank" it. We had wooden planks that steak houses used to hold the sizzling metal steak platters (something like Fajitas are served on today), and they were well oiled and "seasoned" so that a fast baking fish would cook very evenly on these planks. Then we piped mashed potatoes all around the edges of the finished, baked redfish, sprinkled it all over with chopped fresh parsley, and feasted. It was like a fisherman's "Shepherds' Pie". Somehow over the years and the many moves, we have lost our "planks" and our steak platters, and there doesn't seem to be any time for mashing and piping potatoes, although we were certainly not living a life of leisure back then with babies and jobs and driving car pools, etc. This recipe is an adaptation of "Planked Redfish", and actually any white fish would do. Salmon, tuna, and the like are just too oily to bake like this, but trout, pompano, snapper, bass, and redfish (a type of a bass), if you can find it, are excellent. Allow about 10 minutes to the pound to bake a stuffed fish. Since it is a bread stuffing, we no longer use potatoes of any kind here. This is how foods and recipes change until they are hardly recognizable years later, and we often wish we "had time" to go back to that good "planked redfish" that we used to have.

> 1 large whole fish, 4 to 5 pounds, cleaned and gutted but with the head on
> 2 tablespoons oil
> 2 large onions, chopped
> 4 stalks celery, chopped
> 3 cloves garlic, chopped
> 2 teaspoons each: thyme, tarragon, basil and chives
> 4 cups dry seasoned bread crumbs or cornbread or herb stuffing mix
> ½ cup dry white wine or vermouth
> 1 to 2 cups chicken broth to moisten the stuffing
> salt and pepper to taste
> 2 cans Creole tomatoes

1. Heat the oil in a Dutch oven, and add the onions, celery, and garlic, and cook until just sweated. Add the herbs, bread crumbs, white wine or vermouth, and enough chicken broth to moisten thoroughly. It should be a very moist dressing mixture. Cook for about 5 minutes over medium high heat, stirring constantly to blend all the flavors and cook the alcohol out of the wine or vermouth. Remove from heat and let cool.

(Creole-Baked Fish, continued on next page)

(Creole-Baked Fish, continued)

2. Put the cleaned and gutted fish on foil in an oven-proof pan. Use enough foil to completely wrap the fish on all sides. You may have to use two long pieces of foil in a cross-shape.
3. When the dressing is cool enough to handle, spoon the dressing into the cavity of the fish. Pour the tomatoes around the outside of the fish, and salt and pepper the fish.
4. Bring the foil up over the fish making an airtight package, and put in a 375° oven for about 10 minutes to the pound. A 5-pound fish will take about 50 minutes.
5. To test for doneness, peel back a small piece of the skin and press with the back of a fork. The fish will feel very firm, and the inner flesh will all be opaque. Any juices that come from the cooked fish will also be opaque and milky in color.
6. To serve: Carefully cut the foil from around the fish, leaving it on the serving platter in which it was cooked. Remove the skin while the fish is hot with a table knife or fork, being careful not to shred the flesh. The skin will come off easily. Discard the skin. Baste with some of the tomato liquid and serve each person some of the fish, stuffing, and tomatoes. Serve with a green salad and French bread.

Serves 4 to 6

JAMBALAYA

This is a good Cajun dish that really means "mixture." Our yearbook at Tulane was called the "Jambayala," which was appropriate for a large port city's in-town university. Jambalaya, the dish, always has rice, some kind of fish, or shellfish, tomatoes, and, of course, garlic. It is usually a very good recipient of whatever is left over. This recipe assumes that your house is like mine in that no left overs are ever compatible, thus it is a recipe that starts from scratch. If you have a cup or so of cooked English peas, stewed tomatoes, sautéed mushrooms, then, by all means, add them.

Jambalaya is not a formula that must be rigidly followed. You can substitute almost any cooked meats for the chicken and sausage called for here: duck, ham, shrimp, oysters, crab (carefully picked and cleaned), and almost any kind of sausage that you particularly like.

> **6 chicken breast halves (3 whole breasts)**
> **water to cover, about 1 quart**
> **2 stalks celery, washed and left whole**
> **1 small onion, peeled and cut in half**
> **½ cup dry white wine or vermouth**
> **2 pounds Italian sausage**
> **1 large yellow onion, chopped**
> **3 cloves garlic, smashed flat and chopped**
> **1 small green bell pepper, chopped**
> **1 red bell pepper, chopped**
> **½ cup additional dry white wine or vermouth**
> **1 large (16 ounce) can tomatoes, with their liquid**
> **1 teaspoon each: thyme and tarragon**
> **2 leaves fresh basil, chopped, or 2 teaspoons dry basil**
> **2 bay leaves**
> **1½ cups long-grain rice, uncooked**
> **salt and pepper to taste**
> **2 teaspoons Tabasco sauce**
> **1 tablespoon Worcestershire sauce**

1. Cook the chicken breasts in enough water to cover with the uncut celery stalks (with some of the leaves), the halved onion, 1 teaspoon salt, until the breasts are done. This should take about 20 minutes on medium-high heat in a 3 quart pot. Let cool in the broth.
2. If the Italian sausage is in casings, cut the casings with a sharp knife and remove the sausage, discarding the casings. Heat a deep skillet and add the sausage. Continue cooking the sausage

(Jambalaya, continued on next page)

(Jambalaya, continued)

until it is completely done. Remove with a slotted spoon to paper towels and drain. Pour out all but 1 tablespoon of the fat from the sausage.

3. Heat the oil from the sausage and add the chopped onion, celery, peppers, garlic, and cook until wilted. Lower the heat and add the white wine or vermouth, the tomatoes and their liquid, all of the herbs, including the whole bay leaf. Cook over medium high heat for about 20 minutes, stirring occasionally.

4. Drain the chicken breasts through a colander, reserving the broth. Discard the celery and onion. Let the chicken breasts cool while preparing the rice.

5. Measure 3 cups of chicken broth, or add hot water to equal 3 cups liquid. Add salt and pepper. Bring to a boil and pour in the 1½ cups rice all at once. Bring to a rolling boil, cover, and reduce the heat, cooking the rice for about 25 minutes or until it is done. This will depend on the size of your pan. The larger it is, the faster the rice will cook.

6. While the rice is cooking, shred the chicken breasts with your hands (this is "pulled chicken"), or chop very coarse with a knife into bite-size or larger pieces.

7. Add the chicken and cooked sausage to the tomato sauce. Keep warm.

8. When the rice is cooked, stir it well to fluff it up, and add it to the chicken, sausage, and tomato sauce. Add the Tabasco sauce and Worcestershire sauce. Stir well. Taste for seasonings. Add salt and pepper if necessary.

Serves 4 to 6

Note: This can all be done ahead to this point and kept in the refrigerator overnight. It is much better the next day.

CRAWFISH PIE

2 baked pie shells (8")
½ cup vegetable oil
½ cup flour
2 onions, chopped
3 garlic cloves, chopped
3 stalks celery, chopped
1 red bell pepper, chopped
2 tablespoons tomato paste
4 cans tomatoes (can use those called "Cajun Style")
1 tablespoon Creole seasonings
2 teaspoons each: thyme and tarragon
2 bay leaves
3 pounds crawfish tails, raw

1. Make a roux from the oil and flour and cook until it is the color of tobacco. Do not burn it.
2. Add the onions, garlic, celery, and stir carefully to barely wilt the vegetables. Add the tomatoes and seasonings. Cook for about 20 minutes or more uncovered over medium-high heat to reduce and thicken. Taste and correct the seasonings.
3. Sauté the crawfish tails in a very little oil. Drain well and add to the thickened tomato mixture. Mix carefully, but thoroughly.
4. Fill the pie shells with the crawfish-tomato mixture. Can do ahead up to this point. Refrigerate and cook within 24 hours.
5. Heat on a cookie sheet at 375° until bubbling.

Serves 6 to 8

DEVILLED OYSTERS

If you can get fresh oysters on the half-shell, and you know how to open them, they are by far the best. Most of us, however, who are inland have to buy our oysters by the pint or quart. Oysters are highly perishable, so be sure you know your vendor. When you get them, whether in the shell or in the plastic, the oysters should be carefully cleaned of any pieces of shell that may cling to them, by gently washing under cold water. For this recipe, dry them on paper towels before breading them, or the breading won't stick. Allow about 6 per person.

3 dozen oysters
½ stick unsalted butter
½ cup good olive oil (Tuscan, if possible)
1 tablespoon Dijon mustard
2 teaspoons thyme
salt and pepper
3 cups bread crumbs

1. Clean the oysters by running them under gently flowing cold water. Put them on paper towels to dry completely.
2. Melt the butter and olive oil together, add the mustard, thyme, salt and pepper, and mix well. Dip the oysters in this mixture until they are completely coated. Then roll them in the bread crumbs and put on a foil-lined cookie sheet.
3. When all of the oysters are breaded, run them under a broiler and broil for several minutes or until the breading is golden brown, but not burned. Watch them carefully.
4. Remove and serve with Béarnaise sauce or see the section on eggs for a Hollandaise sauce.

BÉARNAISE SAUCE

½ **cup tarragon or cider vinegar**
1 teaspoon dried tarragon
1 stick melted unsalted butter
1 teaspoon pepper
1 teaspoon salt
1 teaspoon dry mustard
2 whole eggs
1 teaspoon Tabasco sauce

1. Combine the vinegar and tarragon in a small non-reactive saucepan. Bring to a boil and reduce to 3 tablespoons.
2. Add the hot butter and pepper to the vinegar mixture and stir well.
3. Beat the eggs in a blender until they are light yellow. Remove the cap from the lid, and with the motor running, pour the hot butter into the blender in a thin, steady stream and blend until thick.
4. Add salt and pepper and Tabasco sauce to taste.

Makes 1 cup

Oysters and Béarnaise Sauce: 6 servings

SCALLOPED OYSTERS

This could come under any of the decades in this book. It has remained popular ever since my childhood fifty years ago, but it was usually served with Thanksgiving or Christmas dinner. In New Orleans, scalloped oysters were served as a side-dish any time of the year. Usually, it accompanied some kind of veal or meat dish, but occasionally, it appeared in the hot summer months with a fruit salad, French bread, and fresh asparagus.

½ cup butter or low-fat margarine
1½ cups cracker crumbs
1½ pints fresh oysters
salt and pepper
Tabasco sauce
½ cup oyster liquor
½ cup cream or low-fat sour cream
1 cup buttered bread crumbs
½ bunch fresh parsley, chopped fine

1. Drain the oysters, reserving the liquor from them. Wash the oysters gently under cold water to remove any pieces of shells. Let drain dry or pat dry with a dish cloth.
2. Layer cracker crumbs and oysters in a baking dish. Dot each layer with the butter or low-fat margarine. Add salt and pepper to each layer.
3. You should have at least two layers, preferably three, depending on the size of your dish. Add the cream (or low-fat sour cream), oyster liquor, and Tabasco sauce to the entire dish, and top with the additional buttered bread crumbs.
4. Bake 25 to 30 minutes at 400° until bubbling. Remove from the oven and sprinkle with the chopped parsley.

Serves 4 to 6

POMPANO EN PAPILLOTE

This could be any fish, even salmon or tuna. When it is steamed like this in either parchment paper or foil, the fish stays moist, smells heavenly when the little packets are opened at the table, and can be prepared in advance. It looks and sounds hard, but it is really very simple, and as of now, a little unusual. Allow 1 pound of fish per person, because it will cook down to about ¾ of a pound or 12 ounces which is not too much fish.

> **1 large sheet parchment paper or several small sheets heavy-duty tin foil**
> **4 pounds boneless fish filets (pompano, trout, scamp, salmon, mackerel, flounder, etc.)**
> **5 tablespoons unsalted butter or good olive oil**
> **1 bunch green onions, chopped with some of the green**
> **1 pound fresh mushrooms, washed and chopped**
> **4 small cloves garlic, smashed and chopped**
> **½ cup good white wine or vermouth or good brandy**
> **salt and pepper**

1. Fold a 24" piece of parchment paper in half, and cut half of a heart-shape. This will be the baking and serving paper. If no parchment is available, cut pieces of heavy-duty tin foil into 24" sections, and fold in half. Set aside.
2. Heat 1 tablespoon of the oil in a skillet and add the green onions, mushrooms, garlic, and sauté until they are wilted, but not limp. Add the white wine or vermouth or brandy, stirring well.
3. Put each fish filet in the folded parchment on a cookie sheet with sides or a jelly-roll pan. Remove ¼ of the mushrooms and onions from the wine sauce with a slotted spoon and top each fish filet with ¼ of the mushrooms, and onions. Add salt and pepper to each filet.
4. Fold each little packet over to make ½ of a heart, and crimp the edges of the paper or foil to seal, leaving 1" open at the top. Put the packages on the sheet-pan, and add a little of the wine sauce through the 1" opening in each packet. Seal the last 1" by crimping. You can do ahead to this point.
5. Put the packets into a 350° preheated oven and bake for 15 minutes or until the parchment gets brown. If using foil, carefully open one packet and test the fish with a fork to see that the fish is milky white and opaque. Serve at once.

Serves 4

Note: This is good served with baked or boiled potatoes or pasta.

SHRIMP SAUTÉ

1 pound medium to large raw shrimp (26-30 or larger)
1 tablespoon oil
1 bunch green onions, chopped
3 cloves garlic
½ cup dry white wine or vermouth
½ cup cream or low-fat sour cream
salt, pepper and fresh basil

1. Shell the shrimp if necessary, and split the shrimp down the back where the vein is. (This is "butterflying" the shrimp).
2. Heat the oil in a skillet and add ⅓ of the shrimp, ⅓ of the green onions, and 1 clove garlic, stirring constantly to keep the onions from burning and to cook the shrimp. Remove from the skillet to a heated platter, and cook the remaining shrimp, green onions, and garlic in small batches in order to cook the shrimp, and not to toughen them by steaming them (which is what would happen if you dump them all in at once), adding more oil as necessary and allowing it to get hot before adding the next batch.
3. When all of the shrimp and vegetables are cooked and removed to a heated platter, remove the skillet from the heat, and slowly add the ½ cup white wine or vermouth to the skillet, scraping any bits that adhere to the bottom of the skillet. Return to the heat and stirring constantly, cook for about 5 minutes or until the wine loses its sharp alcohol smell and taste.
4. Add the cream or low-fat sour cream to the wine, beating constantly with a wire whisk to incorporate the cream into the wine. Return the shrimp to the sauce in the skillet and heat thoroughly.

4 to 6 servings

Note: Serve over white rice, wild rice, or pasta.

SMOTHERED CRAWFISH

½ stick butter, margarine, or 4 tablespoons good olive or
   vegetable oil
3 large yellow onions
4 green onions, chopped
2 cloves garlic, chopped
1 large red bell pepper, chopped
1 large green bell pepper, chopped
1 can tomatoes (Cajun-Style)
1 small can mild chilis, chopped
½ bunch fresh parsley, chopped
1½ pounds fresh crawfish tails, cleaned
salt and pepper to taste

1. Heat the oil in a heavy Dutch oven, and add the onions, red and
   green peppers, garlic, and cook until the vegetables are wilted.
   Add the tomatoes, chilis, and chopped fresh parsley, and cook
   for 8 minutes stirring frequently.
2. Add the crawfish, cover, and cook over low heat for about 15 to
   20 minutes. Taste and correct seasonings.
3. Serve over rice topped with a little more chopped fresh parsley,
   if desired.

Serves 4 to 6

TROUT AMANDINE

Traditionally, this is trout, but today there are many wonderful fish available that we can substitute that are often better than trout. Try scamp, Spanish or king mackerel, or any other white fish. The original Trout Amandine was too heavy on butter for today's taste, so I have cut back somewhat on that, too. This is a 90's version of a 60's tradition.

6 trout filets (or any other fresh white fish)
½ cup white flour
1 teaspoon each: thyme, tarragon, salt and pepper
½ stick butter or margarine or ½ cup good olive or vegetable oil
1 clove garlic
1 cup sliced, blanched almonds
¼ cup white wine or vermouth
salt and pepper

1. Dry the filets carefully with a towel. Remove any bones.
2. Heat half of the butter, margarine, or oil in a large skillet, re-serving the other half for the almonds.
3. Mix the flour, thyme, tarragon, salt and pepper in a bowl. Dredge the fish filets in the flour and add to the hot oil in the skillet. Cook the filets a few at a time until they are golden brown, then carefully turn to the other side and cook until the second side is golden and the fish is firm and opaque. Do not overcook or it will be too dry. Over-crowding the skillet will also make the fish dry.
4. Remove the filets to a warm platter and keep warm uncovered in a very low oven (180°). Add the rest of the butter, oil, or margarine to the skillet, and when it is hot, add the 1 cup of sliced, blanched almonds, the one clove of garlic, and cook stirring constantly until the almonds are browned. Add the ¼ cup white wine or vermouth and scrape and stir all of the bits into the sauce, and cook for about 5 minutes until the alcohol is cooked out of the wine, and the wine is reduced by about half. Serve the almonds and white wine sauce over the warm fish filets. Season as necessary with salt and pepper.

Serves 4 to 6

MEAT & POULTRY MAIN COURSES

COQ AU VIN (Chicken in Red Wine)

This is a classic French dish, but, of course, in New Orleans, we had to personalize it and that was usually with lots of garlic and onions; occasionally, some cooks added tomatoes, none of which was in the original. This was and is the essence of not just New Orleans cuisine, but also of all of American food: we tend to take the original and incorporate it into what we have on hand locally and what we like personally and with no apologies. It always seemed odd to me that you would cook chicken in red wine like this, which, of course, makes the chicken pieces dark red; but with boneless, skinless chicken breasts rather than the original whole stewing chicken, somehow, the finished product looks a little better to me. The boneless, skinless chicken breasts cook to a mahogany color, rather than the plum color of the whole chicken. Ideally, we like to top the cooked chicken with a tablespoon or so of Béarnaise sauce, but in today's faster world, somehow the Béarnaise sauce never gets made. The results are just as good without it, and few of us now-days can remember ever having had Béarnaise sauce on it, not even for company.

> 4 whole, boneless, skinless chicken breasts (8 halves)
> ¼ cup oil, butter, or margarine
> 1 box fresh mushrooms, washed and sliced
> 1 medium onion, chopped
> 3 green onions, chopped with the green
> 2 cloves garlic, chopped fine
> 1 cup rich chicken broth (or 1 can chicken broth)
> 1 cup beef stock or consommé
> 1 tablespoon Worcestershire sauce
> 2 cups red wine (Burgundy)
> salt and pepper to taste

1. If the chicken breasts are whole, cut them into halves. Pound them to tenderize them, taking care not to tear the flesh.
2. Heat the oil in a large Dutch oven, and add the chicken breasts a few at a time to prevent their getting tough and drying out. Cook on both sides, and remove to a platter when they are just done.
3. When all of the chicken is browned and just cooked, add the mushrooms, green onions, regular onions, and garlic to the Dutch oven, and cook until they are just limp. Add the Worcestershire sauce and stir well.

(Coq au Vin, continued on next page)

(Coq au Vin, continued)

4. Add the chicken back to the Dutch oven. Add the chicken and beef broths and the red wine. Cover and cook over medium heat or in a 350° oven for 45 minutes or until the chicken is tender. Add salt and pepper and taste and correct seasonings.
5. Serve over buttered Holland Rusks, potatoes, rice, or pasta with or without Béarnaise sauce. (See index for Béarnaise sauce recipe).

Serves 4 to 6

CHICKEN CREOLE

The following recipe can be made with cooked shrimp, left-over cooked turkey, or as a sauce for pork chops, fish, or cooked vegetables. It is a great buffet-dinner recipe because it can be increased easily. In our "early marital days" of entertaining with tight budgets, and little time, we served either chicken or shrimp Creole in one footed silver chafer, borrowed a second one from a friend, and put the cooked rice in it. We garnished the tops of the chicken or shrimp and the rice with lots of chopped parsley and green onion tops. A big green salad with mixed lettuces or all spinach, hot French bread left in long loaves and tied with a damask napkin around the middle of the bread, and it looked the part of a dinner party. For dessert, chess pie, fresh fruit, and cheeses made a colorful, uncomplicated dinner.

> **5 to 6 whole boneless, skinless chicken breasts**
> **salt and pepper**
> **1 cup chicken stock**
> **¼ cup dry white wine**
> **2 tablespoons vegetable or olive oil**
> **2 medium onions, chopped**
> **4 stalks celery, chopped**
> **3 cloves garlic, minced**
> **1 red bell pepper, chopped**
> **1 green bell pepper, chopped (optional)**
> **3 cups cooked tomatoes (or canned Creole tomatoes)**
> **1 can tomato paste**
> **2 teaspoons each: thyme, tarragon, basil**

1. Cook the chicken in the broth, white wine, salt, and enough water to cover until they are tender, about 25 minutes. Let cool in the broth. Chop or tear into pieces.
2. Heat the oil in a Dutch oven and add the chopped vegetables and sauté until they are just limp. Add the tomatoes, tomato paste, and herbs. Let cook uncovered for about 30 minutes or until reduced by one-third and fairly thick.
3. Let the Creole sauce cool, add the chopped cooked chicken, and refrigerate for several hours, preferably overnight. Season as necessary with salt and pepper and more thyme. Heat gently the next day. Serve over cooked rice.

Makes 8 to 10 servings

GRITS & GRILLADES

This is a typical New Orleans meal. Grillades are the small strips of either veal or beef that are pounded for tenderness, then stewed in a tomato, onion, mushroom sauce (with lots of garlic, of course) and served over grits. Every good cook in New Orleans is convinced that he or she makes "the best" grits and grillades, gumbo, red beans and rice, jambalaya, dirty rice, etc., which only means that there are countless variations on each recipe. Any one of the above dishes is not only family-fare, but stands up rather effectively for company too. They are all usually best done the day before. The grillades part of this dish certainly benefits from a night's rest getting to know its other ingredients. The grits practically self-cook the day you serve them; just follow the recipe on the box or bag.

    4 pounds veal or beef rounds
    3 tablespoons oil
    1 medium onion, chopped
    1 medium bell pepper, chopped
    4 stalks celery, chopped
    1 box fresh mushrooms, chopped
    3 cloves garlic, chopped
    1 large can (16 ounce) tomatoes
    2 tablespoons beef extract (Bovril, etc.)
    2 tablespoons tomato paste
    1 cup red wine
    2 bay leaves
    2 teaspoons each: thyme and tarragon
    3 tablespoons Worcestershire sauce
    2 teaspoons Tabasco sauce
    salt, pepper to taste
    ½ bunch fresh parsley, chopped

1. Pound the veal or beef to tenderize it. Cut the meat into long, 2-inch strips.
2. Heat the oil in a Dutch oven, and add the meat pieces, being careful not to over-crowd the skillet and toughen the meat. When the pieces are all cooked, remove them to a platter, and set aside.
3. To the oil and drippings in the Dutch oven, add the onion, celery, bell pepper, mushrooms and garlic, and sauté, stirring until they are all limp, but not at all burned. Add the tomatoes with their liquid, the beef extract, red wine, and tomato paste. Add the bay leaves, thyme, tarragon, Worcestershire sauce, and Tabasco sauce. Stir constantly to incorporate the extract and the tomato paste.

(Grits & Grillades, continued next page)

(Grits & Grillades, continued)

4. Add the cooked veal or beef pieces. Refrigerate over night if possible. Otherwise, cook the veal and beef pieces over medium heat, covered, for about 3 hours for the beef, and 2 hours for the veal, adding more red wine or hot water half-way through the cooking if the mixture is so thick that it begins to stick. Taste and adjust seasonings as necessary.
5. Serve over cooked grits (or rice or pasta).

Makes 6 to 8 servings

OSSO BUCCO

The Italian population in New Orleans lends as much, if not more according to some, flair and pizazz to the cuisine of the region as any of the other cultures there. The markets in the 1960's, when my family and I were living there, as well as today, of course, and through many decades, were filled with fresh artichokes, large and tiny; tomatoes of every shape, including the wonderful Roma tomato; pots of fresh herbs like rosemary, oregano, marjoram, thymes, basil; strings of garlic, peppers, and bay leaves. The shops with their breads, pastas, cheeses, oils, vinegars, sausages and, of course, the wonderful desserts and cookies- all were and are a cook's heaven. This veal dish is one that also has as many variations as New Orleans has cultures. The following one is our family favorite that you can easily adjust to your style with all tomatoes, or all mushrooms, etc. It's the long, slow cooking and doing it ahead that makes it great.

  4 veal shanks with a lot of meat on them
  ¼ cup good olive oil (Tuscan if possible)
  3 tablespoons tomato paste
  2 onions, chopped
  3 green onions, chopped with the green
  1 box fresh mushrooms, chopped
  4 stalks celery, chopped
  3 cloves garlic, chopped
  1 large (No. 16) can stewed or crushed tomatoes
  2 cups veal or chicken broth
  1 cup red wine
  2 teaspoons each: thyme, tarragon, rosemary and oregano
  3 or 4 leaves fresh basil (or 2 teaspoons dry)
  salt and pepper to taste

1. Heat the oil in a large Dutch oven, and add the veal shanks, browning on both sides. Remove to a platter.

(Osso Bucco, continued next page)

(Osso Bucco, continued)

2. Add the chopped vegetables and garlic to the oil and cook over medium heat until they are limp and not at all brown. Add the tomato paste and stir carefully to incorporate it. Add the tomatoes with their liquid, the stock, and the red wine. Stir carefully, and bring to a boil.
3. Add the herbs, including the basil leaves, and taste for seasonings, adding more if necessary.
4. Add the veal shanks to the tomato mixture, cover and cook over medium heat or at 350° for 2 to 3 hours or until the veal is tender but not falling off the bones. Let cool and refrigerate overnight, if possible.
5. Heat before serving, taste for salt and pepper, and add 1 or 2 tablespoons of the following "gremolata" to each serving.

Serves 4

GREMOLATA

This is sort-of an Italian "salsa." It is wonderful on soups, beans, and is a necessary part of Osso Bucco. You can make it up ahead and keep it for several days if the parsley is fresh. The parsley keeps the raw garlic from over-powering the dish or the diner.

3 cloves garlic
1 bunch parsley, washed and drained very dry
1 large lemon, whole

1. Cut the whole lemon in quarters, and remove any seeds.
2. Put the garlic and the parsley in a processor and process. While the motor is running, drop the lemon quarters peel and all through the feed tube one at a time, and process until all of the lemon is finely chopped.
3. Remove from the processor, scraping the sides to get all of the parsley. Refrigerate covered until needed. This keeps several days.
4. Put 1 to 2 tablespoons on each serving of Osso Bucco (or on minestrone, black or red beans, etc.).

Makes about 1 cup (8 tablespoons)

PORK CHOPS & SOUR CREAM

Pork chops German-style may seem off-beat from the Creole and Cajun fare of New Orleans, but Kolb's restaurant in the first block off of Canal Street on the old street-car line, was one of our early encounters with German fare during our years in New Orleans. This dish can also be made with some of the wonderful sausages that are available today, bratwurst, kielbasa, even the Cajun andouille. To substitute sausages, we like to take them out of their casings before cooking them, which makes the finished dish look a little more presentable and easier to eat in our opinion. It's a shame to have to do that, because some poor butcher has knocked his lights out trying to get the sausage in the casings, but since I'm the one cooking, serving, and eating it, I always remove them. Pork tenderloin, boneless pork chops, and butterflied boneless pork chops are a little easier to eat than bone-in pork chops, but if it's just family, the bone-in chops are the best.

> **4 thick pork chops**
> **1 tablespoon light vegetable oil**
> **1 medium onion, sliced medium thin**
> **1 clove garlic**
> **2 teaspoons thyme**
> **2 teaspoons dill weed**
> **cracked black pepper**
> **½ cup dry white wine or vermouth**
> **1 cup low-fat sour cream**
> **1 cup good rich chicken broth (or 1 can chicken broth)**
> **salt and pepper to taste**

1. Trim the chops of excess fat if necessary. Heat the vegetable oil over medium-high heat in a deep skillet or Dutch oven, and add the pork chops two at a time in order not to over-crowd the skillet. Brown the chops on both sides, remove to a platter and brown the remaining chops. Grind the black pepper over the chops. Sprinkle the thyme and dill over each chop.
2. Pour off all but 2 tablespoons of any fat that remains in the pan, reserving any browned bits of pork. Heat the fat and add the sliced onions and garlic and heat until the onions are limp. Remove the pan from the heat and carefully add the dry white wine or vermouth. Return to the heat, and cook over medium-high heat for about 5 to 8 minutes or until the wine loses its sharp alcohol taste and smell.
3. Add in the 1 cup sour cream, and whisk or stir until smooth. Add in the chicken broth, stirring well to incorporate. Put the

(Pork Chops & Sour Cream, continued on next page)

(Pork Chops & Sour Cream, continued)

pork chops in the sauce, sprinkle again with a little dill and thyme. Cover and cook in a 350° oven for about 1 hour or until the chops are well done. If the liquid cooks out too much before the 1 hour is up, add an additional ½ to 1 cup chicken broth. Add salt to taste. Serve hot with some of the sauce.

Serves 4

Note: Serve with potatoes or wide egg-pasta and sprinkle with chopped fresh parsley, if desired.

VEAL STEW

This is a "blanquette de veau" of sorts in that this is a "veal stew", but we have lightened it up from the wonderful, rich creamy-white "blanquette" of classical French definition. It is with much regret that we do too, because veal and cream get along beautifully. If you use fresh herbs, the best veal, mushrooms, and brandy to be found, and season it all with lemon juice, it's still a good stew. However, if your waist and your heart can stand it, a cup or so of real cream will make all the difference.

4 pounds veal stew meat, cut into ½" cubes
¼ cup good olive oil
2 large onions, chopped
4 stalks celery, chopped
1 box fresh mushrooms, washed and chopped
4 carrots, peeled and cut into 2" or 3" strips
1 cup dry white wine
3 cups veal or chicken stock, or canned chicken broth
2 teaspoons each: thyme, tarragon and cilantro
2 bay leaves
salt and pepper to taste
¼ cup good brandy
juice of 1 medium lemon

1. Cut the veal into small cubes of about ½" each. The smaller they are, the faster they will cook, and the more tender they will become.
2. Heat the oil in a large Dutch oven, add the veal cubes a few at a time in order not to over-crowd the pan and toughen the meat. Remove to a platter as they are done, and continue until all are cooked.
3. After all of the veal is cooked, add the onions, celery, mushrooms, and carrots to the Dutch oven, and cook until limp. Add the veal, stock or broth, white wine, thyme, tarragon, cilantro, and bay leaves to the pot and stir well.
4. Cover tightly with foil and then a lid and cook on top of the stove over medium to low heat or in a 325° oven for 1 hour or until tender.
5. Remove the covers from the Dutch oven, and cook over high heat for about 8 to 10 minutes, stirring to prevent sticking and burning, and until the sauce is reduced by half. Add the ¼ cup brandy, stirring it in well. Taste and season for salt and pepper. If the brandy has too much alcohol for your taste, continue to heat the stew over medium heat until the alcohol is cooked out and the brandy flavors remain. Add the juice of one lemon, and stir well. Serve with potatoes, rice, or pasta.

Serves 4 to 6

RICE DISHES

Almost every culture has its rice dishes, and to many of the poorer countries, it is called the "pearl of life." Louisiana and its bayous is agriculturally perfect for growing rice. It is one of the largest rice-producing states in the U.S. Rice readily absorbs other flavors, therefore it is very useful in highly seasoned dishes, as well as in delicately flavored desserts. These are some of our favorite rice recipes for main courses. We have included rice pudding under the desserts of the '60's.

BROWN RICE

Brown rice has not been "polished" as some of the long-grain white rices are, and the debate about which rice, the brown or the white, has the most food value rages still. We find that brown rice adds a nice change from the long-grain white or even the short-grain white rice. Here we actually cook it in beef stock to enhance its brown color and to enrich the taste. If you add left-over cooked chicken, beef, sausage, turkey, duck, etc., you can have a wonderful "Jambalaya" from brown rice. Left-over brown rice also makes a wonderful cold salad with an oil and lemon juice vinaigrette, a few sliced or cherry tomatoes, sliced cucumbers and a little chopped celery.

> **2 cups brown rice**
> **2 cups good beef stock (or 2 cans beef bouillon or beef**
>   **consommé)**
> **2 cups hot water**
> **1 tablespoon light vegetable or olive oil (Tuscan, if possible)**
> **4 green onions, chopped**
> **3 stalks celery, chopped**
> **½ cup pitted black olives, sliced**
> **1 cup sliced almonds, toasted**
> **salt and fresh ground pepper to taste**
> **4 slices bacon, cooked and crumbled**

1. In a large boiler with a lid, bring the beef stock and hot water to a boil. Add the 2 cups brown rice, gradually. Cover and cook on medium-high heat for 25 minutes or until all of the liquid is absorbed.
2. Heat the oil in a heavy skillet and add the green onions and celery and cook until they are limp but still have some texture. Lower the heat and add the olives and almonds. Toss about in the pan to mix thoroughly. Remove from the heat until the rice is cooked.
3. Add the sautéed onions, celery, olives and almonds to the

(Brown Rice, continued on next page)

(Brown Rice, continued)
brown rice when it is completely cooked and mix well. Taste
and correct seasonings.
4. Serve topped with the cooked crumbled bacon.

Makes 4 to 6 servings

CREOLE RICE

2 cups white long-grain rice
1 14½ ounce can tomatoes
2 or 3 cups hot water
1 tablespoon Worcestershire sauce
2 teaspoons Tabasco sauce
2 bay leaves
2 teaspoons each: thyme and oregano
1 tablespoon vegetable or olive oil
3 green onions, chopped with the green
1 clove garlic, chopped
1 red bell pepper, chopped
1 green bell pepper, chopped
salt and pepper to taste

1. Drain the tomatoes in a colander reserving the juices in a measuring cup. Add enough hot water, the Worcestershire, and
   Tabasco sauce to the tomato juices to make 4 cups. Bring the 4
   cups tomato juices and hot water to a boil. Add the rice, bay
   leaves, thyme, oregano, salt and pepper. Stir and bring back to
   the boil. Cover the pot, and cook until tender for 25 to 30 minutes.
2. Heat the oil in a large skillet, and add the green onions, garlic,
   red and green peppers, and cook over medium heat until they
   are limp, but still have some texture.
3. When the rice is tender, add the cooked vegetables to the rice,
   and stir well. Taste and correct the seasonings as necessary.

Makes 4 to 6 servings

"DIRTY RICE"

The finished rice dish looks "dirty" because of all the browned additions. The traditional addition, and really the main ingredient to make it "dirty rice", is sautéed chicken, duck, or wild bird livers. If livers aren't in your repertoire, you can always replace them in this recipe with bits of cooked meats from those birds, but then it would probably have to be called "Not-So-Dirty Rice."

> **1 pound chicken livers**
> **½ pound gizzards**
> **1 large onion, cut into slices**
> **2 cloves garlic smashed**
> **2 stalks celery, cut in ¼'s**
> **water to cover**
> **2 cups long-grain rice, uncooked**
> **1 tablespoon butter or oil**
> **1 medium onion, chopped**
> **2 cloves garlic, chopped**
> **3 stalks celery, chopped**
> **4 green onions, chopped with the green**
> **½ bunch fresh parsley, washed and chopped fine**

1. Cook the livers and gizzards (the giblets) in enough hot water to cover, the sliced onion, smashed garlic cloves, and celery quarters until the giblets are tender, about 30 to 45 minutes.
2. While the giblets are cooking, heat the oil in a heavy skillet, and add the onions, green onions, garlic and celery and sauté until just limp.
3. Drain the livers, reserving the liquid. Add enough hot water to the liquid from the giblets to make 4 cups.
4. Bring the 4 cups liquid to a boil, and add the uncooked rice, stirring well, and returning to the boil. Cover and cook until tender, about 25 to 30 minutes on medium-high heat.
5. Chop the giblets and add to the sautéed onions, celery, and garlic. Keep warm while the rice is cooking.
6. When the rice is tender, add the giblets and vegetables to the rice, and season with salt, pepper, and mix well. Taste and correct seasonings.

Makes 4 to 6 servings

Note: Serve with the chopped parsley sprinkled on top.

LEMON-HERB RICE

3 cups uncooked long-grain rice
3 cups rich chicken broth (or 3 cans chicken broth)
3 cups hot water
2 teaspoons each: thyme and tarragon
2 bay leaves
salt and pepper to taste
2 lemons, grated and juiced
2 or 3 leaves fresh basil, chopped or shredded into pieces

1. Bring the 3 cups chicken broth and the 3 cups hot water to a boil. Add the rice, thyme, tarragon, bay leaves, salt and pepper. Cook covered until tender, about 25 to 30 minutes.
2. While the rice is cooking, grate the peel from the 2 lemons, being careful not to include the bitter white that is just under the peel. After grating the lemons, squeeze the juice into a small cup removing the seeds.
3. When the rice is tender, remove from the heat and add the juice and peel of the lemon, the basil and more salt and pepper, if necessary.

Serves 4 to 6

PECAN RICE

There is a rice called "pecan rice," that has no pecans in it at all, which you treat just like brown rice in that it takes a bit longer to cook than the long-grain white rices. This recipe is for brown or wild rice or a mixture with added pecans. It is especially good with wild game.

3 cups brown rice
2 cups good beef broth (or 2 cans bouillon or consommé)
1 tablespoon Worcestershire sauce
enough additional water to make 6 cups
1 tablespoon butter or olive oil
4 stalks celery, chopped
1 medium onion, chopped
2 green onions, chopped with the green
1½ cups toasted pecan pieces
salt and pepper to taste

1. Measure the broth, Worcestershire sauce and hot water to make 6 cups. Bring to a boil, and add the brown rice. Cover and cook until tender, about 30 to 40 minutes.
2. In a large skillet, heat the butter or oil and add the onions and celery, and cook until they are just limp. Add the pecans and toss around in the skillet until they are well mixed. Turn off the heat until the rice is ready.
3. When the rice is tender, add the celery, onions, and pecans with their butter or oil into the rice. Mix well. Add an additional 1 or 2 tablespoons butter (or margarine) if necessary. Taste for seasonings, and add salt and pepper.

Serves 4 to 6

RED BEANS & RICE

1 1 pound bag of dried red beans
1 large onion, chopped
4 stalks celery, chopped
4 cloves garlic, chopped
2 bay leaves
2 tablespoons Worcestershire sauce
salt and pepper
4 to 6 cups cooked white rice

1. Wash the beans in a colander, then put them in a 3 quart pot and cover the beans with boiling water. Put a lid on the pot and let the beans sit for at least one hour.
2. Drain what water is left. Fill with hot water until the beans are covered by several inches. Put on high heat and bring quickly to a boil. Do not cover.
3. Put another pot of water on the stove and cover it with a lid (so that the water won't boil away quickly), bring to a boil, then reduce to a simmer. This is the water to replenish the "big bean pot" as it boils down.
4. Boil the beans until they begin to burst, which usually takes about two hours. Add in the chopped celery, onion, bay leaf, and the garlic. Continue to cook over medium heat just above a simmer, watching carefully for the water not to boil out.
5. As the water is reduced in the pot, bring the second pot of simmering water to a full boil and add the boiling water to the beans. If you add cold water or water that is not boiling to the beans, the beans will be toughened by stopping the boiling each time you add additional water.
6. Continue to cook the beans watching very carefully until half of the water is gone, and the beans are not beginning to stick to the bottom of the pot. Stir occasionally to make sure.
7. When the water has cooked half-way down, add the salt, pepper, ham, Worcestershire sauce, Tabasco sauce, and continue cooking until the beans are tender and some have burst. (If you add the salt, ham, Worcestershire before the beans are almost done, the salty additions will make the beans tough.)
8. Taste and correct seasonings, adding more Worcestershire, Tabasco sauce, and ketchup, if desired.

Serves 4 to 6

Note: Serve over white cooked rice.

RICE STUFFING

It is not surprising to find "stuffing" for poultry, game, pork chops, or fish made out of rice instead of bread, because rice is so readily available in Louisiana. This is a nice change from our Alabama cornbread stuffing.

    4 cups cooked white rice
    ¼ stick butter or 4 tablespoons light vegetable oil
    1 medium onion, chopped
    1 box fresh mushrooms, chopped
    3 stalks celery, chopped
    2 teaspoons each: thyme, sage, marjoram
    ½ bunch fresh parsley, washed, chopped fine, and drained
      well
    ½ cup good chicken broth

1. Heat the butter or oil in a Dutch oven, and add the onions, celery, and mushrooms. Cook until they are barely limp. Add the rice all at once, and cook over medium heat until the rice is hot.
2. Add the thyme, sage, marjoram, chopped fresh parsley and the chicken broth, and cook uncovered another 5 minutes stirring well. Let cool before stuffing fish, poultry, game, etc.

Makes 5 cups stuffing

WATERCRESS RICE

For years the following rice recipe was about the only "fancy" rice dish I ever fixed for company, and no one complained about it. Somehow, it rotated off of my repertoire, and I have missed it. I used to load it up with unsalted butter, but now I find the olive oil or even just half of the butter I used to use is just as good. You can substitute margarine, but it isn't quite as good.

> 2 cups long-grain rice
> 2 cups chicken broth
> 2 cups hot water
> 2 bay leaves
> ½ stick unsalted butter (or ¼ cup good olive oil)
> 3 stalks celery, chopped
> 1 bunch green onions, chopped with the green
> ¼ cup dry white wine or vermouth
> 1 bunch watercress, washed and chopped with some of the
>   stems
> salt and pepper to taste

1. Cook the rice in the broth and hot water with the bay leaves for 25 to 30 minutes or until all of the liquid is cooked out, and the rice is tender.
2. In a skillet or sauté pan, heat the butter or oil, and add the green onions and their green, and the celery and cook until they are just sweated and still have texture. Lower the heat and add the white wine or vermouth, and cook for about 5 or 6 minutes or until the wine loses it alcohol taste and smell.
3. When the rice is cooked and tender and still hot, add the sautéed vegetables, watercress with some of their peppery stems, butter and white wine to the rice. Stir well. Taste for salt and pepper. Remove the bay leaf before serving.

Serves 4 to 6

Note: This can be done ahead and refrigerated. It can easily be doubled.

WILD RICE, TOMATOES, & MUSHROOMS

This is one of our favorite dishes. When we ran the restaurant and take-out shop in the '80's, we offered this as an alternative for cornbread dressing at Thanksgiving and Christmas. It was very popular, but so much easier to make than the dressing that we usually had some of the wild rice left over after all the orders had gone out. Many a Thanksgiving and Christmas morning during those shop years found me frantically getting all the left-over wild rice orders for my own family. After a while, it grew to be a tradition for us as strong as cornbread dressing had been. It, obviously, can be done ahead, and even at the last hour, it's not too taxing. If you use all wild rice, however, it does take almost twice as long to cook as the wild rice mixture, so don't be too cavalier.

> **1 package wild rice or wild rice mixture**
> **1 cup chicken broth (or 1 can chicken broth)**
> **2 tablespoons unsalted butter, margarine or olive oil**
> **1 box fresh mushrooms, sliced**
> **6 to 8 very pretty tomatoes, or 1 can tomatoes**

1. Cook the wild rice or the wild rice mixture according to the directions on the package, substituting the chicken broth for part of the water.
2. Sauté the mushrooms in the butter or olive oil, and add the tomatoes. Cook down gently until most of the liquid is gone. Add to the rice.

Serves 4 to 6

DESSERTS FROM THE 60's

BANANAS FOSTER

This is a Brennan's-for-Breakfast hallmark, and as many times as I fix it at home now years later, it never tastes quite as good as theirs does. I have even served it on the patio at home, surrounded with flowers, etc., but there is just something about Brennan's that can't be duplicated. This is a good try, though. The best ice cream is essential, and I don't think anything substitutes for the butter in this. It IS dessert, so if you are opposed to desserts, just eat the banana and feel good about it.

> **4 ripe bananas, sliced lengthwise**
> **4 tablespoons unsalted butter**
> **½ cup dark brown sugar**
> **1 teaspoon each: cinnamon and nutmeg**
> **juice of 1 small lemon**
> **½ cup banana liqueur**
> **½ cup good brandy**

1. Melt the butter in a skillet and add the brown sugar, cinnamon and nutmeg, stirring until the sugar is completely melted. Add the ripe bananas and cook until they are hot and well coated, but not mushy.
2. Carefully pour in the banana liqueur and brandy. If the butter is very hot, they will flame on their own. If not, either: Cook over medium heat stirring until the alcohol cooks out. (Lowering the heat and stirring, it will not flame up, and the alcohol will cook out.) OR: Flame the liqueur and brandy in the pan with the bananas with a match and cook until the flame dies out and the alcohol is thus cooked out.
3. Add the juice from the lemon and stir to incorporate. You can do ahead to this point and heat it later.
4. Serve the bananas and sauce warm over the best vanilla ice cream available. (Wine glasses or brandy snifters or a large glass bowl).

Serves 4

BREAD PUDDING

The ultimate bread pudding is made with real croissants and heavy cream. But in New Orleans, we almost always made our bread pudding with left-over French bread, which was good and nowhere near as rich. Here we have substituted part whole milk for all cream, and leave the choice of bread up to you. Today's "light" breads just don't work. They tend to "melt away" under the baking time. Whenever we had extra strawberries or fresh pineapple, dried apricots, golden raisins, or good pears, we added them. Any one of them or one or two in combination are wonderful. This recipe makes a lot, but you can easily half it.

1 loaf French bread or the equivalent in dry, rich bread
6 eggs beaten in
1 quart milk or ½ milk, ½ cream
3 tablespoons vanilla
2 teaspoons each: cinnamon and nutmeg
1 cup sugar
pinch of salt

1. Cut the bread into slices and line the bottom of an oven-proof baking dish with them. (Add fruit on top of the bread if you are using it.)
2. Mix the eggs, sugar, vanilla, milk (and/or cream) cinnamon and nutmeg, and salt, and pour over the bread slices. The bread should float, but be totally covered.
3. Bake uncovered at 325° until a knife comes out clean in the center. Depending on the depth of the bowl, this will take from 45 minutes to an hour. The more shallow the bowl, the faster it will bake (and the easier it is to serve). Serve with Bourbon Sauce.

Serves 6 to 8

Bourbon Sauce:
1 pound softened unsalted butter
2 cups confectioners sugar
2 teaspoons salt
½ cup bourbon

1. Beat all together well.

CRÈME BRULÉE

A crème brulée is served cold with a hard sugar crust on the top. In the years we lived in New Orleans, the crème brulée was only the vanilla flavor, but now with the advent of new and young cooks and chefs, crème brulées are flavored with lots of things: chopped candied ginger is my personal favorite, but orange, lemon, raspberry, and lots of others abound. I like to serve little small ramekins of two or three flavors per person, but that is only workable if we don't have too many people. The small 4- or 6-ounce size ramekins are just right for this rich, heavenly dessert.

> **4 egg yolks**
> **2 whole eggs**
> **1 cup sugar**
> **2 cups milk**
> **1 cup cream**
> **1 teaspoon vanilla**
> **pinch of salt**
> **10 to 12 tablespoons dark brown sugar**
> **optional additions: chopped crystallized ginger, fresh raspberries, dried chopped glazed apricots, dried cherries or cranberries, grated lemon peel**

1. Mix all of the ingredients together.
2. If using any of the optional ingredients, divide them among all of the small ramekins.
3. Carefully pour the custard into the ramekins dividing equally.
4. Put the individual ramekins in a baking pan, and half fill the pan with warm, not hot, water.
5. Bake in a 325° oven about 25 minutes or until they are set, and a knife in the center of the ramekin in the middle of the baking dish comes out clean. Carefully remove them from the oven and the water and chill covered.
6. Spoon 2 tablespoons of the brown sugar over the top of each ramekin. Two or three hours before serving, run the brown-sugared ramekins in the baking dish under the broiler just until the brown sugar is totally melted and caramelized. Keep chilled until serving time. Serve in the ramekins. The sugar will be very hard, and each person is to break through the caramel crust with a spoon to the cold custard.

Serves 6 to 8

CUP CUSTARD

Cup custard can be made in little Pyrex ramekins or in a larger charlotte mold or soufflé dish. This can be unmolded successfully, and it usually is served unmolded. The caramelized sugar on the bottom melts during the baking so that when you reverse the custard onto a plate, the caramel is on the top. The baking of the custard must be done at least 6 hours in advance for the custard to chill enough to unmold. "Cup custard" is probably one of the most traditional desserts in New Orleans, and for us, it is a real "comfort food."

¾ **cup white sugar to caramelize the mold(s)**
1 tablespoon hot water
1 cup cream
6 whole eggs
½ **cup sugar**
1 teaspoon each: vanilla and nutmeg
pinch of salt
2 cups milk

1. To caramelize the mold(s): Melt the ¾ cup sugar and the hot water in a small heavy saucepan and stir just enough to moisten the sugar well. Cook over medium-high heat until the sugar turns golden brown and is not at all dark. Pour the hot caramelized sugar into the mold or molds completely covering the bottom of each mold. Set aside while making the custard.
2. Scald the cream, and let cool a bit in order not to cook the eggs.
3. In a large separate bowl, mix the eggs, ½ cup sugar, salt, vanilla, and nutmeg and mix until smooth. Add the cream and milk and stir carefully.
4. Strain the mixture into the caramelized mold or molds, and put them in a large baking pan in the preheated 350° oven.
5. When the baking pan filled with the mold or molds is in the oven and before it begins cooking, fill the baking pan ⅔ full with warm water.
6. Bake at 350° for 45 minutes to 1 hour for the large mold, and about 25 minutes for the smaller ones, or until a knife in the center comes out clean. Carefully remove them from the oven and from the hot water bath. Let cool 30 minutes.
7. Refrigerate covered for at least 6 hours before unmolding onto a platter or individual plates. The caramel will be melted and will be on the top of the inverted unmolded custard.

Serves 6 to 8

Note: This can be done and kept molded for 2 or 3 days before using. Unmold several hours before serving.

CRÊPES

Crêpes are fun to serve: they can be done ahead of time and even frozen, they can be used for dessert or a fast lunch or even an hors d'oeuvre. They always look so festive, and they are not at all hard to do. This is the master recipe, and it makes about 20 8" crêpes. You can double it if you need to. A small seasoned iron crêpe pan is easy and quick, but any skillet with short sides that has been treated or sprayed so not to stick works just as well. You can cook two at once in a larger skillet, just take care to make them thin.

> **1 cup white flour**
> **3 whole eggs**
> **1 teaspoon each: salt, nutmeg and cinnamon (for dessert crêpes)**
> **2¼ cups milk**
> **3 tablespoons melted unsalted butter (or margarine)**

1. Put the eggs, salt, nutmeg, cinnamon, and 2 cups of the milk in a blender and blend until smooth. Add the flour and blend, scraping the side of the jar occasionally. The mixture should be smooth and the consistency of cream. Let rest for at least 30 minutes for the bubbles to subside from the blender and for the flour to expand. Add the ¼ cup milk after the 30 minutes if the mixture seems too thin. Stir well.
2. Heat a crêpe pan or any skillet with low or sloping sides with 1 teaspoon butter or margarine. Pour in enough batter to coat the bottom of the pan. Pour any excess back into the mixer jar.
3. Cook over high heat until the crêpe begins to have bubbles forming, and the crêpe is easily turned. This takes just a few minutes. Turn and cook the other side until it slides out easily.
4. Keep warm on a platter, not stacking the others while they are hot or they will stick together. To freeze them, place wax paper between each one and wrap tight in foil.

CRÊPES WITH STRAWBERRIES

Brennan's Restaurant in New Orleans calls these crêpes "Crêpes Fitzgerald". It is really a favorite there and at home. Make the crêpes up in advance, and the filling and sauce a day ahead, and dessert is ready to be heated.

If you can't find strawberry brandy or liqueur, use brandy or dark rum. Strawberries marinated in sugar produce a wonderful liquid that can always be used with or instead of the brandy and liqueurs. Just supplement the strawberry liquid with a little orange or apple juice being careful not to overwhelm the strawberry taste with the juices.

> **12 8" crêpes**
> **1 16 ounce package of cream cheese (or Neufchâtel, a low-fat cream cheese)**
> **1 cup confectioners sugar (10 X)**
> **4 tablespoons sour cream (or low-fat sour cream)**
> **grated peel and juice of 1 lemon**
> **pinch of salt**
> **1 carton fresh strawberries, washed and hulled**
> **2 tablespoons unsalted butter**
> **¼ cup sugar**
> **½ cup strawberry liqueur (or orange juice)**
> **½ cup brandy (or apple juice)**

1. Mix together in a mixer or a processor the cream cheese, confectioners sugar, sour cream, grated lemon peel, lemon juice, and the pinch of salt until they are smooth but not runny. Refrigerate for 10 minutes or so if the processor got it too runny.
2. Spoon some of the cream cheese mixture into each crêpe, and roll the crêpe in a pencil shape. If you are serving at once, put in an oven proof dish and keep warm. Otherwise, keep them in the oven-proof dish in the refrigerator, covered. Heat in a low oven (200°) while making the sauce.
3. Heat the butter in a skillet and add the strawberries and sugar. Heat the strawberries only; if they over-cook, they will become mushy. Add the liqueurs and brandy or fruit juices, and cook stirring just until the alcohol is cooked out. Put two filled, warmed crêpes on each plate and serve the strawberries and the sauce over and around them.

Serves 6

CHOCOLATE-CHOCOLATE-CHOCOLATE CRÊPES

Every part of this dessert except the whipped chocolate cream can be made ahead of time and assembled early in the day you are to serve it. Heat the sauce and spoon it over the crêpes, or puddle it and then put the crêpes on top of it, just before serving. Decorate each plate with one pretty red strawberry if you have it.

Chocolate Crêpes:
1 cup white flour
3 tablespoons cocoa
3 eggs
1 tablespoon sugar
2 tablespoons melted unsalted butter (or vegetable oil)
1 teaspoon salt
¾ cup milk

1. Put all ingredients into a blender container and blend until it is completely mixed, scraping down the sides of the container occasionally. The mixture should be the consistency of heavy cream. Add more milk if it is too thick. Let rest at least 30 minutes to deflate the bubbles from the blending and to let the flour expand.
2. Heat a seasoned crêpe pan or an oiled skillet with low sides, and pour enough batter just to cover the bottom of the pan. Pour back any extra batter into the blender container. When the top side is cooking around the edges, and little bubbles appear, turn the crêpe to the other side and continue cooking the second side until it is lightly brown. Remove from the pan and keep on a platter, not stacking the hot crêpes on top of each other or they will stick together.

Chocolate Sauce:
1 cup cocoa
1 cup sugar
3 tablespoons light corn syrup
1 cup cream
4 tablespoons unsalted butter
½ teaspoons salt

1. Put all ingredients in a small boiler and over low heat, bring to a boil, stirring to melt the butter and incorporate all the

(Chocolate-Chocolate-Chocolate Crêpes, continued on next page)

(Chocolate-Chocolate-Chocolate Crêpes, continued)

ingredients. Cook for another 2 minutes. Remove from heat and
let cool.

Makes 1½ cups

*Note: This keeps for weeks in a glass jar in the refrigerator. Heat in
warm water or microwave to warm it for the crêpes.*

CHOCOLATE CREAM FILLING

2 cups whipping cream
½ cup confectioners sugar
4 tablespoons cocoa
2 teaspoons vanilla

1. Sift the cocoa into the confectioners sugar and blend well.
2. In a mixer whip the cream, adding the confectioners sugar and
   cocoa gradually until all the cream is whipped being careful not
   to over-whip it (or it will turn to butter). Add the vanilla and
   stir in carefully with a spoon.

*Note: This will hold about 3 hours before it begins to separate. It can
be frozen and even served frozen, if desired.*

To assemble and serve:
1. Fill each crêpe with either the frozen or the unfrozen whipped
   cocoa cream, and serve with the warmed chocolate sauce.
2. A few toasted almonds, a big, pretty strawberry, are good
   additions.

Serves 6 (2 crêpes each)

CRÊPES WITH APPLES & RUM

12 cooked 8″ crêpes
6 medium to large apples, Granny Smith, York, etc., peeled
** and sliced**
4 tablespoons unsalted butter (or margarine)
¼ cup brown sugar
2 teaspoons each: cinnamon and nutmeg
1 cup dark rum (or apple juice)
1 cup apple juice or cider
juice of 1 lemon
4 tablespoons cream (optional)

1. In a large skillet, melt the butter (or margarine) and add the brown sugar. Stir until the sugar is completely melted.
2. Add the peeled and sliced pieces of apples, the cinnamon and nutmeg, and sauté until the apples are tender but not mushy.
3. Add the rum and apple juice or cider and cook over medium heat, stirring constantly for about 5 minutes until the rum has lost the strong alcohol taste and smell. Add the juice of the lemon, stir well. Add the cream now if you are using it. Stir well.
4. Let cool and fill each crêpe with the apples, rolling in a pencil shape. Reserve the sauce. Keep the filled crêpes on a platter and either refrigerate or keep warm in a 200° oven, uncovered, if serving at once. These keep well in the refrigerator for several days.
5. Serve 2 crêpes per person with some of the sauce.

Makes 6 servings

FROZEN CAPPUCCINO

A strong dark roast coffee is important for this recipe. If you usually don't have it, you can make-do with a good instant like Medalia d'Oro. Don't use the instant cappuccino mixes, they are not strong enough to stand up to freezing. Don't go overboard with the bourbon, etc., either because too much alcohol will keep it from freezing.

5 cups strong, dark roast coffee
1¼ cups dark brown sugar
4 tablespoons white corn syrup
1 tablespoon of any of the following: bourbon, vanilla, coffee
** liqueur, chocolate liqueur**

(Cappuccino Ice, continued on next page)

(*Frozen Cappuccino, continued*)

1. Heat the coffee, dark brown sugar, and corn syrup over medium heat until the sugar is completely melted and the corn syrup is blended in with the rest. Taste and add more brown sugar if it is not sweet enough, heating and stirring until the brown sugar is melted.
2. Add the bourbon, vanilla, etc., if desired.
3. Pour into 6 coffee cups, wine glasses, or sorbet glasses and freeze overnight.
4. Top with sweetened whipped cream*

Serves 6

*Note: Sweetened whipped cream: to 1 cup whipping cream add 4 tablespoons confectioners sugar and beat until stiff.

FROZEN COFFEE MERENQUE

1 tablespoon dark-roast instant coffee (Medalia d'Oro)
3 tablespoons mini-size chocolate chips, melted
3 tablespoons mini-size chocolate chips, not melted
1 can condensed milk
¼ cup milk
1½ cups whipping cream
3 tablespoons confectioners sugar

1. Put the coffee, melted chocolate, and condensed milk in a double boiler, and heat stirring until thick and smooth.
2. Add in the ¼ cup regular milk and the unmelted chocolate chips, and stir to incorporate. Chill for several hours.
3. Whip the 1½ cups whipping cream with the confectioners sugar until stiff and fold it into the coffee mixture. Chill overnight.

Serves 4 to 6

Note: Serve in wine glasses with shaved chocolate over the top.

ORANGE-RICE PUDDING

Rice Pudding is another "comfort food" that is good any time of day, month or year. Once in a culinary class in Paris, the instructor made and served a similar version of this after the class, and all through the room in a chorus of every language from French to Russian to German and more, each person said :"Ummm. I love rice pudding." We didn't have to speak the language to know what was being said, it was clearly understood. Any white rice (not instant) can be used for this, but the fat, short-grained Italian Arborio rice is our favorite. It takes a bit longer to cook, but it turns out creamier than other rices.

> 1 cup Arborio rice (or 1 cup long- grain rice)
> 1 cup cream
> 1 cup milk
> pinch of salt
> vanilla bean, split (or 2 teaspoons vanilla)
> 4 eggs, beaten
> 2 cups milk
> pinch salt
> 1 cup sugar
> 4 large oranges, grated and juiced
> 1 lemon grated
> 1 tablespoon Grand Marnier (or other orange liqueur),
>   optional
> 1 cup whipping cream
> 3 tablespoons confectioners sugar

1. In a colander, wash the Arborio rice under very hot water for about 3 minutes (If using long-grain rice, omit this step).
2. Bring the cream and milk to a boil, add the rice, salt, vanilla bean or vanilla, stirring constantly. Put a lid on the rice, lower the heat to medium, and cook for 30 to 45 minutes or until the rice is tender. If the milk boils out before the rice is tender, add hot milk or cream in order not to stop the cooking. Set aside when done to cool.
3. While the rice is cooking, beat the eggs, 2 cups milk, salt, and sugar together, and cook in the top of a double boiler until the custard coats a spoon. Stir occasionally to keep it from curdling. Remove from the heat and add in the grated peel of the oranges and the lemon, the orange juice, and Grand Marnier, and mix well. Cover with plastic wrap touching the custard to avoid a skin forming on the top. Let cool in the refrigerator or over a bowl of ice.

(Orange-Rice Pudding, continued on next page)

(Orange-Rice Pudding, continued)

4. When the rice and the custard are cool, whip the cream and add in the confectioners sugar, beat until stiff.
5. In a large bowl, put the rice and the custard, and fold in the whipped cream. Fold it in carefully in order not to deflate the cream. Chill for at least four hours. Serve with additional sweetened whipped cream if desired.

Serves 6 to 8

THE 1970s

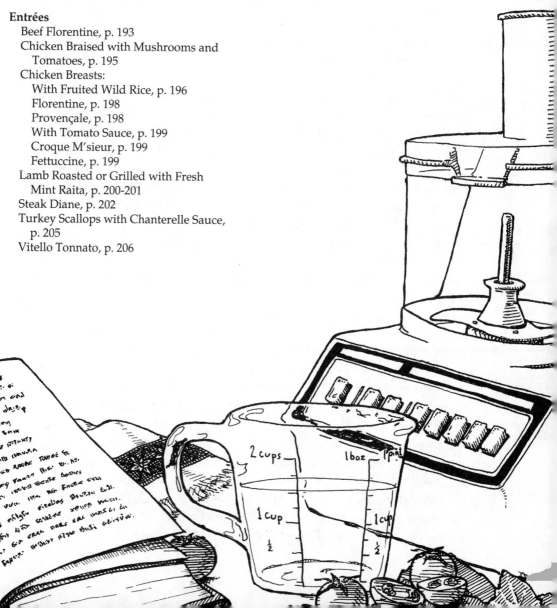

The 1970's will always seem to me to have been the high noon of my life. My generation was just turning 30, and where 30-year-olds get all their energy is still an enigma to me. Although there were some "surprise-caboose-babies" born to my friends who married early or late in our 30's, generally speaking, our lives were no longer totally bounded by babies and diaper service. (Remember, we didn't have disposable diapers back then, and as Erma Bombeck says, in the days of diapers in a hamper for a week, you could easily lose an eye from the ammonia if you opened that hamper carelessly at any given time.) Like young mothers today, we drove, and we drove, and we drove. Our low-slung station wagons were excellent examples of the impossible task of putting a quart in a pint jar: children, dogs, groceries, carpools, cleaning to drop off, cleaning to pick up, school books, musical instruments, costumes for plays and holidays: all in bumper-to-bumper traffic with the radio and the children blaring.

When my husband had finished all ten years of his medical training, plus two compulsory years in the armed forces, he made the decision to move us all to Birmingham, Alabama, my own hometown, for him to pursue academic medicine at the University of Alabama in Birmingham Medical Center. We moved into a house that my uncle had built from the G-I bill in the 1940's after World War II ended. All my life I had loved that house, and although we hated to leave 15 years of friends in New Orleans, we were glad to be "back home." We moved into our house on our tenth wedding anniversary, and I was so happy that I often thought that had I known ten years before when we had gotten married that I would be moving into my favorite house in Birmingham, I might have been tempted just to camp out there for ten years and wait, knowing the wait was worth it. But then, I sure would have missed a lot.

In Birmingham, a friend asked me to teach cooking to her high school students' Fine Arts class, and the 12th graders were so creative, so enthusiastic, so successful that it made me look pretty good. Soon, their parents were asking me to teach them, and my cooking school years were launched in 1974.

A new organization of cooking teachers had formed because of the need for standardization and accountability in this new exciting field of cooking classes in America, and this group which then called itself, the International Association of Cooking Schools (the IACS), began with their first meeting in New Orleans, Louisiana. The first annual meeting I attended was in Chicago at The Drake Hotel. I checked in and went up the elevator with Julia Child and her husband, Paul, and I was totally speechless. The IACS was fairly small then, compared to today when it has become the International Association of Cooking Professionals, the IACP, and it was very encouraging to be in such illustrious company, then and now.

Julia Child warned us back in the early 70's at the meeting in Chicago that things were inevitably going to get worse before they got better in the culinary world. Technology was producing all sorts of strange hybrids such as imitation cheese, imitation vanilla, imitation milk, imitation chocolate, imitation restaurants, and imitation cooks. She wisely predicted that such aberrations would not endure, and we were admonished not to compromise our values for a seemingly easier road. In the long run, we all knew then, and it is beginning to come to light now, twenty years and more later, that chemicals are not food, and fresh food unsauced, unadulterated, and real, will always produce healthier people.

Perhaps many of us became near-Francophiles in the 70's, despite Julia and others calling us back home to our abundant natural resources in America, because of our disregard for America's rapidly expanding "fast-food industries." However, we soon found that our own gardens, our own herbs, mustards, oils and vinegars that were our heritage from our own history were not so easily forgotten or lost in the fast lane that was gaining on us.

Cooking classes were quickly and eagerly filled, and what better way to learn than to teach. We all learned together, and more and more teachers soon came into our lives. Technology joined our purists' forces as well in the advent of the food processor. Kitchen shops were elated from selling several expensive processors a day, and after a year or two of practice, most cooks were not serving pureed dinners as often, but rather through classes and raw experience learning to use these revolutionary machines to do a lot more than mush. Our "tammis" (sieves) and wooden mashers were put away as relics of an earlier time. They were not especially missed either.

The following recipes from the decade of the 70's are ones that have, once again, stood the test of time. We have tried to up-date them, and simplify them, but they never were very complicated to begin with. We followed the Julia-Child-admonition to her disciples: we were to keep it simple, pure, and enjoyable. Good food for good health. Once again, these are intended for family or formal entertaining, because they are not too fancy, and most can be done ahead.

SOUPS & STARTERS

BELGIAN CHICKEN OR FISH STEW

Myriam Guidroz in New Orleans was my first and favorite cooking teacher. She preceded Julia Child's television programs by several years in the 1960's, and I really credit Ms. Guidroz with my career in food. She was a single mother in New Orleans, a food-writer for The New Orleans STATES-ITEM, and she taught classes in her home. She supported herself and her children in those days with her classes and her newspaper column. Therefore, economy and efficiency in the kitchen were her basic concepts of teaching, making her an excellent first teacher for any one. The soup recipe here is called "Waterzooie" in Belgium, and you can use either chicken or fish. Here we used chicken, but any good white fish could be substituted.

> 2 tablespoons vegetable oil or unsalted butter
> 6 boneless, skinless chicken breast halves, cut into cubes
> 1 small box fresh mushrooms, chopped
> 4 green onions, chopped
> 2 carrots, peeled and cut into 1" sticks
> 3 stalks celery, chopped
> 2 teaspoons each: thyme and tarragon
> 2 bay leaves
> ½ cup dry white wine
> 1 cup chicken broth
> ½ cup cream (optional) or low-fat sour cream
> juice of 1 lemon
> ½ bunch fresh parsley, washed and chopped
> salt and pepper to taste
> 4 medium-size boiled potatoes, cut into large slices or chunks

1. Heat the oil in a large Dutch oven, and add the chicken, the chopped vegetables, herbs and bay leaves, and cook until the chicken is almost completely cooked.
2. Add the dry white wine, broth, and the cream, lemon juice, salt and pepper. If using the sour cream instead of the cream, whisk carefully to incorporate, and stir it in well. Cover with a lid and cook over low heat for another 10 minutes until the chicken is tender.
3. Add the chopped parsley and salt and pepper to taste. Cook for another 5 to 10 minutes over medium heat. Serve in soup bowls over the boiled potatoes with plenty of the liquid from the stew.

Serves 4 to 6

CARROT & GINGER SOUP

2 tablespoons unsalted butter or light vegetable oil
1 medium onion, chopped
3 stalks celery, chopped
6 large carrots, peeled and chopped
3 cloves garlic, chopped
1 medium fresh ginger root, grated
6 cups chicken or veal stock
2 cups dry white wine
grated peel of 1 lemon
juice of 1 lemon
2 teaspoons each: thyme, basil, and cilantro
salt and pepper to taste

1. Heat the oil in a Dutch oven or large boiler. Add the chopped vegetables, garlic, and ginger root. Sauté over medium heat, stirring until they are wilted.
2. Add the stock and dry white wine, the lemon peel, and the herbs. Cover and cook over medium heat for about 45 minutes or until the vegetables are very tender. Puree in a blender or food processor.
3. Taste for seasonings, adding the lemon juice and salt and pepper as necessary. Garnish with 1 tablespoon per serving of sour cream and a sprinkling of chives. This soup can be served hot or cold.

Serves 6 to 8

CORN CHOWDER

2 teaspoons vegetable oil or unsalted butter
8 to 10 large ears white corn, cooked and cut off the cob
  (to equal about 4 cups corn)
1 red sweet bell pepper, seeded and chopped
1 large onion, chopped
4 stalks celery, chopped
2½ cups chicken or veal stock
2½ cups milk (regular or low-fat)
2 teaspoons each: thyme, cilantro and basil
2 medium tomatoes, peeled, seeded and chopped
salt and pepper
1 cup sour cream (low-fat or regular)
4 or 5 chopped fresh chives or green onion tops, chopped

1. Clean the cooked white corn of all silks, and set aside.
2. Heat the oil or butter in a Dutch oven or large boiler, and add all of the chopped vegetables except the tomatoes and corn, and sauté until they are just limp.
3. Add the stock, milk, and the herbs. Reduce uncovered over high heat until reduced by about one-half for about 20 to 25 minutes.
4. Add the corn, tomatoes, salt and pepper, and cook covered over medium heat for another 20 minutes. Taste for seasonings, adding more salt, pepper, and herbs if necessary. This is best if made and refrigerated overnight.
5. Top with 2 teaspoons of sour cream (low-fat or regular) and a few chopped chives.

Makes 4 to 6 servings

Note: We have cut down on the fat and the calories from the original recipe which used all cream instead of milk. It is still good, but there is nothing quite as good as cream if your weight and cholesterol can stand it.

GREEN ONION BISQUE

Originally, this soup was made with 5 kinds of onions (red, white, yellow, leeks, and green onions), but as all things are wont to do, it soon ended up just with green and yellow onions. No one ever really knew the difference, because the green onions hold up fine with just a little help from their yellow cousins. Onions actually have a fairly high sugar content which makes an excellent soup when paired with heavy cream. Here again, however, we have omitted the cream, added in potatoes, broth, and a little white wine, and we think the results are excellent. Maybe it's because we have a more clear conscience both for our weight and for our budget than if we had used all cream.

> 2 teaspoons unsalted butter or good quality olive oil (Tuscan, if possible)
> 4 bunches green onions, washed and chopped
> 2 yellow medium yellow onions, chopped
> 2 medium potatoes, peeled and cubed
> 4 cups chicken or veal stock
> ½ cup dry white wine, or vermouth
> 2 teaspoons thyme
> 1 teaspoon grated fresh nutmeg
> 2 bay leaves
> salt and pepper to taste
> 1 cup sour cream (low-fat or regular)
> 1 cup Parmesan or Romano cheese, grated

1. Heat the butter or oil in a Dutch oven or in a large boiler, and add the whites of the chopped green onions, the chopped yellow onions, and the peeled and cubed potatoes. Sauté until the vegetables are beginning to wilt. The smaller the cubes of the potatoes, the faster they will cook.
2. Cover and cook over medium heat for about 8 more minutes, stirring occasionally, until the potatoes are tender. Add all but ½ cup of the green onion tops, the broth, wine, herbs, nutmeg, and bay leaves, and cook covered over medium-high heat for about 45 minutes. Let cool slightly off the heat, uncovered.
3. Process or blend the soup a little at a time until smooth. Taste and correct seasonings. The soup is best done one day ahead. Serve heated with 1 tablespoon each of the sour cream, reserved chopped green onion tops, and grated Parmesan or Romano cheese on each serving.

Serves 4 to 6

MUSHROOM CREAM SOUP

2 tablespoons vegetable oil or good quality olive oil (Tuscan, if possible)
1 pound fresh mushrooms, chopped
1 medium onion, chopped
2 celery stalks, chopped
2 cloves garlic, minced
1 tablespoon tomato paste
6 cups beef stock (or consommé or bouillon)
3 green onions, chopped with the green
½ bunch fresh parsley, washed, chopped, and towel-dried
2 teaspoons tarragon (fresh if possible), chopped
salt and pepper to taste
¼ cup dry sherry
1 cup sour cream (low-fat or regular)

1. In a Dutch oven or a large boiler, heat the oil and add the mushrooms, onion, celery, and garlic. Sauté until they are wilted.
2. Add the herbs, tomato paste, and stir to incorporate them. Add the stock and cook over medium-high heat for about 30 minutes, uncovered, to reduce by about one-third and to allow the tomato paste to thicken it. The mixture should be fairly thick. If not, reduce another 5 to 10 minutes or until it is no longer watery.
3. Mix the chopped green onions, parsley, and tarragon together. They must be thoroughly dried or they will clump together. Add to the mushroom mixture about 5 minutes before the reduction is complete.
4. Taste for seasonings, and add salt and pepper if necessary.
5. To serve: Add about 1 or 2 tablespoons dry sherry to each individual bowl, with a tablespoon of sour cream. The soup must be very hot or the sherry will cool it off.

Serves 4 to 6

PUMPKIN BISQUE

The idea of pumpkin soup must conjure up nutmeg, cinnamon, etc., in some people's minds, but pumpkin is a member of the squash family, and squash is excellent with onions, garlic, etc. If you still have qualms about Pumpkin Soup, call it "Harvest Chowder."

> 2 teaspoons light vegetable oil
> 1 medium onion, chopped
> 2 cloves garlic, minced
> 3 stalks celery, chopped
> 1 cup cooked cubed ham, or chicken, or smoked turkey (or a combination of all 3)
> 3 tomatoes, peeled, seeded, and chopped
> grated peel of one lemon
> 1½ cups cooked pumpkin puree
> 2 tablespoons tomato paste
> 2 teaspoons thyme
> 3 cups chicken or veal broth
> 1 cup milk
> salt and pepper to taste

1. Heat the oil in a Dutch oven or large boiler and sauté all of the chopped vegetables except the tomatoes until they are wilted.
2. Add the cubed ham, chicken, or smoked turkey, and cook over medium heat stirring for a few minutes. Add the tomatoes, lemon peel, pumpkin, and stir until thoroughly mixed.
3. Add the thyme, broth, and milk, and cook over medium-high heat for about 30 to 45 minutes, uncovered, to reduce and thicken. The pumpkin and tomato paste are thickeners, so stir the soup occasionally to prevent sticking, and remove it from the heat when it is as thick as pea soup. Taste and correct seasonings with salt, pepper, or any of the above herbs already added, or a teaspoon or so of fresh lemon juice.
4. This is best the next day. Serve hot with garlic croutons.

Serves 4 to 6

TOMATO SOUP WITH FRESH TOMATOES

2 teaspoons good olive oil, Tuscan, if possible
3 onions, chopped
4 stalks celery, chopped
3 garlic cloves, minced
3 pounds ripe tomatoes, peeled, seeded, and chopped
1 cup dry white wine or vermouth
5 cups chicken or veal broth
1 cup low-fat cottage cheese
2 teaspoons thyme
3 or 4 fresh basil leaves
salt and pepper
juice of one small lemon
½ cup low-fat sour cream

1. In a Dutch oven or large boiler, heat the olive oil and sauté all of the chopped vegetables except the tomatoes.
2. Add the white wine or vermouth, the chicken stock, the thyme, and the tomatoes. Cook over medium heat uncovered for about 30 minutes.
3. Process the cottage cheese, the fresh basil leaves, salt and pepper and lemon juice until the cottage cheese is smooth. Taste and add more salt and pepper if necessary. Add to the tomato soup slowly and stirring constantly to blend. Continue to cook the soup, stirring constantly for another 5 minutes. Correct seasonings.
4. This soup is best made the day before, but you can serve it right away. Add 1 tablespoon low-fat sour cream to each serving, and top with a few chopped fresh chives or green onion tops.

Serves 4 to 6

WATERCRESS-CREAM SOUP

1 medium bunch fresh watercress
2 tablespoons unsalted butter or good quality olive oil
  (Tuscan, if possible)
2 stalks celery, chopped
5 green onions, chopped with the green
2 medium potatoes, peeled and diced
2 cups chicken or veal stock
2 cups milk (or cream, or 1 cup milk, 1 cup cream)
salt and pepper
2 teaspoons fresh grated nutmeg

1. Wash the watercress and reserve 12 large leaves for garnish. Chop the watercress with some of the stems very fine. Set aside.
2. In a Dutch oven or large boiler, heat the olive oil and sauté the chopped green onions with their green, the celery, and the diced potato until they are sweated and the potatoes are almost tender. The smaller the dice, the faster the potatoes will cook.
3. Add the watercress and cook for another 3 to 4 minutes. Add the broth, milk (or cream), salt, pepper, and nutmeg, and cook uncovered over medium-high heat 25 to 30 minutes or until reduced by about one-half.
4. Let cool slightly and process or blend until very smooth. Strain through a strainer if necessary to remove any fibers from the watercress stems. Taste and correct the seasonings, adding more salt, pepper, nutmeg, or a few drops of fresh lemon juice if necessary. Garnish with the reserved watercress leaves.

Serves 4 to 6

VEGETABLES

ARTICHOKES FLORENTINE

1 package (10 ounce) frozen spinach, cooked and drained
2 tablespoons olive oil
1 bunch green onions, chopped
1 package fresh mushrooms, sliced thin
2 cloves garlic, minced
salt and pepper
2 teaspoons each: oregano, thyme and basil
1 (15-ounce) can artichoke bottoms, or 4 to 6 fresh cooked
   artichoke bottoms
¼ cup dry white wine or vermouth
1 additional tablespoon olive oil
¼ cup grated Parmesan or Romano cheese

1. In a Dutch oven, heat the olive oil and sauté the green onions, mushrooms, and garlic until they are sweated.
2. Add the spinach to the vegetables and cook until the spinach is very hot and all water has cooked out from it. Season with salt, pepper, and the herbs. Taste and correct seasonings.
3. If using canned artichoke bottoms, drain them well and trim the bottoms so that they sit flat. Trim fresh ones of their large stem.
4. Fill each artichoke bottom with the spinach mixture, dividing it equally. Put them in an oven-proof dish.
5. If doing ahead, refrigerate until serving time.
6. To heat, pour ¼ cup dry white wine or vermouth, 1 additional tablespoon olive oil in the bottom of the oven-proof dish, cover with foil, and heat in a 350° oven for 20 to 30 minutes or until bubbling. Top with grated Parmesan or Romano cheese.

Serves 4 to 6

ASPARAGUS WITH ORANGE

2 pounds fresh asparagus (the smaller, the better)
1 whole egg
2 teaspoons Dijon mustard
1 teaspoon salt
¾ cup light vegetable oil
2 tablespoons frozen orange juice concentrate
2 teaspoons fresh lemon juice
2 teaspoons lemon thyme (or thyme)
salt and pepper
3 oranges, Valencias or "blood oranges"
½ bunch fresh watercress, washed and drained

1. If small asparagus are not available, cut the big stumps off of the very bottom of the large asparagus, and peel the thick stalks with a vegetable peeler all the way up to the points. This is not necessary with the baby fresh asparagus.
2. Fill a skillet with boiling water and 2 teaspoons salt, place the asparagus in the hot water all lying in one direction, and lower the heat to a simmer. Cook uncovered until a fork barely goes through the stem, but not until they are limp. Drain under cold water to stop the cooking. Put on a towel to cool and dry.
3. Make a mayonnaise from the whole egg in a bowl or in a blender. Beat the egg, salt, and the Dijon mustard until it is light-lemon colored. Add the oil one teaspoon at a time, whisking or processing the entire time. As soon as 2 tablespoons oil have been added into the egg, you can add the oil a little faster, continuing to stir or process until all of the oil is used up. Stop the stirring or the machine, add in the orange juice concentrate, the lemon juice, and the lemon thyme, and whisk or process until they are incorporated. Taste and add salt, pepper, and more thyme if necessary.
4. Section the orange and arrange on individual salad plates or on one serving platter with the cooked, drained asparagus. Spoon a wide ribbon of the orange mayonnaise over the asparagus and oranges, and serve with a sprig or two of fresh watercress.

Serves 4 to 6

BULGAR BAKED WITH FRESH MUSHROOMS

Bulgar, or cracked wheat, is cooked exactly like long-grain regular rice. Bulgar is a very high fiber, cracked wheat that is also high in nutrition and taste. It makes a welcome change from rice, potatoes, and pasta.

4 cups chicken or veal broth
2 cups dry cracked wheat
2 teaspoons salt
3 tablespoons unsalted butter or olive oil
1 large onion, chopped
1 box fresh mushrooms, sliced thin

1. Bring the broth to a boil. Add the cracked wheat and salt and stir so that it does not stick. Cover and cook until tender, about 20 to 25 minutes depending upon the size of your pan. The bulgar should be tender and all of the liquid should be absorbed.
2. Heat the unsalted butter or olive oil in a skillet and add the onion and fresh mushrooms and sauté until they are sweated and slightly limp. Add to the cooked hot bulgar. Stir well, and taste for seasonings, adding salt and pepper if necessary.

Serves 4 to 6

CHEESE PUDDING

This is really what my grandmother's generation called a "fondue," but as the years rolled on, a fondue was more well defined than this dish. The fondue from Switzerland, which was not the one my grandmother knew, is a cheese and kirsch "dip" for bread cubes, or chocolate sauce for fresh fruits, etc. The title "Cheese Pudding" or "Mock Soufflé" is far more descriptive of what we had as children and what we resurrected for cooking classes. The cheese pudding smells wonderful when guests or family arrive, and it holds very nicely too, should all not be as coordinated as planned. Be creative with other ingredients to go into this pudding: cooked crabmeat, shrimp, 2 or 3 kinds of olives, sautéed celery and green onions, etc., just as you would with a real soufflé. Everything that goes in it must be cooked, and it can take a lot of seasoning.

> 6 slices "heavy" bread (Pepperidge Farm or homemade white bread)
> 2 cups grated New York sharp cheese
> 4 eggs, beaten
> 2½ cups milk
> 3 tablespoons Worcestershire sauce
> 2 teaspoons Dijon mustard
> 2 drops Tabasco sauce
> salt and pepper

1. Remove the crusts from the bread, and cut into small cubes. Put in a oven-proof dish and cover with the grated cheese.
2. In a large measuring cup, add the beaten eggs to the milk, and the rest of the ingredients. Mix well and pour over the bread and cheese. Let rest overnight.
3. Bake uncovered in a 350° oven about 1 hour and 15 minutes or until puffed and golden. Serve hot.

Serves 6 to 8

MUSHROOMS MEDITERRANEAN

1 large carton fresh mushrooms, left whole
½ cup good quality olive oil or vegetable oil
3 tablespoons white vinegar
1 small onion, sliced into rings
4 or 5 sprigs fresh parsley, chopped
2 cloves garlic, minced
1 teaspoon sugar
2 teaspoons each: oregano and fresh cracked pepper
4 whole coriander seeds
3 or 4 leaves fresh thyme and tarragon

1. Wash and dry the mushrooms to remove any grit. Put in clean Mason jars or a deep glass bowl.
2. Heat all the rest of the ingredients in a boiler over medium heat until the vegetables are barely limp. Pour over the mushrooms, and let marinate overnight. Serve as an appetizer, relish, or salad.

MUSHROOM SUKIYAKI

These mushrooms are not as Oriental as they sound, but it makes a wonderful and different vegetable side-dish. You can add cooked chicken, shrimp, or lobster for a main course for luncheon or dinner. We like it as an accompaniment to grilled fish or meat, and that is how we taught it in our cooking classes.

> 1 tablespoon vegetable oil
> 3 stalks celery, chopped
> 3 green onions, chopped
> 2 large red bell peppers, chopped
> 1 medium onion, chopped
> 1 small piece fresh ginger, peeled and chopped
> 1 carton fresh mushrooms, sliced
> ½ cup soy sauce
> 1 tablespoon sesame oil
> 1 tablespoon dry sherry
> 2 teaspoons Dijon mustard
> 2 teaspoons sugar

1. In a skillet or Dutch oven, heat the oil and add the vegetables and the ginger, and sauté until they are just wilted.
2. Add the rest of the ingredients. (Note: if you are using this as a main course, add the cooked shrimp, lobster, or chicken at this point with the soy sauce, etc.) Cook covered over medium heat for another 8 to 10 minutes. Taste and correct seasonings.

Serves 4 to 6

Note: Serve over buttered Holland Rusks, rice, or pasta.

VEGETABLES IN WHITE WINE

Myriam Guidroz, my teacher in New Orleans, was again the inspiration for this pretty and delicious vegetable dish. The vegetables are good if you cut them up in a coarse, peasant-style, and very frou-frou looking if you feel like balling them all up with a melon baller, or "turned" in the French manner. ("To turn" vegetables is to trim them attractively in neat oval and/or oblong shapes.) The vegetables should be about the same size, chopped, chunked, or turned so that they will cook more evenly. Personally, we like the peasant-chunks, even for an elegant dinner. If your knife skills are great, and you have the time, by all means, turn 'em.

> 2 cups potato chunks or ovals
> 4 to 6 Jerusalem artichokes ("sunchokes"), peeled and
>   trimmed
> 4 large carrots in chunks or ovals
> 1 bunch radishes, trimmed into nice shapes
> 3 stalks celery, cut on the bias
> 8 small onions, peeled
> 1 box fresh mushrooms, stemmed and left whole
> 3 tablespoons good quality olive oil (Tuscan, if possible)
> 2 teaspoons salt and fresh cracked pepper
> 1 cup chicken or veal broth or stock
> ½ cup dry white wine or vermouth
> 1 bunch fresh basil
> 3 or 4 sprigs fresh tarragon

1. Trim all of the vegetables into about two-inch ovals, rounds, or chunks (See discussion above). Quickly rinse and dry the mushrooms leaving them whole, but removing their stems.
2. Heat the oil in a Dutch oven or heavy stove-top casserole, and add the vegetables, salt and pepper. Sauté until the vegetables begin to sweat, but are not at all limp.
3. Add the rest of the ingredients. Cover and cook over low heat, adding more broth or hot water only if the vegetables begin to stick. Simmer over low heat for 25 to 30 minutes or until the hard vegetables are tender. The smaller they were trimmed, the faster they will cook.
4. Taste and correct seasonings.

Serves 4 to 6

ENTRÉES

BEEF FLORENTINE

During our cooking school years, we taught a lot of garden clubs and other groups cooking classes. Beef Florentine was one of the favorites. We taught it for special entertaining at home, Christmas or New Year's Eve, or for an easy-but-glamorous dinner. Some of the womens' groups were my mother's friends and were quite accomplished cooks, and even they liked this recipe, and they actually prepared it themselves at home. We felt like that gave us an "A". It is very pretty, and very easy. It can also be served cold in the summer, just season it highly.

> 1 whole beef filet, trimmed (about 4 to 6 pounds)
> 2 teaspoons good olive oil, Tuscan, if possible
> 2 cloves garlic, minced
> 1 bunch green onions, chopped
> 1 box fresh mushrooms, chopped
> 1 box frozen chopped spinach, or 3 pounds fresh cooked and drained
> 1 8-ounce package low-fat (Neufchâtel) or regular cream cheese, softened
> salt and pepper to taste
> 1 package puff pastry dough, thawed
> egg wash: 1 whole egg beaten with 1 tablespoon water

1. Roast the whole filet at 400° on a foil-lined pan for 8 to 10 minutes until the filet is firm to the touch and registers 140° to 160° on a meat thermometer. Let cool completely.
2. Heat the oil in a large skillet, and sauté the garlic, chopped green onions, and mushrooms until they are sweated and slightly limp. Add the well-drained spinach to the skillet and cook stirring constantly over high heat until the spinach is dry, about 3 or 4 minutes. Add the softened cream or Neufchâtel cream cheese and completely mix the ingredients. Taste and add salt and pepper. Let cool.
3. When the filet is cool to the touch, "butterfly" the entire length of the filet, being careful not to cut it into two pieces.
4. Fill the slash in the filet with the cooled spinach and vegetable mixture.
5. Remove the thawed puff pastry to the work counter and carefully stretch the edges slightly to make it large enough to wrap around the filled filet.
6. Put the filet with the spinach filling on the puff pastry rectangle

(Beef Florentine, continued on next page)

(Beef Florentine, continued)

and pull the edges up around the meat and spinach, covering it completely and neatly. Trim any excess pastry, which you can use for decorations if desired (ribbons, leaves, monograms, etc.) You can do ahead to this point and refrigerate for 24 hours.

7. Brush the entire puff pastry package with one whole egg beaten with 1 tablespoon water. If using decorations from the puff pastry, stick them onto the egg wash at this point, and then egg wash them, too.

8. Preheat the oven to 400°, and bake the filet in its pastry for about 30 to 40 minutes or until the puff pastry is golden brown and all layers of the flaky pastry are done. (It looks done before it is. Test with a fork to see if the pastry layers are all baked.)

9. Let rest 10 minutes. Serve whole in its pastry, slicing 1" pieces slightly on the diagonal.

Serves 6 to 8

Note: This is a pretty presentation on a plate with the circles of golden pastry, red meat, and green spinach. Serve with pasta, potatoes or rice.

CHICKEN BRAISED WITH MUSHROOMS & TOMATOES

2 teaspoons olive oil
1 whole chicken cut into parts
3 cloves garlic, minced
3 onions, chopped
1 package fresh mushrooms, chopped
5 fresh tomatoes, peeled, seeded, and chopped
1 cup green or ripe olives (or ½ cup of each), sliced
2 teaspoons each: thyme, basil, tarragon, salt and cracked pepper
1 cup dry white wine

1. Heat the oil in a Dutch oven or oven-proof casserole, and add the chicken pieces a few at a time until they are brown, but not completely cooked. Remove to a platter as they brown.
2. When all of the chicken is browned, add the garlic, onions, and fresh mushrooms to the Dutch oven, and sauté until they are sweated. Add the tomatoes, olives, herbs, and dry white wine, and stir well.
3. Add the chicken pieces back to the casserole with enough hot water to cover. Bring to a boil, cover, and simmer over low heat for 35 to 40 minutes or until the chicken is tender. Remove the chicken to a serving platter, and with the casserole uncovered, reduce the sauce over high heat for about 5 minutes or until thickened. Taste and add salt and pepper. Spoon the sauce around the chicken.

Serves 4

CHICKEN WITH FRUITED WILD RICE

Stuffed, filled chicken breasts, breaded and roasted were great favorites of our cooking school classes, and when we went into the take-out business later, we used to make these by the hundreds. We would have the stuffings, or fillings, completely ready and cooled, the sauce(s) made, and cooled, and the whole, boneless, skin-on chicken breasts laid out on our long prep table at the shop. We covered the chicken breasts with parchment paper to keep them from tearing while we pounded them with a meat pounder. We removed the paper, then all of us would fill each pounded whole breast with about ½ cup filling, roll the chicken breast into a neat little package, dip each one in beaten egg and milk, then in croissant crumbs, and put them on a sheet pan. We baked them for about 45 minutes or until they were firm. Put them in the take-out pans on the appropriate sauce, let them cool, lidded them, labeled them, and sold them. Customers could see in our big picture windows into the kitchen, and on Wednesday afternoons when we did these chicken breasts, people would line up and watch us. It was fun and fairly easy, and as one man said, "Better than the car wash." You can begin with 8 or 10, and only use one filling at first, and freeze what you don't use that week. They don't need to be tied up into bundles, the chicken is quite gelatinous and sticks to itself nicely. To serve, cut the cooked, cooled breast into circles, rather than leaving them whole, so that you can see the white chicken, the green, red or rice filling, and the golden crust. A tomato sauce is easy and wonderful, and a white wine sauce is excellent, but a little more time-consuming.

> **4 whole chicken breasts, boneless with skin ON**
> **1 small box wild rice mixture (Uncle Ben's)**
> **2 teaspoons olive or vegetable oil**
> **3 green onions, chopped**
> **2 Granny Smith apples, peeled and chopped coarse**
> **2 stalks celery, chopped**
> **1 cup milk mixed with 1 whole egg**
> **2 cups dry bread crumbs**

1. Cook the wild rice mixture as directed using the seasoning package.
2. Heat the oil in a skillet and sauté the green onions, apples and celery. Add to the cooked wild rice mixture and let cool.
3. Put the boneless, whole chicken breasts skin-side down on a counter or table. Cover with plastic wrap or waxed paper, and pound lightly with a meat pounder or the flat-side of a hammer wrapped in a dish towel. (The head of a hammer or the flat-side not wrapped in a dish towel will tear the chicken flesh to pieces,

(Chicken with Fruited Wild Rice, continued on next page)

(Chicken with Fruited Wild Rice, continued)

and it will not hold the filling). Remove and discard the plastic or wax paper.

4. Sprinkle the pounded breasts with salt and pepper and a pinch of thyme. Put about ½ cup of the completely cooled apple and wild rice mixture on each breast in a neat line along the center-line of each breast. Roll each breast into a neat cylinder, tucking the ends on both sides in neatly. Put on a tray until they are all finished.

5. Dip each rolled, filled breast into milk and egg, then into the bread crumbs. Place on a sturdy cookie sheet or jelly-roll pan with at least an inch between each package. Bake at 350° for about 45 minutes or until very firm to the touch.

6. Let cool slightly and slice into about 4 to 6 circles so that the breaded chicken encircles the filling. You can also cut them when they are slightly cooled into quarters, but the circles are prettier. Serve with the white wine sauce below.

Serves 4

White Wine Sauce:
2 tablespoons unsalted butter
2 tablespoons flour
2 cups liquid: milk, cream, wine, broth, or any combination

1. Heat the butter and add the flour all at once. Cook for about 5 minutes, stirring until they are incorporated, and the flour is cooked.

2. Add the liquid, and stir constantly or whisk to prevent lumps. Cook 8 to 10 minutes or until thickened to sauce consistency.

3. Add salt, pepper, and any herbs like thyme, tarragon, or a pinch of fresh grated nutmeg.

VARIATIONS ON STUFFED CHICKEN BREAST:

CHICKEN FLORENTINE:

Use the spinach filling in the "Beef Florentine" for the chicken, following the directions under Chicken and Fruited Wild Rice." You can use either the White Wine Sauce or the Tomato Sauce (see Italian Chicken Stuffing) for the Chicken Florentine.

CHICKEN PROVENÇALE:

2 teaspoons vegetable or olive oil
1 medium onion, chopped
2 stalks celery, chopped
2 cloves garlic, minced
½ bunch fresh parsley, chopped fine
2 cups dry bread crumbs
½ cup chicken broth
¼ cup dry white wine or vermouth
salt and pepper
2 teaspoons each thyme, basil and tarragon

1. Heat the oil, and sauté the vegetables until they are cooked. Add the rest of the ingredients and mix well. Cook over medium heat uncovered to reduce all of the liquid, stirring constantly.
2. Taste and season with salt, pepper and herbs. Let cool completely before filling each chicken breast with about ½ cup each along the center line of the whole breast.
3. Proceed as in the recipe for Chicken Stuffed with Fruited Wild Rice. Serve with the following Tomato Sauce.

TOMATO SAUCE:

2 teaspoons olive or vegetable oil
3 green onions, chopped
2 garlic cloves, minced
3 red or yellow bell peppers, chopped
3 cups cooked tomatoes
2 tablespoons tomato paste
½ cup dry white wine
1 cup chicken or veal broth
2 teaspoons each: thyme, basil, cilantro
salt and fresh cracked pepper

1. Heat the oil in a large boiler or Dutch oven, and sauté all of the vegetables except the tomatoes.
2. When the vegetables are cooked but not limp, add the rest of the ingredients. Cook over medium high heat uncovered until reduced and thickened.
3. Taste and correct seasonings.

Other Variations:
1. For Fruited Wild Rice, use chopped dried apricots, mandarin oranges, golden raisins, or a combination, instead of the sautéed apples in the wild rice, OR
2. Fill each pounded whole chicken breast with 1 slice Monterey Jack cheese, 1 slice smoked turkey, and 2 teaspoons red or green pepper jelly, for "CHICKEN CROQUE M'SIEUR," OR
3. Fill each pounded whole chicken breast with cooled cooked fettuccine pasta mixed with chopped, sautéed, fresh mushrooms, green onions, and garlic, and bound with 2 tablespoons low-fat or regular sour cream, chives, and salt and pepper for "CHICKEN FETTUCCINE."

LAMB ROASTED OR GRILLED WITH FRESH MINT RAITA

5 to 6 pound deboned leg of lamb
½ cup good quality olive oil
juice of 3 lemons
1 tablespoon dried rosemary
fresh cracked pepper
3 cloves garlic

1. Have the butcher bone the lamb leg for you. It will weigh about 8 or 9 pounds with the bone in. Do not tie it up, but leave it "butterflied."
2. Marinate the lamb leg in all of the ingredients overnight.
3. Remove from the marinade and broil flesh side up 6 to 8 inches from the broiler watching carefully for about 8 to 10 minutes. Carefully turn the lamb over with a large, heavy kitchen fork or tongs and broil for another 5 to 8 minutes to sear the skin side of the lamb.
4. Turn the oven to Bake and roast the lamb for another 10 to 12 minutes at 375° or until the thickest part of the lamb registers 140° to 160° on a meat thermometer, depending on your preference. This can also be done on a grill.
5. Let rest 10 minutes before carving. Turn the lamb to the flesh side and carve very thin on a slight diagonal. Serve with the following Mint Raita.

FRESH MINT RAITA

A raita is almost mandatory with hot Indian food. Spearmint makes the best raita, but you can use any other fresh mint too.

1 teaspoon cumin seeds
1 teaspoon coriander seeds
3 to 4 green onions, chopped
1 cup fresh mint leaves, tightly packed
juice of one small lemon
½ teaspoon dried hot pepper (or Tabasco sauce)
2 teaspoons salt
1 cup plain yogurt

1. Toast the seeds in a skillet. Grind them together or smash with the bottom of a skillet until pulverized.
2. Process with all of the rest of the ingredients except the yogurt.
3. If you prefer a thin raita, or sauce, add the yogurt in the processor. For a thicker one, add the processed ingredients to the yogurt in the bowl.

Serves about 6 to 8

STEAK DIANE

"Table-top cooking" was quite in vogue in the "cooking school years", and we taught it in a men's class in my home. The men were each given a portable cooktop upon which to cook, a tray of ingredients all neatly lined up, an apron, a wooden spoon, a set of directions, and a "fire extinguisher" (a lid to a large pot and a bowl of salt). We had one instructor-assistant for each two "chefs." There were about 24 "chefs," plus 12 teachers, and 2 dishwashers. Absolute organization was essential. The class was a great success. Miraculously, there were no disasters. (We had also had a fire-drill in the very beginning, just in case). Of course, we prayed a lot before, during, and after. It was one of the only participation classes that our cooking school ever had, because our nerves were shattered. The other two or three times that we taught this particular men's class, we taught it in the cooking school in our shop, The Highland Gourmet, as a demonstration class. The "Men's Class" became a popular Christmas, birthday, and anniversary present for a lot of men, because, obviously, the women enjoyed it as much as the men did. For four to six people at home, it is very easy, because it has to have everything ready beforehand, or as the French say, "mise-en-place." Chicken Diane, in this day of low-or-no-fat meats, is equally as good as the beef, but our family has always liked beef the best here. We allow 6 ounces per person of beef, and about 8 ounces per person for chicken; thus for 6 people, you will need 36 ounces (2¼ pounds) beef, or 48 ounces (3 pounds) of chicken. (There are 16 ounces in a pound, remember). If you are the fearful sort, you can easily fix this in the kitchen by yourself, and serve it without all the pomp.

> **2¼ pounds filet mignon, cut into 36 strips about 1" long (or see above)**
> **4 tablespoons olive oil or butter**
> **4 green onions, chopped**
> **1 box fresh mushrooms, washed and sliced thin**
> **2 teaspoons Dijon mustard**
> **1 tablespoon Worcestershire sauce**
> **1 tablespoon A-1 Sauce**
> **2 tablespoons brandy**
> **salt and pepper**

1. These are to be done in 3 batches so that you do not overcrowd the skillet and thus steam the beef (or chicken) instead of sautéing it. Steaming it will make it dry and tough by pulling all of the juices out of the meat into the pan.
2. Divide the beef strips, mushrooms, green onions, and minced garlic into 3 separate batches.

(Steak Diane, continued on next page)

(Steak Diane, continued)

3. Heat the sauté pan, or skillet, with 1 tablespoon of the oil or butter until sizzling. Add the first batch of beef strips, mushrooms, green onions, and garlic into the hot pan, and cook over high heat stirring lightly, being careful not to pierce the meat with a fork (and lose the juices) or to burn the garlic and green onions.
4. Remove the first batch to a platter and keep warm in a very low oven (200°) while cooking the last two batches.
5. Repeat step #2 with the second and third batches, removing each to the same heated platter.
6. After the last batch is finished, remove the sauté pan from the heat, add the brandy and enough hot water to allow scraping of all of the browned bits on the bottom and sides of the pan. To this, add the rest of the ingredients: the Dijon mustard, Worcestershire sauce, and the A-1 Sauce, and stir well. Add salt and pepper to taste.
7. Return to low heat and cook stirring all the while until sauce is bubbling. Pour over the warm beef strips and serve at once over rice or pasta or Holland Rusks.

Serves 6

Note: If you need to "hold" this dish for a while, put the cooked strips in the sauce, remove from the heat, cover and set aside or refrigerate. Heat gently on top of the stove so as not to cook the meat further, and serve.

204 : Remembrances of Things Passed

TURKEY SCALLOPS WITH CHANTERELLE SAUCE

Chanterelles are "wild" mushrooms that are available fresh in the better grocery stores and markets. During our cooking school days, a co-teacher of ours, Sue Richards, would pack up her children here in Alabama and head to the northwest United States where she ran a business cutting and supplying up-scale restaurants with these and other wonderful wood treasures. The chanterelles and morels she brought to our cooking classes and taught us to use were our favorites. They were packed in beautiful boxes layered with fern fronds. Her classes were always filled with men and women of all ages. Chanterelles and morels are not good raw, but intensify in flavor as they are cooked and permeate the foods around them. They are somewhat like truffles in that respect, and yet far more available, and quite a bit less expensive.

> **12 small turkey scallops**
> **salt and pepper**
> **flour**
> **4 tablespoons unsalted butter**
> **1 tablespoon good quality olive oil**

1. Pound the scallops to flatten to ¼ inch, sprinkle with salt, pepper, and flour lightly.
2. Heat the butter and olive oil and sauté the turkey scallops for 4 or 5 minutes on each side. Remove to a platter while making the sauce.

CHANTERELLE SAUCE

2 tablespoons unsalted butter or good quality olive oil
1 cup chanterelle mushrooms
3 green onions, chopped with some of the green
4 sprigs fresh parsley, chopped
2 teaspoons tarragon, fresh if possible
2 cups chicken or veal stock
¼ cup cream
¼ cup good brandy

1. Heat butter or olive oil, add the mushrooms, green onions, and tarragon. Sauté for several minutes. Remove the mushrooms with a slotted spoon to a platter.
2. Add the rest of the ingredients and cook over high heat for about 15 to 20 minutes or until it is reduced to about 1 cup liquid. Return the mushrooms to the pan, and cook another 3 or 4 minutes uncovered over low heat. Season with salt and pepper as needed.

Serves 4 to 6

VITELLO TONNATO

In our early cooking school years, Vitello Tonnato, a cold veal and tuna summer dish, was almost a hallmark, because Spring and Summer classes were very popular in those days. Veal is usually quite expensive, but you can substitute some of the many turkey products available today instead of the veal. A small boneless turkey breast is an excellent substitute for a veal roast, or you can buy the turkey breast scallops and sauté them in olive oil instead of using a whole roast and serve the scallops with the tonnato sauce. Although this is a traditionally summer meal, it can be served warm any time of the year.

> **3 to 5 pound veal roast (or see above)**
> **1 can oil-packed anchovy filets, drained**
> **salt and freshly ground pepper**
> **⅔ cup good quality olive oil**
> **2 carrots, peeled and cut into small strips**
> **1 large onion, chopped**
> **4 celery stalks, chopped**
> **2 cups dry white wine**
> **2 cups beef, veal, or chicken stock**

1. Slit the roast in three places and insert the anchovy filets in the roast.
2. Heat the oil in a Dutch oven or roasting pan, brown the roast on all sides, add the vegetables, and cook until the vegetables are limp.
3. Cover the roast and vegetables with the liquids and enough hot water to cover the roast. Cover the casserole and cook over low heat or in a 325° oven for about 2 hours or until the roast is very tender. Cool the meat in the broth, uncovered. Refrigerate until cold.
4. Make the tonnato sauce while the meat is cooking and refrigerate. Serve the roast sliced very thin with about 2 tablespoons of the sauce on the side of the slices, and top with capers, cornichons, and chopped fresh parsley.

TONNATO SAUCE

1 teaspoon each: dry mustard, salt, freshly ground pepper and thyme
juice of one lemon
1 7-ounce can tuna, drained well, or 1 cup cold, cooked fresh tuna
1 cup vegetable oil
½ cup broth from the roast
8 cornichons (tiny, sour pickles)
¼ cup good quality capers

1. Process the salt, pepper, mustard, tuna, and lemon juice in the processor.
2. With the machine running, slowly add the oil to create an emulsion of mayonnaise-like consistency.
3. Add the broth, and process completely. Taste and correct seasonings.

Serves 6 to 8

Note: The sauce can be made and held in an airtight jar for two days.

DESSERTS

These desserts from the 70's, our cooking school era, were a little reminiscent of the 40's in that they were often more complicated than our mothers had attempted in the 50's. They were not, however, so Southern-American as the 40's in that the cooking schools, magazines, etc., of the 70's were practically Francophiles. Classic French cuisine in America that was popularized by Julia Child's books and t.v. programs opened the floodgates for French cuisine and with it came such elaborate desserts as charlottes, Bavarians, and things flambéed even at home-dinner parties. In the South, those of us enamored with such challenges soon began to substitute our own local ingredients rather than search out the esoteric. For example, French cassis made from black currants was soon replaced with our own fresh raspberries and homemade liqueurs; cranberries were often used in linzer tortes around Thanksgiving and Christmas because cranberries were so plentiful then; yogurt soon substituted rather well for crème fraîche; and gradually, we began to be more and more confident in our own markets and in our own abilities rather than the more exotic ones of Europe and New York. These recipes from the 70's were then and now our favorites, and needless to say, we have simplified them greatly over the years. They are like old friends that we have missed, and always elicit a smile of remembrance when they show up.

APPLE GRANITE

This came from The Greenbrier Cooking School which began at the end of the 70's and continued for many years after that. This "granite" or "ice" was served just before the main course of their elaborate "Gold Service Dinner" at the end of the cooking school week. We have served it for dessert especially at the end of a heavy meal. It is wonderfully light which just goes to show that our cooking school years weren't all cream, butter and eggs.

6 to 8 Red Delicious or Golden Delicious apples
¼ cup fresh lemon juice
½ cup water
½ cup sugar
¼ cup of the best apple brandy (Calvados) or frozen apple juice concentrate, undiluted

1. Hollow out the apples taking care not to puncture the bottoms, and reserve all of the flesh. Reserve the apple shells and squeeze enough lemon juice in the cavities of the apples to keep them from discoloring.
2. If the apple shells do not sit level, carefully cut a small piece from the bottom of the apple to level the apple. Put all of the shells in a 9" x 13" dish and cover well with plastic wrap and freeze.
3. Bring the water and sugar to the boil and cook long enough to dissolve the sugar. Let cool and add the apple pulp and lemon juice. Pour into a shallow dish and freeze.
4. When the apple pulp is frozen, chop with a fork into an icy slush and fill each frozen apple shell with the "granite" (the icy mixture) and freeze. Spoon 1 tablespoon apple brandy (calvados) or the undiluted apple juice concentrate over each apple and return to the freezer (Neither the brandy or the undiluted apple juice concentrate will freeze hard because of their respective alcohol and sugar content, and the granite will remain icy).
5. Serve with a sprig of mint in the top of each apple.

Serves 6 to 8

Note: Depending on the size of the apples you use, you may need to add one or two more apples to get the amount of flesh necessary to fill every apple.

BABA AU RHUM/SAVARIN

A "baba" or "savarin" is actually a sweet bread "imbibed" in rum and a sugar syrup. "Babas" are small straight-sided cakes of the same dough as a savarin. A savarin is traditionally baked in a 1-quart ring mold, decorated with candied fruits, almonds, and filled in the center with sweetened whipped cream. This recipe makes 1 large 1-quart ring mold, or about 8 to 10 of the smaller baba molds or cups. The ring mold takes a little less time to fill, obviously, than the smaller ones.

> 1 teaspoon yeast
> 1 cup warm milk (no hotter than body temperature)
> 1 tablespoon sugar
> 4 cups flour
> 6 eggs
> 1 teaspoon salt
> 1½ sticks softened unsalted butter
> ¼ cup sugar
>
> *Rum Syrup:*
> 1 cup sugar
> 1 cup hot water
> ½ cup dark rum
> 1 tablespoon vanilla

1. In a mixer bowl, dissolve the 1 tablespoon sugar in the warm milk, and add the yeast and allow the yeast to proof.
2. Add the flour, eggs, ¼ cup sugar, and salt, and beat on low to medium speed until the dough is very sticky and clings to the flat beater. Add the softened butter gradually and continue beating for another 2 minutes. Cover with a warm cloth and set aside to rise.
3. When the dough is doubled in bulk, return to the mixer and beat for 1 or 2 minutes until the dough is deflated. Remove from the mixer (it is very sticky) and put into the oiled 1-quart ring mold. Let rise another 30 minutes or until the dough is almost doubled in bulk.
4. Bake in a preheated 375° oven for 30 to 45 minutes or until the cake begins to pull away from the sides of the pan, and it is springy to the touch. Let cool in the pan for 10 minutes.
5. To make the rum syrup, heat the 1 cup sugar, 1 cup hot water, and the dark rum together until the sugar is dissolved. Add 1 tablespoon vanilla. Let cool to room temperature.
6. Remove the cake from the pan and put on a rack over a cookie

(Baba au Rhum/Savarin, continued on next page)

(Baba au Rhum/Savarin, continued)

sheet with sides to catch the dripping syrup. Let the cake cool completely at room temperature.

7. As soon as the cake and syrup are thoroughly cooled, spoon the syrup over the cake, reserving all the drippings. Repeat at 10-minute intervals until the cake is very moist and "imbibed."
8. Decorate the cake with candied fruit such as cherries, pineapple, apricots, etc., and toasted almonds. Fill the center just before serving with the sweetened whipped cream.

Makes 1 1-quart ring mold or 8 to 10 smaller baba molds

QUICK "SAVARIN"

Technically, this is not a "savarin" in that it does not have any yeast in the dough, but it is a good substitute. Since there is no yeast, the cake will not hold up as well as a "real" savarin to a lot of "imbibing" of the rum syrup, so baste it only once or twice with the cooled syrup . The cake must be completely cooled also before you begin to baste it with the syrup.

> 1 cup flour
> 1 stick unsalted butter
> 1¼ teaspoons baking powder
> 3 eggs, separated
> ½ cup sugar
> 4 tablespoons cream
>
> *Rum Syrup:*
> 1 cup sugar
> 1 cup warm water
> ½ cup dark rum
> 1 tablespoon vanilla

1. Cream together the butter, sugar, and egg yolks. Stir in the cream. Mix the baking powder with the flour, and add in gradually to the butter-sugar mixture, mixing well.
2. Beat the egg whites to a soft peak, and carefully fold into the batter. Pour into a well-oiled and floured 1-quart ring mold and bake at 375° for 35 to 40 minutes or until a straw in the center comes out clean. Let cool in the pan for 10 minutes. Remove to an oiled rack over a cookie sheet with sides to catch the dripping syrup.
3. Make the rum syrup by boiling the hot water, sugar, and dark rum until the sugar is dissolved. Add the 1 tablespoon vanilla and let cool completely.
4. When the cake and the rum syrup are cooled, spoon or drizzle the rum syrup over the cake to baste it. Repeat once.
5. Decorate with candied fruit, and almonds. Just before serving, fill the center with sweetened whipped cream if desired.

BAVARIAN CREAM

The Bavarian cream recipe here actually came from my grandmother's collection, and it is a little lighter than the French versions we made during the 70's. You can add any fresh pureed fruit, such as peaches or pears, or just garnish with them if desired.

> **5 teaspoons gelatin**
> **¼ cup sugar**
> **¼ teaspoon salt**
> **4 egg yolks, beaten**
> **3 cups whipping cream**
> **¼ cup brandy or 2 teaspoons vanilla**
> **4 egg whites, unbeaten, at room temperature**
> **pinch salt**
> **½ cup sugar**

1. In the top of a double boiler, combine the gelatin, ¼ cup sugar, salt, egg yolks and cream. Cook over boiling water, stirring until the custard coats a spoon. Refrigerate the custard covered with plastic wrap touching the custard to prevent a skin forming on the top. Chill until the custard mounds when dropped from a spoon. Add brandy or vanilla (and 1 cup pureed fresh fruit such as peaches, pears, raspberries, etc., if desired).
2. Beat the egg whites and salt until soft peaks form, then gradually add the ½ cup sugar, and beat until stiff peaks form.
3. Gently fold the egg whites into the chilled custard until combined. Turn into a lightly-oiled 2-quart mold, and refrigerate until firm. Unmold onto a serving plate and garnish with sweetened whipped cream and any fresh fruit.

Serves 8

CHARLOTTE RUSSE

My grandmother also made this version of a charlotte russe, and it, like the Bavarian, is a somewhat lighter version than the classic French charlottes. "Charlottes" are lovely pans that come in many sizes, but we molded this in a pretty glass bowl and omitted any cake or lady-fingers. Years ago, there was a local caterer who made a wonderful version of this recipe, and we never tired of it. Instead of lady fingers, she used crushed almond macaroons that had been toasted a bit to keep them from becoming soggy. She flavored the dessert with almond liqueur, amaretto, which was not as overwhelming as almond flavoring. Charlottes are especially pretty at Christmas, but I find that with lemon and fresh berries, they are equally as lovely in the summer, too.

> 2 tablespoons unflavored gelatin
> 1 cup sugar, divided
> ¼ teaspoon salt
> 4 eggs, separated
> 2½ cups milk
> 1 tablespoon brandy, bourbon, rum, or amaretto (almond
>   liqueur)
> ½ cup chopped maraschino cherries
> ¼ cup sliced almonds, toasted
> 1 cup whipping cream, whipped

1. Mix gelatin and ½ cup of the sugar and the salt in a large boiler. Beat egg yolks and milk together and add to the gelatin mixture. Cook over low heat, stirring constantly until the gelatin is dissolved, about 6 minutes.
2. Remove from the heat and add the 1 tablespoon brandy. Chill until the mixture mounds slightly when dropped from a spoon.
3. Beat the egg whites stiff but not dry. Gradually add in the remaining ½ cup sugar and beat until very stiff. Fold into the gelatin mixture.
4. Carefully fold the cherries, nuts, and whipped cream into the rest of the mixture, turn into a glass serving bowl and chill until firm. Garnish with additional sweetened whipped cream and shaved chocolate if desired. In the summer garnish with fresh mint leaves and grated lemon peel.

Serves 12

ÉCLAIRS

Éclairs are usually filled with a crème pâtisserie, or pastry cream, and topped with a chocolate sauce, but a plain frozen sweetened and flavored whipped cream is our favorite. The frozen, sweetened whipped cream can be made up days ahead as can the éclairs and the chocolate sauce, and then all that needs to be done is assembled just before serving. This pastry, pâté à choux, is very versatile, however, and can be the base for fritters; seasoned with salt, Tabasco, cheese, etc., and it becomes a "gougère", an appetizer or soup accompaniment; filled with chicken salad for luncheons or cocktails, etc. The recipe here is seasoned more for dessert than for savories, but you can adjust the flavorings accordingly. They are wonderfully simple to make.

> 1 cup water
> 4 tablespoons unsalted butter
> 1 teaspoon each: salt, nutmeg, cinnamon and vanilla
> 1 cup flour
> 3 large eggs

1. In a large saucepan, bring the water, butter and flavorings to a boil. Add in the flour all at once, beating vigorously with a heavy spoon. Keep over the heat until it begins to ball up, and the bottom of the pan has a "spidery" look.
2. Remove from the heat. Let cool just slightly. Add the eggs one at a time, beating each egg in very thoroughly before adding the next one. The consistency should be like very stiff mayonnaise, holding a shape when dropped from a spoon, and very glossy in appearance.
3. Pipe or spoon into round puff shapes or elongated, finger-like, éclair shapes.
4. Bake in a hot 400° oven for 10 minutes or until they are puffed and brown. Lower heat to 325° and allow them to dry out. Don't open the oven for the first 5 minutes to keep them puffy.
5. Remove the éclairs from the oven and pierce the sides with a sharp knife to let the steam out. Return to the oven and dry for another 5 minutes or so depending on the size of the éclair.
6. Let cool and store in an airtight container until ready to use, or they can be frozen for several weeks.
7. Fill with frozen sweetened whipped cream just before serving and with chocolate sauce on the side. Garnish with fresh strawberries if desired.

FROZEN ITALIAN MERINGUE

Not only is this coffee meringue delicious, it is also very beautiful in its satiny texture. Occasionally, we add toasted slivered almonds for texture, but it is not necessary. Once, by mistake, we inadvertently put the finished meringue in the refrigerator instead of the freezer. It was still good, but freezing it makes it much, much better. It is a wonderful ending to a heavy meal, and it can be done days in advance and frozen.

> **6 egg whites**
> **2 cups granulated or super-fine sugar**
> **1½ cups very strong dark roast coffee**
> **2 cups cream, whipped**
> **2 teaspoons vanilla**

1. Make a syrup of coffee and sugar. Boil to 230° on a sugar thermometer or until the syrup spins a thread. This takes about 20 minutes or more at high heat. Do not stir while it is cooking or it will crystallize.
2. As soon as the syrup begins to reach 230°, beat the egg whites at high speed until they begin to mount and look like marshmallow, but not until they break apart (If they do, add one more egg white to smooth it back out again). With the machine running, add the syrup in a steady stream taking care not to get the hot syrup on you. Beat at high speed until the bottom of the mixer bowl feels cool.
3. As soon as the meringue is cool, stop the machine and fold in the whipped cream. Freeze covered overnight before serving.

Note: If you are adding toasted almonds or coconut, fold them in at the same time you fold in the whipped cream, or garnish the top of the bowl or the individual serving glasses. This is very pretty in a large glass bowl or in individual red wine glasses.

FRUIT TART WITH PASTRY CREAM

Tart Crust:
1 cup flour
1 egg plus 1 yolk
½ stick unsalted butter, room temperature
1 teaspoon salt
6 tablespoons sugar
½ cup tart jelly (red currant, guava, apple, etc.)

1. Put the flour in a large bowl and make a well in the center. Put the room temperature butter, egg yolk, salt, and sugar in the well. Mix together starting from the center until you have a soft dough. Refrigerate for at least 2 hours.
2. Roll the dough out on a lightly floured counter to an even ⅛" thickness.
3. Lightly oil an 8" quiche pan with removable bottom, and put the pie crust in it, lightly pressing the crust into the fluted sides of the oiled pan. Prick the crust all over with a fork, and bake in a 350° oven until the crust is golden all over, which should be about 8 minutes. Watch during the first few minutes that the center does not rise, and prick with a fork if it does. When the crust is golden and still hot, brush the bottom with the melted red currant (or guava) jelly. Let cool.

CRÈME PÂTISSERIE (PASTRY CREAM)

3 eggs
1½ cups milk
½ cup sugar
2 teaspoons vanilla
3 tablespoons flour

1. Scald the milk and let cool.
2. Beat together the flour, sugar, and eggs. Pour the cooled milk over the flour, sugar, and eggs, and return to the pan, and cook over medium heat, stirring constantly, until thick. Stir in the vanilla.
3. To assemble: Strain the custard through a sieve into the pie shell that has been brushed with the melted jelly. Chill until set. Garnish the top with strawberries, grapes, etc., in a pretty design, and fill in with fresh mint, if available. Serve within 24 hours.

Makes about 2½ cups

LEMON TART

The above pastry shell is a rather basic one that can be filled in a number of ways. Lemon Curd, which is a lemon-butter, is not only excellent tasting, but it also can be done days in advance. It keeps for a week or so in a glass jar with a lid. Garnish the tart or tarts with fresh fruit, toasted almonds, coconut, or just serve it plain as it is. You can substitute orange, lime, or grapefruit juice for the lemon juice. Do not cook this in a reactive pan such as aluminum, but in Creuset Ware or any nonreactive pan.

> **4 large lemons**
> **2 sticks unsalted butter**
> **2 cups sugar**
> **6 eggs, beaten**
> **½ teaspoon salt**

1. Juice the 4 lemons and add to the butter and sugar in the top of a double boiler over medium heat. Heat just until the butter is melted, but not boiling.
2. Add the beaten eggs and the pinch of salt and cook over medium heat until the mixture is thick and coats a spoon.
3. Cover the top of the custard with plastic wrap touching the custard to prevent a skin from forming.
4. Let cool over a bowl of ice, stirring occasionally. Refrigerate when cool in an airtight glass jar.

Makes about 2½ cups

LINZER TART

A good linzer tart is hard to beat, and even though it is usually a winter dessert, no one objects if it is served any time of the year. Traditionally, ligonberries or raspberries are the fruit filling, but sweetened cranberries or apricot puree are wonderful substitutes. Linzer dough has cinnamon, nutmeg, cloves, and other spices (some even put cocoa in the dough) and sugar, so a tart fruit filling makes a better contrast than a sweet one. Strawberries, in our opinion, usually don't have enough flavor by themselves, but they mix well with any other berries for the filling. The dough keeps for several days in the refrigerator and almost indefinitely in the freezer. When we are in a hurry, especially at Christmas, we make little thumb-print cookies from the dough and fill the thumb-print with a teaspoon of raspberry or apricot preserves. Then bake them for about 8 to 10 minutes or until golden brown. Remove them carefully, because the preserves get very hot.

LINZER TART DOUGH

    1 cup almonds, toasted and processed
    1¾ cups flour
    ½ cup sugar
    ½ pound unsalted butter at room temperature
    3 egg yolks
    2 teaspoons each: grated fresh lemon peel, cinnamon, nutmeg, cardamom, vanilla and salt

Filling:
    1 jar (10 oz.) of the best raspberry (apricot, etc.) preserves available
    3 tablespoons fruit liqueur (Cassis, Grand Marnier, etc.)
    2 teaspoons fresh lemon juice

1. Mix all of the tart dough together in a mixer on low speed. It will be very sticky. Chill for at least 1 hour.
2. Heat the filling ingredients together, and stir until melted. Strain while hot through a strainer to remove the seeds, if desired.
3. On a well-floured counter or board and with a floured rolling pin, roll out the tart dough and fit into the oiled tart pan or pans. Fill ½ full with the fruit filling and bake on a cookie sheet at 375° until the dough is golden brown and the filling is bubbling. Remove from the oven and let cool slightly. Insert a sharp

(Linzer Tart, continued on next page)

(Linzer Tart Dough, continued)

knife point around the fluted edges of the tin(s) to loosen the crust from the sides before the sugar cools completely. Let cool, and remove from the baking pan, reheating slightly if the tart has adhered to the tin from the hot preserves.

4. Serve with whipping cream whipped with 3 tablespoons confectioners sugar per half-pint of cream, 2 teaspoons vanilla, and fresh nutmeg grated over the top.

Makes two 8" tarts or six 4" tarts. This recipe can be doubled.

Note: Any left-over tart dough scraps can be rolled out and cut into shapes such as leaves, apples, turkeys, bells, pumpkins, etc., for the season, and baked on the tops of the tarts.

THE 1980s

What happened in the 1980's with American food was probably inevitable, but certainly welcomed by many of us. In California, Alice Waters and a stellar group opened "Chez Panisse," which, despite its French name, was American-through-and-through. In New York, Julee Rosso and Shiela Lukins combined to revolutionize us all with The Silver Palate, a miniscule take-out shop in Manhattan. Again, in California, Alice Medrich and her "Cocolot" shop with all kinds of chocolate delicacies, came onto the scene. Food magazines and news-letters about every kind of food imaginable crowded our lives, and many of us read them avidly. There were newer and bigger than ever "Fancy Food Shows," where we somehow always managed to put chocolate on our pasta samples, and become totally overwhelmed with all the fare displayed there. Wine shows, wine talks, and tastings were rampant, or so it seemed.

Wonderful bakeries with croissants of every shape and kind, rye and whole-grain breads, desserts to sing about came into existence. The owners and bakers were at first elated, but after many, many cold dawns, more than the day began to dawn. I know, I was in the middle of it with The Highland Gourmet, Inc.

The Highland Gourmet, Inc., began as a dream for Birmingham to have a Solari's of New Orleans, an Oakville Grocery of California, and a cooking school in the one thousand square feet in the back of the shop: A quiet, friendly, controlled little jewel of a business. It was friendly, and it was a jewel, we thought, but quiet and controlled?

The building had been an old pizza parlor on the then "wrong-side-of town", but I had gone to high school in that neighborhood, and I loved it. It was an open, exciting location, though perhaps at the time a bit tired. We began the process of opening a "small little take-out shop" in November, 1982, and finally opened in March, 1983. Unfortunately, no one had heard of a "take-out-shop" in those days. They wanted and got a restaurant. We had left some of the old chairs and tables from the pizza parlor which we used for a few days, but before the first week was up, we called the carpenter back and put tables and chairs everywhere. We even put a counter and stools in the long hallway. The newspapers gave us great reviews, and we nearly killed ourselves in general. Someone gave us a sign that said "We don't know what we are doing, but we are getting better at it." That became our motto.

In April of that same year, the Chamber of Commerce of Birmingham needed a place for their Festival of Arts cooking school, and we volunteered the Highland Gourmet. The cooking school was then opened, and from then on, it was an integral part of our business.

Tuesdays were not busy enough, so we launched "High Tea" on Tuesday afternoons and evenings, a "home-type, working-person's supper", not anything big and fancy, and we were booked up for four months in advance.

Evans, the youngest of our three sons, was the maître d' (at age 14), of High Tea, and John, the middle son, was the baker.

After cooking classes, everyday business, High Tea, we should have realized that we were headed right towards the off-premise catering business. Actually, we hired a very capable and competent sure-enough chef from culinary school to take care of the catering business entirely. We lined him up with every group who called for help, and there were quite a few. He made all kinds of concrete plans, complicated foods and all, and then headed to California leaving us wide-eyed.

Gwen Henry (who was as much a part of The Highland Gourmet in many ways as my family and I) and I called a meeting: Gwen, myself, my husband, and William, our best friend and dishwasher. The men said we could do it, I cried a lot, and Gwen said she could handle it. It was a very, very big business for us. We made everything, breads, mayonnaises, vinaigrettes, everything from "scratch" every day, not only for the shop, but then also for the catering business. We supplied Macy's with salads and take-out dinners for their "Cellar" when they moved to town, and breads, real French bread, honey-wheat, and others, to about seven or eight local restaurants. The wedding cake business was a natural spin-off from catering, and that was my personal responsibility no matter how hard I tried to give it to others. It was a beautiful, joyful part of the business, but it took the most time of all, and we had learned to work fast.

The accountants told us that we could put in the private dining room that we had always dreamed about where the cooking school was, keeping the cooking school which we loved, and open a private dining room for parties of up to 30 people. We did, and it was beautiful. One of our favorite catering clients, an architectural and design company, designed it for us, and it was our pride and joy. We got our wine, beer, and liquor license, and the private dining room became a reality.

The next time the accountants called to tell me I could add on something else, I asked them if I could take the money instead, and in one year, close the shop. After eight years, I felt like a one-armed juggler, and so did Gwen. Our sons had helped us for the first five years, but they were off in colleges and graduate schools, our husbands travelled all the time with their jobs, and for me, the dog died. I found myself coming home late to an empty house with no lights on, and then, no dog. It didn't help to know that in only six hours I had to go turn on the proofers and start again.

The accountants agreed, and at the end of the first quarter of 1989, The Highland Gourmet, Inc., the restaurant, cooking school, catering business et al, closed its doors. Gwen and her husband are retired now, and loving it. She and I both have grandsons, and are disgustingly indulgent and attentive to them.

It's taken me three years to get this book written since my retirement. I feel like my mentor from the 60's, Peg Bracken, who said a cookbook is the hardest of all books to write, and next time, she is going to write a Western, with one cowboy and one horse. Maybe I'll just read hers instead. She should have run a restaurant.

You hear this all the time, but it is true: "Where did the time go? How did it happen so fast?" (Especially when most days were not 12, but more like 18 hours long.) Julee Rosso and Shiela Lukins sold their Silver Palate at about the same time we closed The Highland Gourmet, and so have quite a few others who were in the same type of small business.

The only thing most of us miss is the people: the many, many friends who were always so supportive and kind. Maybe these recipes from our Highland Gourmet Days will rekindle something of the old friendships that are now such treasured memories. We taught these recipes in our classes, shared them over the phone, at parties, and on the streets with people while we were in the business. (We knew we were so apt to change the recipes or forget them completely that by sharing them, we knew we had someone to call when we needed the original again.) The recipes here were our favorites, and even we held on to them. Feel free to adapt them yourself, we sure did, and you loved them! Thank you again, to: my family, Gwen and her family, William Gilmore and his family, to my employees, and our customers. They were wonderful years for us.

APPETIZERS & HORS D'OEUVRES

BLACK-EYE PEA PÂTÉ

The Service Guild of Birmingham brought Martha Stewart to our city for a demonstration lecture, and our shop catered the patrons' party for her. The tables were all covered with quilts and baskets, so our food could not compete in colors. We also wanted our food to be totally Southern. The pâté from black-eyed peas was quite a success, and we later incorporated it into a class that we called "Haute Down: Southern Entertaining."

    4 cups cooked black-eyed peas, drained
    1 medium onion, chopped and sautéed
    3 cloves garlic, minced
    1 cup ketchup
    3 tablespoons Worcestershire sauce
    ½ pound unsalted butter, room temperature (or low-fat margarine)
    2 teaspoons Tabasco sauce
    salt and pepper

1. Process all but the butter until smooth and not liquid. Add in the softened butter through the feed-tube. Taste and correct the seasonings.
2. Line a bowl or bread-loaf pan with plastic wrap. Put the pâté in the lining. Weight down. Let chill at least 6 hours.
3. Unmold and smooth sides with a table knife or spatula. Serve with mild jalapeño peppers in lieu of crackers. Garnish with chopped chives.

Serves 20-25

GARLIC ROASTED

This is the best "butter" we know. When the very large elephant garlic is roasted, it becomes very mild and sweet. It is excellent on toasted rounds of good French bread to serve with pâtés, cheeses, or spreads.

> **4 heads "elephant" garlic**
> **¼ cup best quality olive oil**
> **salt and freshly cracked pepper**
> **4 ounces chèvre cheese, plain or herbed**
> **2 teaspoons fresh basil, chopped**
> **2 teaspoons dry thyme**
> **1 red bell pepper, roasted, peeled and sliced into thin strips, or**
> ** 3 sun-dried tomatoes, sliced into thin strips**

1. Peel the whole heads of the elephant garlic and cut them in halves. Sprinkle with the olive oil, salt and cracked pepper.
2. Cover and bake at 375° for about 1 hour or until the garlic is very soft and spreadable.
3. Let cool and mix with the softened chèvre and the herbs. Spread on rounds of toasted sliced French bread. Top each slice with a thin strip of roasted red bell pepper or sun-dried tomatoes.

Note: To roast red bell peppers: Broil whole red bell peppers on all sides until totally black and charred. Put in a small dish covered with foil while the pepper is still very hot so that it will steam. Leave covered for 15 minutes. Remove from the bowl, and with a very sharp paring knife, scrape all of the black and charred skin off of the pepper, saving the juices from the roasted pepper in the bowl. Slice into thin strips.

PALMIERS AS SAVORIES

Palmiers are technically crisp palm-shaped cookies made from puff pastry dough. They are wonderful with fruits, custards, sorbets, etc. The sweet ones have been around for decades because of the classic French cuisine. Savory palmiers are appetizers, usually filled with a sweet and sour mustard, ham, cheeses, pesto, etc. They are wonderful with cocktails or tea or brunches, etc. Use your imagination on the fillings. They freeze well too, and all that is needed at the last minute is to cook them in a very hot oven for 10 to 15 minutes even from the frozen state. Classic puff pastry is not very difficult to make, just time-consuming. A fairly good commercial one is made and sold through grocery stores. It is always frozen, and the directions on the package are self-explanatory. Usually, commercial puff pastry is not made with all butter as home-made puff pastry is, which means that the commercial brands are not as good "left-over" or reheated as your own, but they are still quite good. To make your own puff pastry, refer to any good classic French cookbook, especially those with step-by-step pictures. To make ahead and freeze any of the puff pastry products, savory or sweet, keep in mind that you freeze them unbaked, which means that they have been frozen twice and must, therefore, be wrapped air-tight and then baked from the frozen state to retain their "puffiness."

> **1 sheet thawed puff pastry**
> **1 tablespoon good quality olive oil, Tuscan, if possible**
> **¼ cup Roquefort or blue cheese, crumbled into small bits**
> **3 slices cooked bacon, finely crumbled**
> **¼ cup toasted pecans, finely crumbled**
> **1 whole egg beaten with 1 tablespoon water**

1. Put the puff pastry rectangle on a counter on wax or parchment paper. Lightly brush with the olive oil. Press the crumbled cheese, bacon, and pecans into the oiled pastry, distributing them evenly over the surface and into the corners.
2. Roll the two long sides of the puff pastry sheet towards each other so that they meet in the middle, forming two identical "tubes" on each side. Freeze until just before baking.
3. Cut through the frozen tubes into ¼" slices, and put cut-side down on a foil-lined cookie sheet. Brush each palmier lightly with the egg wash. Bake in a preheated 400° oven for 10 to 12 minutes until golden-brown and every layer is flaky. They will look done before they actually are, so test for flakiness. Remove and let cool. Serve within a day, reheating in a low (200°) oven uncovered for 8 to 10 minutes. Microwaving tends to toughen them.

Makes about 2 dozen

VARIATIONS:

Classic Basil Pesto Filling:
2 cups fresh basil leaves
4 cloves garlic
1 cup walnuts
1 cup Parmesan cheese
¼ cup Romano cheese
salt and pepper
1 cup Tuscan olive oil

1. Process basil, garlic, walnuts. Slowly add oil. Add cheeses and seasonings.

Honey-Mustard Filling:
2 tablespoons honey mustard
1 cup grated Parmesan cheese
½ cup smoked turkey or baked ham, slivered

1. Spread the honey mustard on the puff pastry sheet, and press the grated cheese and slivered turkey or ham into the pastry. Roll, freeze, egg-wash, and bake as described above.

Sun-dried Tomato Filling:
1 small jar marinated sun-dried tomatoes (approximately 6 ounces)
1 tablespoon olive oil from the marinated sun-dried tomatoes
3 to 4 sun-dried tomatoes, drained and chopped fine
3 ounces feta or blue cheese, crumbled fine
½ cup ripe or Greek olives, drained and sliced or shredded into pieces
2 teaspoons thyme

1. Brush the puff pastry rectangle sparingly with the olive oil, and crumble and press the rest of the ingredients into the puff pastry sheet. Roll, freeze, egg-wash, and bake as described above.

SAUSAGE PUFFS

1 sheet puff pastry
1 pound bulk sausage, mild or spicy
1 whole egg beaten with 1 tablespoon water

1. Cut the thawed puff pastry rectangle into 4 long strips.
2. Put a long tube of sausage along each strip, and completely encase the raw sausage in the pastry, making a long cylinder. Freeze.
3. The day it is to be served, cut the sausage and puff pastry cylinders into one-inch circles, and put on a rack on a foil-lined jelly-roll pan, so that as they cook, the drippings from the sausage will drain away from the savories. Brush with the egg beaten with the water and bake in a 375° oven for 10 to 15 minutes, or until the sausage is fully cooked and the puff pastry is golden. Drain on paper towels if necessary, and reheat in a conventional oven at 300° for about 10 minutes. Serve warm.

Makes about 5 or 6 dozen tiny sausage puffs

SHRIMP PÂTÉ

Gwen, our catering director and co-teacher at The Highland Gourmet, Inc., made this pâté almost every day during the holiday season between Thanksgiving and Christmas. It is relatively easy to make because it is bound with butter (or low-fat margarine) rather than with gelatin. Use it within 24 hours of making it.

> **2 pounds shrimp, cooked, peeled and deveined**
> **1 small onion, chopped fine**
> **⅓ cup mayonnaise**
> **2 teaspoons each: thyme, tarragon, Tabasco sauce, salt and pepper**
> **2 sticks unsalted butter (or low-fat margarine), room temperature**
> **1 teaspoon white vinegar or fresh lemon juice**

1. Quickly process all ingredients only until coarse.
2. Press into a lightly-oiled bread pan or decorative mold, refrigerate with a light weight on the top over-night.
3. Unmold. Serve with Cucumber-Dill Sauce.

> *Cucumber-Dill Sauce:*
> **1 large cucumber, peeled, seeded, and chopped**
> **⅓ cup sour cream**
> **2 tablespoons lemon juice**
> **⅔ cup mayonnaise**
> **4 tablespoons dried or fresh dill**
> **salt and pepper**
> **1 teaspoon Tabasco sauce**

1. Combine all ingredients. Refrigerate overnight.

SMOKED FISH SPREAD

Smoked fish are easily available in the better grocery stores today, but when we first began catering in the '80's, we had to "import" them from a "Fancy-Food" supplier from Atlanta. Charles, my oldest son, who managed the shop for me in the summers, received them late one evening from our Atlanta supplier, and tied the entire order of smoked fish (about 3 dozen) in all the reach-in refrigerators, in and under the deli case, in the walk-in so that when we came in the next morning before dawn to begin baking the bread, wall-eyed, whole, dried, smoked trout met us at eye-level everywhere we turned. It scared us to death, but we had to admire his diligence and technical skill because they weren't easy to hang. One or two is all you'll ever need for this recipe, and not having to buy more than you use won't leave any around to tempt your creative offspring.

> **6 ounces smoked fish (trout, salmon, etc.)**
> **6 ounces cream cheese, at room temperature**
> **juice of 1 lemon**
> **salt and cracked pepper**
> **1 teaspoon dried chives**

1. Flake the smoked fish and set aside.

2. Process all of the rest of the ingredients, and add in the flaked smoked fish.

   Makes about 1½ cups

   Note: Serve on cucumber rounds, crisp crackers, or toasted pita bread.

TAPENADE

Charles, our oldest son, was a summer missionary in Southern France near Aix-En-Provence when he was in high school. He was on a "work team" that built, repaired, maintained "L'Eau Vive", a French nondenominational camp for young people from all over Europe. The work teams lived in tents on the hillsides for the whole summer. My husband had business in Czechoslovakia that summer, and since our other two sons, John and Evans, were at summer camp in Alabama, I took the "red-eye special" to Europe to meet my husband and to go to visit Charles. The hillsides in Southern France were like I picture heaven: sunny and cool, a constant breeze from the Mediterranean, and every step taken was on fresh thyme that grew wild there. There were olive gardens and almond trees everywhere around that beautiful hillside. Every time I see "Tapenade" I think of the three of us sitting in an outdoor restaurant in Aix near the beautiful lighted fountains of that city, eating hot French bread spread with the black olives, garlic, etc. of the Tapenade. While my husband and I were there with Charles, there was a food fair displaying all the foods of Provence, and no words or photographs will ever capture the beauty of those days in that place. It was more than the colors, the foods, the smells, and sounds: those "Remembrances of Things Passed," even though Aix is the very city Marcel Proust immortalized in his "Remembrances of Things Past." It was a young man giving what he could of himself to One Who had given everything He had for us, One Who never did a thing wrong in His whole life, and Who loves us for even our smallest gifts to Him. Centuries earlier, another little boy gave his lunch to that One, while all of the adults scoffed, but five thousand were fed from it. Our son gave up a summer of being lazy or working for money, and that "small lunch" of his fed our spiritual lives for years to come. A pot of black olives, garlic, and herbs are strange reminders of Eternal Values, but He spoke of the lilies of the fields being robed in more splendor than the wealthiest king who ever lived. (Garlic, by the way, is a member of the lily family.) Maybe I fix Tapenade once every five years. It doesn't matter, because it is just one of the many, many remembrances that He gives me every day of His gifts to us. I must admit though, it's one of my favorites.

TAPENADE

1 cup pitted black or Greek olives
1 tablespoon capers
juice of 1 lemon
2 anchovy filets
2 garlic cloves
2 tablespoons olive oil
2 teaspoons thyme
cracked fresh pepper
salt to taste

1. Process all the ingredients except for the salt. Anchovies and olives are quite salty. Taste and add salt only if necessary.
2. Refrigerate overnight.

Makes about 1½ cups

Note: Use as a butter or spread for French bread as an appetizer, as a "dip" for fresh raw vegetables, on French bread sandwiches, or on pizzas.

TIROPETAS

Gwen Henry was the only one in our shop who made these. She was the only one with patience and discipline enough to stand there and make these things without getting sidetracked or bored. She just kept on and on and on making them. One particularly large order of 400 that she had personally made went out for a late-afternoon tea. Gwen had left the shop for the day, and I answered the phone call from a frantic cook at the hostesses' home who wanted to know what she was supposed to do with "those things" we sent: She had unwrapped every single one of them, and there was almost nothing in them. We told Gwen about it four years later.

¼ **pound feta cheese**
2 **ounces cream cheese**
1 **egg**
pinch nutmeg
fresh ground pepper
4 **sprigs fresh parsley, chopped**
1 **box phyllo dough (or "filo" dough), thawed in the**
   refrigerator overnight
½ **pound melted butter**

1. Combine the cheeses, egg, seasonings and parsley.
2. Remove the phyllo dough from the box in its wax paper, and lay it flat on a work surface. Keep it covered with a slightly damp dish cloth, and work with only a small portion of it uncovered at one time.
3. Cut the rectangle into 2" long strips. Brush one strip at a time lightly with the melted butter. Put 1 tablespoon filling on the bottom of one strip, fold the pastry over the filling to tuck it in, and continue to fold it the entire length of the strip as you would a flag, going from corner to corner. Brush with melted butter, and put on a cookie sheet to freeze. Proceed until all of the dough or filling is used up, depending on how many you need.
4. Freeze or bake at once at 375° for 15 to 20 minutes or until golden and puffed. Serve warm. The cheese is too hot to serve right out of the oven.

Note: Allow 3 per person for hors d'oeuvres.

(Tiropetas, continued on next page)

(Tiropetas, continued)

VARIATIONS:

The following makes a wonderful pick-up dessert. It is a little strudel-like triangle.

1 cup cooked, drained, and processed apricots
¼ cup cookie or macaroon crumbs
2 teaspoons each: cinnamon, nutmeg and cardamom
1 teaspoon ground cloves
2 tablespoons unsalted butter
1 tablespoon Grand Marnier or fresh lemon juice

1. Mix all until the filling is very thick and holds together easily. You may need to add more cookie crumbs if necessary.
2. Put 1 tablespoon on each 2" phyllo strip, and fold as indicated in the main recipe.

Note: Allow 2 per person.

SOUPS

BUTTERNUT SQUASH SOUP

Even without the cream and butter, this soup is a four-star favorite. It is usually a fall and winter soup, but we find that the butternut squash keep for months, and we enjoy it usually from the Fall to Easter.

1¾ pounds butternut squash
2 teaspoons unsalted butter or good quality olive oil
1 medium onion, chopped
2 cloves garlic, minced
3 stalks celery, chopped
3 carrots, peeled and chopped
4 cups chicken or veal stock
2 cups cooked smoked ham, turkey, or Kielbasa sausage, cubed
2 teaspoons Tabasco sauce
2 teaspoons each: thyme, marjoram, and chives
salt and pepper
1 cup cream, optional

1. Wash the squash and wrap in foil and bake on a cookie sheet in a 350° oven for about 1 hour or until it is soft. Let cool and scrape the flesh, removing all seeds and membranes. You should have about 2 cups.
2. Heat the unsalted butter or oil in a large Dutch oven or skillet, and add the chopped vegetables, cooking until limp. Add the cooked squash and the meat or meats, and mix well. Puree in a food processor if a smooth soup is desired.
3. Add the broth, Tabasco sauce, and herbs, and cook uncovered for 20 to 25 minutes over medium heat until the soup is reduced by about ⅓. Add the rest of the ingredients, and continue cooking over medium heat for another 20 minutes. Taste and correct seasonings.

CHICKEN & WILD RICE SOUP

We made this soup one day with a few left-overs from the day, and it was a tremendous success. People today, years after the closing of the shop, still remember it and ask for the recipe. It is so easy to do that it's easy to keep on hand. It is good, too.

1 box Uncle Ben's wild rice mixture, regular, not instant
3 tablespoons unsalted butter or olive oil
3 tablespoons flour
4 cups chicken broth
1 cup milk or cream
1 cup dry white wine
4 chicken breasts, cooked and chopped or "pulled" into shreds

1. Cook the wild rice mixture according to the directions on the box, omitting the butter or margarine.
2. Heat the butter or oil in a Dutch oven or large pot and add the flour all at once. Whisk together until smooth, and cook for about 5 minutes or until the flour is cooked but not at all browned. Add the broth and milk or cream, and white wine. Stir or whisk to blend completely.
3. Add the cooked wild rice and cooked chicken to the broth. Stir well. Cook over medium heat, stirring occasionally, for about 15 to 20 minutes.

Serves 6 to 8

COLD SHRIMP SOUP

Years before the advent of The Highland Gourmet, Inc., a wonderful cooking teacher in Birmingham, Elberta Reid, taught with us on several occasions in cook shops, in her home, for benefits, etc. This was probably her recipe, but it became such a staple around the shop, winter and summer, and especially at High Tea, that we "claimed" it. It is such a neat and precise recipe that I am positive it was hers. Ours were never so orderly, not even Gwen's, who was far more precise than the rest of us. Thanks Elberta, we think.

1 pound medium shrimp, cooked, peeled, and deveined
1 small cucumber, peeled, seeded, and diced
1 ripe tomato, peeled, seeded, and diced
4 green onions, chopped fine
3 tablespoons red wine vinegar
2 cups chicken stock

1. Mix all ingredients. Taste for seasonings, and add salt and pepper if necessary. Chill well.

Serves 4 to 6

GAZPACHO

When we first opened the shop, a customer asked us for gazpacho, which we had made ourselves in our classes quite often. We were so busy with all we had to do and to learn about the restaurant business that we just made this without consulting anything or anyone. It was very successful, and we finally wrote it down when we realized that the shop was going to live if we took time out to record recipes. This soup travels well, too, and now, in our post-shop life, we often give it to new neighbors, take it on picnics, and to our mountain hide-away. It keeps well for several days in a 1-quart Mason or Ball jar, but with all of the fresh raw vegetables in it, we have never tried to freeze it. When chives are all in blossom, garnish the soup with a tablespoon or so of low-fat or regular sour cream, and a few chive blossoms. The blossoms add flavor as well as color.

> **3 large tomatoes, peeled and seeded**
> **2 small red bell peppers, chopped**
> **1 yellow pepper, if available, chopped**
> **1 small cucumber, peeled, seeded, and chopped**
> **1 small onion, chopped fine**
> **juice of 1 lemon (or lime)**
> **⅓ cup good quality olive oil**
> **1 cup fresh soft bread crumbs**
> **¼ cup red wine, or 3 tablespoons red wine vinegar**
> **4 cups tomato juice (preferably homemade)**
> **1 garlic clove, minced**
> **3 or 4 tablespoons total of chopped fresh herbs: chives, basil, thyme, parsley, tarragon, in any combination**

1. Process half of the vegetables, including all of the garlic, in a processor or blender. Pour the liquid from the processor into a serving bowl, add the lemon juice, and half of the oil.
2. Add the rest of the bread crumbs, and the chopped unprocessed vegetables. Mix carefully, adding the red wine or the red wine vinegar, the rest of the oil and tomato juice. Taste and correct the seasonings.
3. Pack in 1-quart glass Mason or Ball jar. Chill.

Makes 1 quart

LOBSTER & WATERCRESS SOUP

> 2 lobsters, cooked
> 2 quarts fish stock, or court-bouillon (see below)
> 2 lemons: grated peel, and juice
> 1 bunch watercress, washed and chopped
> ½ cup cottage cheese, drained
> 2 teaspoons each: thyme, tarragon, chives, salt and pepper
> 4 fresh tomatoes, peeled, seeded, and cubed
> 4 fresh basil leaves, rolled and cut into julienne strips

1. Remove the meat from the lobsters and cube. Crack the claws and reserve for garnish.
2. Using the shells and appendages from the lobster, make a stock or court-bouillon according to the recipe that follows.
3. Puree the washed and drained watercress with some of the stems with the cottage cheese until completely smooth. Add the grated lemon peel, the lemon juice, all of the herbs except the julienned basil, salt and pepper.
4. Heat the court-bouillon, add the pureed watercress mixture, and whisk or mix well until smooth. Cook uncovered over medium heat for about 20 minutes or until the mixture is slightly reduced. Taste and correct seasonings, adding more salt, pepper, and herbs if necessary.
5. Add the cooked lobster, tomatoes, and julienned basil strips, and continue to cook until the lobster and tomatoes are heated. Do not overcook or the lobster will be tough.
6. Garnish with 1 tablespoon sour cream (low-fat or regular) if desired.

Serves 4 to 6

LOBSTER COURT-BOUILLON

1. Clean the lobster shells of the feathery lungs, and put the lobster shells, appendages, etc., in a large boiler with 2 large onions, peeled, and sliced, 4 stalks celery, 1 bunch washed fresh parsley, 4 green onions, ¼ cup dry white wine or vermouth. Bring to a boil and cook over medium-heat heat for 15 to 20 minutes. Strain and correct seasonings. Reduce over high heat for 5 to 8 minutes if the broth is not strong enough.

MUSHROOM BARLEY SOUP

*Amanda, one of our best cooks, used to make this for me to take
house in the mountains on my Mondays off. I would eat it for br
the screened-in porch while the early-morning train in the valley ...u be
going by below our house. I still make this soup, summer or winter, for
any meal, but mine is never as good as Amanda's was. It's a good Sunday
night supper too. For guests, we serve it with red wine or sherry, but
since, in my mind it was originally a breakfast food, I really prefer having
it with milk. It is a very easy soup, and it freezes perfectly. I give it for
Christmas presents in glass Mason or Ball jars with a loaf of homemade
bread.*

>2 teaspoons vegetable oil
>1 medium onion, chopped
>1 pound fresh mushrooms, chopped
>4 cups beef stock or broth
>1 cup milk (or cream)
>1 cup barley
>1 tablespoon fresh lemon juice
>1 tablespoon Worcestershire sauce
>salt and pepper

1. Heat oil in a Dutch oven or large boiler, and sauté the onions
   and mushrooms until tender. Stir in the broth, the milk, and the
   barley.
2. Cook covered for 15 to 30 minutes or until the barley is tender
   and completely cooked. Add the lemon juice and the Worcestershire sauce.
3. Taste and add salt and pepper if necessary.

Serves 4 to 6

ONION-ONION SOUP

Originally, we made this "Four Onion Soup", but like all things, some were lost over time. The same thing happened to our "Green Onion Bisque" in the '70's, and undoubtedly to any number of recipes. But the results of both the Green Onion Bisque and the Onion-Onion Soup were, oddly enough, not only different, but also better than their respective originals. We had a quiche that we made with five onions, but not only did we somehow lose all the onions in that recipe, but the whole quiche itself. We consider these two soups fine survivors.

    ¼ cup good quality olive oil, Tuscan, if possible
    4 large yellow onions, sliced very thin
    2 large red onions, sliced very thin
    1 pound fresh mushrooms, chopped
    4 cups beef or veal stock
    ½ cup red wine
    2 teaspoons Dijon mustard
    1 tablespoon Worcestershire sauce
    salt and pepper to taste
    4 tablespoons cognac
    6 to 8 slices toasted French bread
    1 cup grated Gruyère cheese

1. Heat the oil in a Dutch oven or large boiler, and add the onions and mushrooms. Cook until the onions are golden.
2. Add the stock, red wine, Dijon mustard, Worcestershire sauce, and cook covered over medium for 45 minutes to an hour. Add the cognac and cook another 3 or 4 minutes. Taste for salt and pepper, adding if necessary.
3. Put one slice of the toasted bread in each bowl. Top with the grated Gruyère cheese, allowing about ¼ cup per bowl. Ladle the hot onion soup into each bowl, and heat on a tray in the oven at 400° or until the cheese is melted.

Serves 4 to 6

SPLIT PEA & SAUSAGE SOUP

1 tablespoon vegetable or olive oil
1 large onion, chopped
2 cloves garlic, minced
3 stalks celery, chopped
1 pound dried split peas, washed under cold water
2 cups chicken or veal broth
2 teaspoons each: thyme, tarragon and chervil
2 bay leaves
1 pound cooked Kielbasa sausage, cut into bite-size pieces

1. Heat the oil in a large Dutch oven or boiler and add the chopped onions, mushrooms, garlic, and celery. Cook until they are limp.
2. Add the washed split peas, the broth, and 4 cups of hot water. Bring to a boil. Add the herbs and bay leaf.
3. Cook covered for two to three hours or until the peas are tender and have begun to burst. Watch carefully the last 30 minutes to prevent the peas from sticking. Stir occasionally. Remove the bay leaf, and taste and correct seasonings, adding salt and pepper and more herbs, if necessary. Puree and return to the pan.
4. Add the cooked Kielbasa, and cook covered another 10 to 20 minutes, watching carefully, stirring occasionally.
5. Add ¼ cup dry sherry before serving. Heat carefully, stirring constantly.

Serves 4 to 6

SALADS

The first thing a customer saw when entering The Highland Gourmet, Inc., was a ten-foot deli case filled with a variety of salads. These salads were the backbone of our business. The favorite foods of my childhood, my years in New Orleans, then my cooking school years, seemed to all come together in the salads we made and served at our shop in the '80's: chicken salad, artichokes, marinated vegetables, fresh fruits, shrimp rémoulade, red beans and rice, and so many others. These were the foods I loved and couldn't buy. Suddenly, or so it seemed, I had almost 3,000 square feet of space, ten employees, walk-in coolers, deliveries from all over the world at my door, and all I knew to do was what my family and I liked. It is still a shock to me that others enjoyed these foods too. The soups, breads, desserts, soon followed, and others added their favorite "Remembrance-foods" and new ideas to ours, and The Highland Gourmet, Inc., was off and running. There were many advantages to a small business: we could make major changes quickly and easily, for example, from a take-out shop to a restaurant overnight, then the catering business, High Tea, the cooking school, the private dining room. If we tried something and didn't like it or found something we liked better to replace it, we could change overnight. The disadvantages were there too: It was a very labor-intensive business that, nevertheless, could only support a minimum of employees. Teamwork was essential. A mother and her three sons running a small business were well received by the public, and we will always appreciate the support our city gave us. The following salad recipes, especially, are only a few of the basic ones we made and served over the seven years, and someday, maybe, there will be an entire book on the recipes from the shop. Maybe. Except for Gwen, none of us were very exacting with our recipes, because things changed every day. Some days the tomatoes were better than other days; if we had more fresh vegetables, we used them, and varied the proportions. The chicken salad with artichokes was fairly standard every day, as were the other basic salads: fresh fruit, pasta Dijon, red potato, tuna salad, and wild rice salad. Vary your own proportions within reason or follow ours here exactly as Gwen would. She is the one who recorded and saved most of these recipes anyhow, so the parameters are safe.

BLACK-EYED PEA SALAD

¼ cup vegetable oil
3 tablespoons cider vinegar
1 cup ketchup
3 tablespoons Worcestershire sauce
1 tablespoon A-1 sauce
1 clove garlic, minced
2 teaspoons Tabasco sauce
salt and pepper to taste
1 medium red onion, sliced into thin circles
4 cups cooked black-eyed peas, completely drained

1. Mix the oil, vinegar, and all of the ingredients except the onion and peas.
2. Remove the very small center circle of the onion and reserve for another use. The center is the strongest part of the onion. Put the separated rings into a bowl with the peas.
3. Add the vinaigrette to the peas, mix thoroughly, and taste and season with salt and pepper as necessary. This is better the next day. It will keep for 3 or 4 days, covered in the refrigerator. Serve cold.

Serves 8 to 10

BEEF & POTATO SALAD

This is an Oriental kind of main course salad that men especially loved. The fresh ginger makes all the difference; powdered ginger is lost in this mixture.

> 2 pounds flank steak
> 5 red potatoes, cooked and sliced thin
> 1 bunch broccoli florets, blanched and drained completely
> 4 stalks celery, chopped or sliced thin on the diagonal

1. Broil the flank steak 5 or 6 minutes on each side until it is firm to the touch and is medium rare. Cool to room temperature. Slice very thin on the diagonal.
2. Combine the red potatoes, blanched broccoli florets, and celery. Add the cooled sliced flank steak. Toss with the ginger vinaigrette. Add salt and freshly cracked pepper to taste.

Note: Serve on Boston or Bibb lettuce.

GINGER VINAIGRETTE

> 1 small fresh ginger root, peeled and grated (or 2 teaspoons
>   dry ginger)
> ⅓ cup soy sauce
> 2 teaspoons Dijon mustard
> 2 tablespoons dry sherry
> 3 tablespoons sesame oil
> ¼ cup cider or white vinegar
> 1 tablespoon hoisin sauce
> fresh cracked pepper

1. Combine all the above ingredients, mixing well.

Serves 6 to 8

CARROT & CELERIAC SALAD

3 carrots, shredded
1 large celeriac, peeled
¼ cup raspberry vinegar
½ cup good quality olive oil
1 teaspoon sugar
2 teaspoons dried or fresh rosemary
2 teaspoons Dijon mustard
salt and pepper to taste

1. Peel and sliver the celeriac into match-stick pieces. Toss with the carrots.
2. Combine the rest of the ingredients in a blender or processor.
3. Pour over the vegetables a little at a time, tossing until well-coated. Taste and correct seasonings.

Serves 6 to 8

Note: Serve chilled on Boston or Bibb lettuce or as a slaw.

CELERIAC DIJON SALAD

2 medium size celeriacs
2 green onions, chopped
2 stalks celery, chopped
6 cherry tomatoes, halved and seeded
1 teaspoon salt
2 teaspoons cracked fresh pepper
1 tablespoon Dijon mustard
1 tablespoon fresh lemon juice
3 tablespoons olive or vegetable oil
2 teaspoons each: thyme and tarragon

1. Peel and slice the two celeriacs into match-stick slices or shred on a grater. Mix with the green onions, celery, and the halved and seeded cherry tomatoes, being careful not to tear up the tomatoes.
2. Make a vinaigrette out of the rest of the ingredients in a processor or blender. Taste and correct the seasonings. Pour over the vegetables, toss lightly. Refrigerate for several hours.

Serves 6 to 8

Note: Serve on Boston or Bibb lettuce or plain as a slaw.

CHICKEN SALAD WITH ARTICHOKES

This was "THE" Highland Gourmet chicken salad. There were a lot of others, but this one was the one that we made forty to fifty pounds of per day every day. It has to be made with homemade mayonnaise to be "our" authentic chicken salad.

6 halves, boneless, skinless chicken breasts
2 large celery stalks, cut into two pieces
1 onion, peeled and sliced
½ cup dry white wine
4 stalks celery, chopped
1 can artichoke hearts, drained, and chopped coarse
1 cup homemade Highland Gourmet mayonnaise
salt and pepper to taste
1 cup toasted, slivered almonds

1. Cook the chicken breasts in a large pot with the celery stalks, onion, dry white wine, and enough water to cover until they are tender. This takes about 30 to 45 minutes over medium heat. Let cool in the broth while preparing the rest of the salad.
2. When the chicken is cool, chop or "pull" the chicken into fairly large pieces. Mix with the chopped celery, the drained and chopped artichoke hearts, and about 1 cup of the mayonnaise. Add salt and pepper to taste. Chill at least 2 hours. Serve topped with toasted slivered almonds.

Serves 6 to 8

Note: Serve on Bibb or Boston lettuce.

HIGHLAND GOURMET MAYONNAISE

3 whole eggs
2 teaspoons dry mustard
2 teaspoons each: chives, tarragon and salt
1½ cups light vegetable oil
3 tablespoons cider or sherry vinegar

1. Put the whole eggs, dry mustard, chives, tarragon, and salt in a processor and process until light yellow.
2. With the machine still running, add the oil 1 teaspoon at a time until ½ cup has been incorporated into the eggs. Then add the rest of the oil, with the machine still running, in a steady stream until all of the oil is used up and the mayonnaise is thick.
3. Turn the machine off, and add the vinegar. Process until the vinegar is just mixed in. Taste and add more salt if necessary.

Makes about 1½ cups

CHICKEN SALAD & HEARTS OF PALM

The artichoke chicken salad was so very popular that it really over-shadowed the following one. I personally preferred the one here with the hearts of palm and oranges. Hearts of palm are usually more expensive than artichokes, so I guess I ought to be glad that my favorite didn't win out.

> **6 halves cooked, boneless, skinless chicken breasts**
> **3 stalks celery, chopped**
> **3 green onions, chopped**
> **1 can hearts of palms drained and cut into circles**
> **2 fresh oranges grated and sectioned, juices reserved**

1. Cook the chicken breasts as described in the Chicken Salad with Artichokes. Chop or "pull" the chicken into fairly large pieces.
2. Mix with the chopped celery, chopped green onions, hearts of palm, and about 1 cup of the following homemade mayonnaise. Taste and add salt and pepper, if necessary.
3. Gently mix the orange sections into the salad taking care not to destroy the orange sections. Chill for several hours and serve on Boston or Bibb lettuce.

ORANGE MAYONNAISE

> **3 whole eggs**
> **2 teaspoons each: dry mustard, chives, lemon thyme (or thyme) and salt**
> **1½ cups light vegetable oil**
> **1 tablespoon of the reserved juices from the orange**
> **1 tablespoon cider vinegar**
> **grated peel from the 2 oranges**

1. Process the whole eggs in a food processor with the dry mustard, chives, lemon or regular thyme, until the eggs are very light yellow.
2. Add the oil 1 teaspoon at a time through the feed tube with the machine running until ½ cup of oil has been incorporated. With the machine still running, add the oil in a steady stream until all of the oil has used up, and the mayonnaise is thick.
3. Stop the machine and add the 1 tablespoon orange juice, 1 tablespoon cider vinegar, and the grated orange peel. Process until all are incorporated. Taste and add more salt and pepper if necessary.

Makes about 1½ cups

CHICKEN SALAD: ORIENTAL CHICKEN SALAD

Someone brought us this salad all made up one day for us to persuade us to add it to our repertoire. We liked it so much that we had it at least once a week. Originally, the recipe called for cooked chicken in it, but all of our employees would avoid the chicken and eat the "good stuff." Since we had no shortage of chicken salads around, it was a natural step to omit the chicken and make a terrific vegetable and pasta salad. You too can leave out the chicken if you like.

3 cups cooked, shredded chicken breasts
1 pound vermicelli pasta
1 cup mayonnaise
1 tablespoon Worcestershire sauce
¼ cup sesame oil
3 tablespoons soy sauce
1 tablespoon hoisin sauce
2 tablespoons cider vinegar
1 tablespoon Dijon mustard
2 cups snow peas, blanched and cut into thirds
1 large red pepper, chopped
4 green onions, chopped with the green
4 stalks celery, chopped
8 ounces marinated baby corn, drained
1 small can sliced water chestnuts, drained
1 cup cooked English peas
1 cup cherry tomatoes, halved and seeded

1. Cook the pasta in boiling salted water, and drain it thoroughly.
2. Mix the mayonnaise with the next 6 ingredients until thoroughly blended. Add the cooked chicken.
3. Add the vegetables, mix in ½ cup mayonnaise mixture at a time, stirring after each addition, until the pasta and vegetables are moistened with the mayonnaise mixture but not overwhelmed. Taste and add salt and cracked pepper if necessary. Refrigerate for several hours, adding more mayonnaise if necessary before serving.

Serves 6 to 8

CUKE-ZUKE SALAD

1 medium cucumber, peeled
1 small zucchini
3 chopped green onions, with the green
salt and fresh cracked pepper
1 cup low-fat plain yogurt
2 tablespoons cider vinegar
2 teaspoons sugar

1. Shred the cucumbers and zucchini in the food processor with the shredder blade or on a mandoline.
2. Mix the rest of the ingredients together and taste for salt and pepper if necessary.
3. Mix ½ of the yogurt mixture with the shredded vegetables until well-coated, adding more only if necessary.

Note: Optional: 1 cup shredded carrots, 1 cup cooked spaghetti squash

JAMBALAYA SALAD

2 teaspoons good quality olive oil
1 medium onion, chopped
1 clove garlic, minced
4 stalks celery, chopped
1 red bell pepper, chopped
4 green onions, chopped with the green
1 medium green bell pepper, chopped (optional)
3 cups raw long-grain white rice
2 cups chicken or veal broth
1 cup white wine
2 bay leaves
2 cups cooked ham, cut into cubes
2 cups smoked turkey, cut into cubes
2 pounds cooked shrimp, peeled and deveined
1 cup black olives, sliced
1 cup cherry tomatoes, sliced in half and seeded
1 cup good quality olive oil
¼ cup tarragon vinegar
2 teaspoons Dijon mustard
2 teaspoons salt and cracked pepper
1 bunch fresh parsley, washed and chopped fine

1. Heat the oil in a Dutch oven or large boiler, and add the chopped onions, the green of the onion, the chopped celery, red and green peppers and cook until wilted.
2. Add the raw rice and continue to cook over medium-high heat until the rice is well coated. Add the chicken broth and white wine and 2 cups boiling water and bring to a boil. Add the bay leaves, cover, and cook over medium heat for 25 to 30 minutes or until all of the liquid is absorbed and the rice is tender. Remove the cover, fluff the rice with a fork, and let cool.
3. Make a vinaigrette by mixing the oil, vinegar, mustard, salt and pepper.
4. When the rice is cool, add the cooked meats, olives, and tomatoes and ½ cup vinaigrette at a time until the rice is fully coated. It may not need the entire 1½ cups of vinaigrette. Taste and adjust seasonings. Serve on Boston or Bibb lettuce, garnished with the chopped parsley.

Serves 8 to 10

JICAMA & ORANGE SALAD

Jicama is a tuber that looks something like a baking potato, but it tastes very much like an apple. It has a wonderful texture that is usually sadly lacking in a lot of salads, and it also absorbs other flavors nicely. They are not very expensive, and are very low in calories. Buy a medium-size one, because the larger ones tend to be a little more fibrous than the smaller ones. Use them anywhere you would use an apple. You pronounce it "Hick-ah-ma."

1 cup jicama, peeled and cut into matchsticks
2 large oranges, Valencia or blood oranges, cut into sections, juice reserved
4 green onions, chopped
1 bunch fresh watercress, chopped with some of the stems
salt and fresh ground pepper
2 tablespoons cider vinegar
2 tablespoons good quality olive oil
2 teaspoons Dijon mustard
2 teaspoons rosemary

1. Section the oranges over a bowl, reserving the juices.
2. Put the jicama sticks, oranges, green onions, in a bowl.
3. Mix the orange juice, salt and pepper, cider vinegar, olive oil, Dijon mustard, and rosemary and mix into the vegetables. Let marinate for several hours.
4. Put the chopped watercress on individual salad plates, strain the oranges and jicama with a slotted spoon and arrange on the watercress.

Serves 4 to 6

Note: Garnish with fresh cracked pepper.

MARINATED VEGETABLE SALAD

> **5 cups total: broccoli, cauliflower, carrot sticks, small green beans, Brussels sprouts, washed and trimmed**
> **2 cups total: zucchini, washed and sliced into 2″ sticks; yellow squash, cut into strips**
> **1 cup small cherry tomatoes left whole**
> **1 cup fresh small mushrooms, washed and drained**

1. Blanch the broccoli, cauliflower, carrots, green beans, and Brussels sprouts in boiling water with 1 tablespoon salt for 5 minutes, drain and run under cold water to stop the cooking.
2. Add the blanched vegetables to the rest of the raw vegetables, and add the following vinaigrette ½ cup at a time until the vegetables are well coated. Add salt and pepper to taste. Serve chilled.

Vinaigrette:
1 cup light vegetable oil
½ cup red wine vinegar
2 teaspoons dill
2 teaspoons Dijon mustard
2 teaspoons salt and fresh cracked pepper

1. Process until well blended.

Makes approximately 1½ cups

PASTA DIJON

1 pound rotelli pasta
5 carrots, peeled and shredded
2 cups commercial mayonnaise
1 cup Zatarain's Creole mustard

1. Cook the pasta in boiling water to which 1 tablespoon salt has been added until the pasta is tender. Put in a colander under cold running water until the cooking has stopped. Drain thoroughly.
2. Mix the pasta and the shredded carrots with the combined mayonnaise and Creole mustard. Mix well.

Serves 8 to 10

PASTA VERDE

1 pound pasta (shells, rotelle, macaroni)
3 stalks celery, chopped
3 green onions, chopped with the green
1 cup black olives, sliced
1 cup sun-dried tomatoes, drained and cut into small strips

1. Cook the pasta in boiling water with 1 tablespoon salt until tender. Put in a colander under cold water to stop the cooking. Drain thoroughly.
2. Mix the pasta and the rest of the ingredients, and bind with 1 or more cups of the following spiced green mayonnaise.

SPICED GREEN MAYONNAISE

1 cup commercial mayonnaise
2 tablespoons green-herb mustard
1 tablespoon horseradish, fresh grated if possible

1. Mix all ingredients and add to the pasta-vegetable mixture ½ cup at a time until well coated.

Serves 8 to 10

Note: Serve on Boston or Bibb lettuce with sliced red tomatoes as garnishes.

RED CABBAGE & CARROT SLAW

½ cup good quality olive oil
2 tablespoons cider vinegar
¼ cup chopped fresh dill
1 bunch fresh parsley, chopped
4 leaves of fresh basil chopped
2 teaspoons Dijon mustard
salt and fresh ground pepper
5 carrots, peeled and shredded
1 medium head red cabbage, outer leaves removed, and
  shredded
8 ounces Roquefort cheese, crumbled

1. Blend or process the olive oil, vinegar, herbs, mustard, salt and pepper.
2. Mix together the carrots, cabbage, and ½ cup or more of the vinaigrette, and mix until well coated. Taste and correct seasonings. Serve with the crumbled Roquefort cheese over the top.

Serves 4 to 6

SAUTÉED SUGAR SNAP SALAD

> 2 teaspoons olive oil
> 1 pound sugar snap peas
> 3 stalks celery, chopped
> 3 green onions, chopped
> 1 pound fresh mushrooms, sliced
> 1 medium red bell pepper, sliced
> ½ cup vegetable or olive oil
> grated peel of one lemon
> juice of one lemon
> 4 leaves fresh basil, rolled and cut into julienne
> 2 teaspoons lemon or regular thyme
> salt and pepper

1. String the peas carefully, and slice into 3 long slivers each.
2. Heat the oil in a skillet, add the peas, and sauté for 3 or 4 minutes or until they are barely cooked.
3. Put in a bowl with the raw chopped vegetables and toss together.
4. Make a vinaigrette from the rest of the ingredients, adding salt and pepper to taste. Mix ½ cup at a time into the vegetables, adding more if necessary to coat. Chill and serve in Boston or Bibb lettuce "cups."

Serves 4 to 6

SKINNY DIP SALAD

The name for this salad came from a take-out shop that used to be in Jacksonville, Florida, called "L.E. Goodstuff, Inc." Ellie, who opened the shop about 6 months before we opened The Highland Gourmet, Inc., was a former model, entrepreneur, and woman of great taste. Her shop really was a take-out shop and never converted to a restaurant the way we did. Her "Skinny Dip" was made with lots of chopped, cooked spinach. Ours is a cottage cheese base made with fresh vegetables and herbs that are seasonally available. My best friend from childhood, who is one of those excellent cooks who makes me swear not to tell it, makes this concoction often, or used to, and it is what made me first eat cottage cheese. That's what best friends are for. Thanks, Brownie.

> 1 8-ounce carton cottage cheese
> ½ cup good commercial mayonnaise
> 1 cup total: chopped celery, green onions with the green,
>   parsley, red bell peppers, chopped or shredded carrots
> 1 small cucumber, peeled, seeded and chopped
> 2 teaspoons each or any combination thereof: chives, basil,
>   tarragon, cilantro
> salt and cracked pepper to taste

1. Mix all the ingredients and let chill for at least one hour.
2. Serve with sliced, peeled tomatoes or in hollowed-out tomatoes.

Serves 4

SHRIMP & AVOCADO SALAD

1 pound 26-30-size shrimp
juice of 1 large lime
1 dried poblano chili pepper, slit open
2 avocados, Haas if available, peeled and sliced
1 bunch fresh cilantro, leaves only
1 bunch fresh watercress

1. Marinate the shrimp and avocado in the lime and poblano chili pepper in the refrigerator for about 30 minutes.
2. Make the following mayonnaise with 2 tablespoons of the lime juice marinade.
3. Arrange a bed of washed and drained watercress on each plate or a platter.
4. Arrange the shrimp and avocado on the watercress, and pour a ribbon of the mayonnaise over all.

LIME MAYONNAISE

3 whole eggs
2 teaspoons salt
2 teaspoons Dijon mustard
1 bunch fresh cilantro, leaves only
1½ cups olive oil, Tuscan if possible
2 tablespoons lime juice from the marinade

1. Process the whole eggs, salt, Dijon mustard, and the cilantro leaves until the eggs are thick and light yellow.
2. Add the olive oil 1 tablespoon at a time through the feed-tube with the machine running. When ½ to 1 cup of the oil has been absorbed by the eggs, add the rest of the oil in a steady stream. Continue to process for another 4 or 5 minutes or until all is incorporated.
3. Stop the machine and add the lime juice. Process only until the lime juice is incorporated. Taste and correct seasonings.

Makes approximately 2 cups

SHRIMP & TORTELLINI

**1 pound shrimp (26-30), cooked, peeled and deveined
1 pound tortellini (spinach, cheese, or any kind)
10 cherry tomatoes, cut in half and seeded
3 stalks celery, chopped
3 green onions, chopped with some of the green
1 cup black olives, chopped
1 cup olive oil
1 tablespoon Dijon mustard
2 teaspoons dill
1 clove garlic, crushed
2 tablespoons cider vinegar
salt and pepper to taste**

1. Cook the tortellini in boiling, salted water until tender. Drain without rinsing to prevent the filling from washing out. Cool.
2. Make a vinaigrette from the rest of the ingredients, blending or mixing well. Remove the garlic clove before adding to the shrimp.
3. Mix the shrimp, tomatoes, green onions, celery, and black olives together carefully, and add about ½ to 1 cup of the vinaigrette. Taste and correct seasonings.

Serves 4 to 6

TUNA SALAD HIGHLAND GOURMET

**1 large can tuna, drained
1 cup mayonnaise
3 stalks celery, chopped
3 green onions, chopped with the green
2 tablespoons cider vinegar
¼ cup sweet pickle relish
1 large Red Delicious apple, chopped but not peeled
2 teaspoons each: thyme, tarragon and chives**

1. Mix all together. Chill 2 or 3 hours before serving.

Serves 4 to 6

TUNA NIÇOISE

1 pound fresh tuna
2 tablespoons olive oil
2 teaspoons rosemary
salt and fresh cracked pepper
1 pound green beans, cooked and drained
4 red potatoes, cooked and sliced thin
6 cherry tomatoes, halved and seeded
½ cup Greek black olives, seeded and chopped
Boston or Bibb lettuce, washed and drained

1. Grill or broil the tuna with the olive oil, rosemary, salt and cracked pepper. Let cool.
2. Marinate the green beans, red potatoes, cherry tomatoes, black olives, and the cooled cooked tuna in the following marinade for at least 2 hours, overnight if possible. Remove from the marinade with a slotted spoon and serve on Boston or Bibb lettuce.

Marinade:
½ cup Tuscan olive oil
1 tablespoon Dijon mustard
5 anchovy filets, drained
¼ cup red wine vinegar
salt and cracked pepper

WILD RICE SALAD

1 box Uncle Ben's long grain wild rice
1 cup chopped celery
1 cup toasted pecans
3 or 4 chopped green onions

1. Cook the rice as directed omitting the butter. Cool to room temperature.
2. Add the rest of the ingredients to the wild rice mixture, and marinate in the following vinaigrette for several hours.

Serves 4 to 6

Vinaigrette:
¼ cup white vinegar
½ cup vegetable oil
juice of one lemon

1. Mix well and add to the cooled wild rice.

ENTRÉES

The following two recipes for our Highland Gourmet main course were the hallmark of our trade. There were many other main courses that we made and sold, and they are distributed throughout this book: Shrimp Creole, Red Beans and Rice, Chicken Stuffed with Spinach, or Wild Rice, etc. The Highland Gourmet years of the '80's would not be complete without these two recipes. When I closed the shop in 1989, Joellen O'Hara of THE BIRMINGHAM NEWS wrote a lovely "farewell tribute" to us, and we gave her the chicken salad recipe and the chicken pot pie recipe for the NEWS. Many, many people have told me that they have the recipes from the NEWS carefully tucked away in a favorite cookbook. The "Mustard Chicken" probably wasn't our original to begin with, but I have no idea from whence it came. It was then, and is now, wonderful for picnics, buffet dinners, or cold and left-over during the middle of the afternoon or night. I send our thanks and tribute to whoever thought it up in the first place. Fresh grouper filets are excellent prepared the exact same way.

CHICKEN POT PIE WITH PUFF PASTRY

**4 or 5 cups cooked chicken breasts, chopped or "pulled"
(shredded)
2 tablespoons unsalted butter or vegetable oil
4 stalks celery, chopped
1 medium onion, chopped
4 carrots, peeled and cut into thin match-sticks
1 pound fresh mushrooms, chopped
2 cloves garlic
2 tablespoons unsalted butter (or vegetable oil)
2 tablespoons flour
1½ cups milk
½ cup cream (or 2 cups milk, total)
¼ cup dry white wine
2 teaspoons each: tarragon, chervil and thyme
4 stalks fresh parsley, chopped fine
1 sheet puff pastry, thawed
1 egg, beaten with 1 tablespoon water**

1. Heat the 2 tablespoons oil and sauté all of the vegetables until
    they are almost completely tender but still have a little texture
    left. Let cool and mix with the cooked chopped chicken.
2. Make a white sauce of the butter and flour and whisk or stir
    until the two are thoroughly incorporated. Add the milk, cream,
    and dry white wine slowly, whisking or stirring constantly until
    all is smooth. Let cook over medium heat, stirring occasionally
    for 8 to 10 minutes to cook the flour. Add the salt, pepper, and
    herbs.
3. Add the white sauce to the chicken and vegetables. Taste and
    correct seasonings. Put in an 8″ x 10″ casserole and cover with
    the thawed puff pastry. Cut 5 decorative slits near the center of
    the pastry for air to escape.
4. "Wash" the puff pastry with the beaten egg and water. Bake in a
    400° oven until the puff pastry is golden and all the layers are
    cooked when tested with a fork. Puff pastry will look cooked
    before it really is. Cooked puff pastry has all the layers flaky.

Serves 6 to 8

Note: This can be doubled, tripled, etc. We made it in big batches.

MUSTARD CHICKEN

1 stick butter or margarine
2 tablespoons vegetable oil
¼ cup Dijon mustard
2 teaspoons salt and cracked pepper
2 teaspoons chives and tarragon
8 boneless, skinless chicken breast halves
2 cups dry bread crumbs

1. Melt the butter and oil and mix in with the Dijon mustard, salt, and pepper, and herbs. Let cool.
2. Pound the chicken breast halves between parchment or wax paper to break down all the tendons which tenderizes them.
3. Dredge the pounded chicken breasts in the oil and herb mixture, then in the bread crumbs. Put on a foil-lined cookie sheet.
4. Bake at 350° until the breasts are golden and firm to the touch. Serve hot or cold.

Serves 4

DESSERTS FROM THE '80'S

These were just a few of our favorites. There were so many that it will take another book just to include all of the desserts and breads especially. Until then, these were the ones we enjoyed the most and that we still make today now that the shop is closed, and we no longer use the commercial equipment of those days. These began at home, and it is fitting that they continue there. Most are quite easy, and as you can tell, a lot lighter and generally less caloric than the desserts of the past decades that we have recorded here. A few are not at all calorie conscious, but after all, they are desserts. We had a sign on the dessert case that read: "Eat dessert first. Life is so uncertain." That's not a bad idea.

Our "Signature Cake" was the "Dome Cake," which my good friend, Rosario Stagno, taught me the year we opened the shop. She moved back to her home of Chile, and thousands of "Dome Cakes" later, we still think of her every time we make it. It caused a lot of trouble for a while. Other bakers in town connived to have my employees tell them how it was done, and only recently, a "volunteer" helper has announced that it is her own original idea and named it after herself! Rosario, a beautiful person and artist, actually learned the technique of forming this cake when she attended LeNotre's in France in the late '70's. She converted it to the chocolate version, using some five different types of chocolate. The directions are lengthy, but if you read over them first, make all of the ingredients except the buttercream the day before, it is not a difficult cake to make. Allow yourself two days. Please, however, please don't cut corners with canned icing and cheaper ingredients. The whole is only equal to the sum of its parts. Do it right. The reward is in the smiles you get when others and yourself see it and taste it.

APPLE CUSTARD PIE

1 unbaked 9" deep-dish pie shell
3 cups apples, peeled and sliced thin
1 tablespoon bourbon
1 teaspoon each: cinnamon, nutmeg, cardamom and salt
grated peel of 1 lemon
3 eggs, beaten
½ cup sugar
1½ cups milk
pinch salt
1 cup sour cream
1 tablespoon sugar

1. Put the peeled and sliced apples in a large bowl with the bourbon, spices, and lemon peel. Toss around until the apples are completely coated. Leave at room temperature while preparing the custard.
2. Mix the beaten eggs, sugar, milk, and pinch of salt until smooth, and cook in a double boiler, stirring constantly until the mixture is the consistency of heavy cream and just beginning to coat a spoon.
3. Put the apple mixture in the unbaked deep-dish pie shell and spread them evenly over the bottom of the crust. Pour the custard over the apples rearranging the apple slices evenly if necessary.
4. Put the pie on a cookie sheet and bake in a preheated 375° oven for about 30 minutes or until the custard is set and a knife in the center comes out clean. Let rest to set up for at least 30 minutes before serving.
5. Serve warm with the sweetened sour cream on the side, or let the pie cool completely and spread the sweetened sour cream on the top and sprinkle with freshly grated nutmeg.

CHEESECAKE from THE HIGHLAND GOURMET, INC.

We must have made thousands of these cheesecakes over the seven years of the shop. They made beautiful presents for Christmas, Secretary's Day, Valentine's, Easter, and even for birthday cakes. We bake them in 8" cake pans that are 3" deep, and put the pans in a water-bath that is two-thirds of the way up the side of the cheesecake pan. Refrigerate the baked cheesecake overnight, unmold the next day. This is actually a baked custard, and we did not use any crust on the bottom. If your pans are sprayed with a nonstick baker's type spray, the cheesecakes come out easily especially without a crust. The cheesecakes baked this way are three inches high with smooth pretty sides. Decorate the tops with chocolate sauce, fresh fruits, crushed peppermint candies, or leave them plain. They freeze perfectly, and this recipe can be doubled if your mixer is big enough.

> 1 pound (16 ounces) cream cheese, softened
> 1½ cups granulated sugar
> 2 tablespoons flour
> 5 large eggs beaten
> pinch of salt
> 1 tablespoon flavoring: vanilla, crème de menthe, bourbon, banana liqueur, etc.

1. Beat the softened cream cheese in a good mixer with a flat beater until all of the lumps are gone. With the machine running, add in the sugar gradually, scraping down the sides occasionally, and continue beating until the sugar is incorporated. Add in the 2 tablespoons flour.
2. With the machine on low, add in the beaten eggs gradually until they are completely incorporated. Add any flavorings at this time.
3. Put in an 8" cake pan that is 3" deep and that has been sprayed with a nonstick baker's spray. Bang the pan on a flat surface to remove all air bubbles from the batter.
4. Put the filled 8" pan into a 10" cake pan, and put in a 325° oven. Fill the 10" cake pan with enough warm water to come two-thirds of the way up the sides of the pan. Carefully close the oven door and do not open it for the first 30 minutes.
5. Bake for 1½ hours or until the cheesecake top is set and the cheesecake is only slightly wobbly when shaken lightly. Do not bake until it is cracked. Remove from the oven carefully and let sit in the hot water for 30 minutes. The cheesecake will continue to cook in the hot water. If the cake is at all cracked, remove it at

(Cheesecake, continued on next page)

The Eighties ❧ 271

(Cheesecake, continued)

once from the hot water, and set in a cool place to stop the cooking.

6. Remove from the water bath and refrigerate lightly covered overnight.
7. Loosen the sides of the cheesecake from the pan with a table knife, and unmold onto a flat platter that has been lightly sprayed with nonstick pan spray. Reverse the cheesecake onto the serving platter right-side up Decorate with fresh fruit, chocolate sauce (see Index), or sweetened whipped cream or sour cream. Cut each slice with a knife dipped in hot water and dried. This will make each cut clean.

Makes approximately 8 to 10 slices

CHOCOLATE CHESS PIE

The plain chess pie recipe is in the desserts of the '70's. The chocolate version of chess pie is quite different from the original, but it is very good, and of course, rich. Small pieces with added sweetened whipped cream and a pretty red strawberry or two make it irresistible.

1 8″ unbaked pie shell
1 stick unsalted butter
4 tablespoons cocoa powder
2 eggs
1 small can Pet milk
2 teaspoons vanilla
pinch of salt

1. Melt the butter and cocoa together. Add the rest of the ingredients and mix thoroughly.
2. Pour into an 8″ unbaked pie shell and bake at 325° for 45 minutes or until the pie is set and the crust is done. Let cool until set.

CHOCOLATE MOUSSE

Our catering director and co-teacher, Gwen Henry, came up with this recipe during our cooking school years in the late 70's. Everyone knew it had to be good, because Gwen is neither a dessert cook nor a dessert eater. This mousse was enormously popular, and usually customers brought us their pretty glass bowls for us to fill and decorate for a party or holiday occasion. It is good, and very, very rich, so it does well for a buffet dinner for a lot of people, because a little goes a long way. People are so chocolate crazy that it is a good idea to have someone serve it for you at a buffet. It looks very pretty too with all its chocolate splendor seen through the glass bowl. A separate bowl or basket of fresh strawberries washed and drained and left whole is a colorful and good companion to this on the buffet. This can be doubled.

1 14-ounce can sweetened condensed milk
6 ounces semi-sweet chocolate bits
3 tablespoons rum, vanilla, or bourbon
1 cup whipping cream, whipped

1. Combine milk and chocolate over low heat. Stir until melted and smooth. Remove to a large bowl. Let cool to room temperature and stir in the rum.
2. When the chocolate mixture is completely cooled, fold in the whipped cream. Freeze.

Makes 6 to 8 servings

Note: This does not freeze hard, but will be a smooth, mousse-like consistency. Decorate the top with additional sweetened whipped cream and shaved chocolate if desired.

SORBETS

As the decade of the '80's wore on, and we had seemingly whipped cases of cream, baked tons of chocolate, eggs, and such, our personal tastes longed once again for fresh fruits, plain or simply fixed. Sorbets became our passion. They are an easy way to "save summer" by putting them in glass Mason or Ball jars, and processing an hour or so before serving to "mush" them up again. They are a welcome surprise in January when watermelons, honeydews, and cantaloupes are not available. If we didn't manage to make the sorbet mixture out of melons that summer, fresh ripe pears, and even a good Cabernet wine make excellent sorbets as well. The amount of sugar used depends on the sweetness of the fruit itself. Keep in mind that anything that is frozen must be a lot sweeter than unfrozen desserts. Freezing the sorbet mixture in the jars makes it turn to a hard icy consistency. Remove it from the jars about two hours before serving, and process in batches until it is mushy and not at all icy. Then put it in a serving bowl and refreeze, or in the individual wine or sorbet glasses, and keep frozen until time to serve. It will reset and stay mushy for about two hours.

CABERNET SORBET

We especially liked this as an alternative dessert on Thanksgiving and Christmas. It can be doubled.

½ cup water
1 cup sugar
1 cup red wine (Cabernet Sauvignon)
juice of 1 lemon
1 cup ginger ale (sugar-free or regular)

1. Bring the sugar and water to a boil, and let boil until all of the sugar is dissolved. Let cool slightly.
2. Add the rest of the ingredients and stir carefully. Freeze in a 10" x 13" Pyrex dish for several hours or until frozen solid.
3. Break the frozen sorbet up into chunks and process in a food processor until it is mushy. Return to the freezer in a deep bowl, a serving bowl, or individual sorbet or wine glasses. Serve within two hours.

Makes 4 cups

MELON SORBET

**8 cups flesh of very ripe melons (cantaloupe, honeydew,
   watermelon)**
4 cups superfine sugar
¼ cup white corn syrup
juice of 1 lemon

1. Process the melon in batches until it is liquid. In a large bowl,
    add in the superfine sugar, corn syrup, and lemon juice, and stir
    until the sugar is melted, and the corn syrup is dispersed
    evenly.
2. Freeze overnight or until the mixture is ice-hard. Break up and
    save in air-tight Mason or Ball jars, leaving some head-room, or
    proceed as follows:
3. In small batches, process the ice-hard sorbet until mushy. Put in
    a decorative freezer-proof glass bowl until two hours before
    serving.

Makes approximately 9 cups

PEAR SORBET

6 to 8 ripe pears
grated peel of 2 lemons
juice of 4 lemons
3 tablespoons pear liqueur or 1 teaspoon lemon extract
1 cup superfine sugar
1 cup water
1 egg white, beaten to soft peaks

1. Melt the sugar and the water over low heat just until the sugar is dissolved. Let cool.
2. Put the grated lemon peel and lemon juice in a large bowl, and add the peeled and thinly sliced pears. Add the cooled syrup, the liqueur, or extract, and mash or process until smooth. Return to the bowl and add the beaten egg white.
3. Freeze in a sherbet or small ice cream maker or in a 9" x 13" Pyrex dish for several hours until hard. If using the Pyrex dish, mash and turn the sorbet several times during the freezing process.

Makes approximately 8 cups

Note: Garnish with strawberries or chocolate leaves or slightly drizzle with chocolate sauce (see Index for chocolate sauce).

INSTANT SORBET

When summer fruits are gone, and the pears don't look so great, the next-best thing is this simple dessert. It is very, very good, and always available.

2 packages frozen strawberries or raspberries, not thawed
½ cup water
6 tablespoons sugar
juice of 1 lemon

1. Process all ingredients in a food processor. The frozen berries will set up immediately.
2. Serve in a pretty glass bowl or wine or sorbet glasses, and top with sweetened whipped cream, if desired.

Makes approximately 6 cups

THE "DOME CAKE"

3 8" or 9" layers of chocolate cake (see Index)
1 recipe buttercream
2 cups raspberry preserves
2 cups toasted almonds
2 cups whipping cream, whipped with 3 tablespoons
   confectioners sugar
1 recipe chocolate ganache
1 deep Pyrex or metal bowl

1. Line the bowl with long strips of plastic wrap with at least two inches extending beyond the bowl so that you can pull the cake out when it is formed.
2. Slice the cake layers horizontally as evenly as possible, saving the bottom of one cake for the bottom of the dome cake.
3. Line the bowl with ¼" layers of the sliced cake, overlapping each slice slightly so that there are no spaces between the cake and the bowl is completely and thinly lined with cake.
4. "Glue" the overlapping cake slices with a thin layer of soft buttercream. Carefully spread the raspberry preserves over the buttercream and sprinkle about ¼ of a cup of toasted almonds over the raspberry preserves.
5. Put one cup of the sweetened whipped cream in the bottom of the cake-lined bowl, and spread the top of the cream smooth. Over the cream, put a trimmed layer of chocolate cake.
6. Put the remaining sweetened whipped cream over the cake layer to make a second layer in the bowl that fills the bowl up to the rim. Put the reserved cake bottom on top of the second cake layer. This will be the bottom of the Dome Cake, so a whole thin slice of cake without any tears or cracks is essential. Put a cardboard cut to the size of the bowl on top of the last cake layer. Weight down with two heavy cans or 2 pounds of butter or any other weight and refrigerate or freeze for at least 6 hours.
7. Using the extending tabs from the plastic wrap, unmold the cake by pulling gently on the tabs, being sure to keep the cardboard circle under the formed cake.
8. Put the dome cake with the cardboard-side down on a rack that is on a tray to catch the drippings from the ganache.
9. With a spatula, spread the buttercream very smoothly over the "dome" of the cake. Let chill for 5 or 10 minutes until the buttercream is set.
10. Quickly pour the room-temperature ganache through a strainer over the butter-creamed dome cake letting the excess drip into

(The "Dome Cake", continued on next page)

(The "Dome Cake", continued)

the tray. By quickly pouring the ganache, rather than a little here and a little there, you will get a more smooth finish. Once the ganache is on, it is difficult to get the ganache any smoother than by the first pouring.

11. Chill the Dome Cake until the ganache is completely set. Reserve all the excess ganache in a glass jar. It will keep for months in the refrigerator, and cold it makes good truffles.

12. Put on a serving platter and decorate the edges with cut strawberries, piped butter cream, or fresh flowers, or ribbons.

Note: To serve: Cut a wedge from the very top of the dome two inches down, and continue on around the top of the cake until the cake is flat. Then cut the second layer in two inch wedges. Do not cut the top section completely off of the cake first. It will collapse.
See page 268 for additional, general instructions.

BUTTER CREAM

4 egg yolks
pinch salt
4 tablespoons sugar
2 tablespoons water
2½ sticks unsalted butter, room temperature
1 cup mini-chocolate chips, melted and cooled

1. Beat the egg yolks and salt in a mixer on high speed until very light. Let them continue to beat while the sugar syrup is cooking.

2. In a very small saucepan, bring the sugar and water to a boil, but do not stir, and let boil over high heat until the syrup spins a thread or reaches 230° on a sugar thermometer.

3. In a steady stream pour the boiling sugar syrup over the eggs that are being beaten. The sugar syrup will cook the eggs. Continue to beat until the bottom of the bowl is cool to the touch. If the mixture is too hot, it will melt the butter that is to be added, and it will not return to its correct consistency for spreading.

4. Add the room temperature butter one tablespoon at a time to the egg and sugar mixture with the mixer still on high. Continue beating until the butter is all incorporated. If it looks "curdled," add a bit more room temperature butter.

5. Add the cooled, melted chocolate, and beat until the consistency of homemade mayonnaise.

Makes about 2 cups

GANACHE

2 12-ounce packages mini-chocolate chips
½ quart whipping cream

1. Melt the chocolate chips over a double boiler and stir until smooth.
2. Scald the cream and add it to the melted chips. At one point it will "seize", but continue adding the cream, stirring over warm water, and it will smooth out.
3. Cool to room temperature.

Serves 10 to 12

Note: If you pour the ganache over the buttercream on the dome cake while the ganache is still warm, the buttercream will slide off of the cake. Let the ganache cool, and the buttercream on the cake chill.

Index

The Highland Gourmet, Inc., Publishers
4212 Caldwell Mill Road
Birmingham, Alabama 35243

Please send _____ copy(ies)   @ $18.95 each _____
Postage and handling   @ $3.00 each _____
Alabama residents add sales tax   @ $1.33 each _____
TOTAL _____

Name _____

Address _____

City _____ State _____ Zip _____

Make checks payable to The Highland Gourmet, Inc., Publishers.

The Highland Gourmet, Inc., Publishers
4212 Caldwell Mill Road
Birmingham, Alabama 35243

Please send _____ copy(ies)   @ $18.95 each _____
Postage and handling   @ $3.00 each _____
Alabama residents add sales tax   @ $1.33 each _____
TOTAL _____

Name _____

Address _____

City _____ State _____ Zip _____

Make checks payable to The Highland Gourmet, Inc., Publishers.

The Highland Gourmet, Inc., Publishers
4212 Caldwell Mill Road
Birmingham, Alabama 35243

Please send _____ copy(ies)   @ $18.95 each _____
Postage and handling   @ $3.00 each _____
Alabama residents add sales tax   @ $1.33 each _____
TOTAL _____

Name _____

Address _____

City _____ State _____ Zip _____

Make checks payable to The Highland Gourmet, Inc., Publishers.

Reorder Additional Copies